INDIAN FASHION

OBRI
.1 |2¹ -

INDIAN FASHION

Tradition, Innovation, Style

ARTI SANDHU

BLOOMSBURY

LONDON • NEW DELHI • NEW YORK • SYDNEY

Bloomsbury Academic

An imprint of Bloomsbury Publishing Plc

50 Bedford Square	1385 Broadway
London	New York
WC1B 3DP	NY 10018
UK	USA

www.bloomsbury.com

Bloomsbury is a registered trade mark of Bloomsbury Publishing Plc

First published 2015

© Arti Sandhu 2015

Arti Sandhu has asserted her right under the Copyright, Designs and Patents Act, 1988, to be identified as the Author of this work.

British Library Cataloguing-in-Publication Data
A catalogue record for this book is available from the British Library.

ISBN HB: 978-18478-8780-1
PB: 978-18478-8779-5
ePDF: 978-1-4725-9084-8
ePub: 978-1-4725-9085-5

Library of Congress Cataloging-in-Publication Data
A catalog record for this book is available from the Library of Congress.

Typeset by Fakenham Prepress Solutions, Fakenham, Norfolk NR21 8NN
Printed and bound in India

CONTENTS

ACKNOWLEDGMENTS

This book is dedicated to my husband, Simon Holland, whose patient and selfless support over the years made it possible to complete. Also included in this dedication are my parents, Amrita Sandhu and Deshvir Sandhu, who never questioned my decision to study fashion design at a time when it was a relatively new field in India. Together they have served as devoted research assistants throughout my field research in Delhi. In addition to diligently mailing me Indian fashion magazines across the world over many years, Amrita Sandhu has also provided the majority of the images in Chapter 2.

Many invaluable discussions on fashion with Asha Baxi were central to the inception of this book's research. I am indebted to Shefalee Vasudev for sharing her deep insight on fashion in India as well as assisting me in approaching various members within the fashion industry. Several people generously gave their time and thoughts across numerous interviews and informal chats through the course of my research that have helped enrich the content in this book. I am deeply grateful to these wonderful and dynamic fashion professionals: Yatan Ahluwalia, Aneeth Arora, Sonu Bohra and Jasleen Kaur Gupta, Meher Castelino, Neeraj Chauhan and Alpana Mittal, Anjali Chawla, Kallol Datta, RK Deora, Anita Dongre, Swarup Dutta, Rohit Gandhi and Rahul Khanna, Sanjay Garg, Gaurav Gupta, Amit Hansraj, Hemani Kashikar, Sangita Kathiwada, Vinod Kaul, Azeem Khan, Tarun Khiwal, Heena Kochhar, Narendra Kumar, Ritu Kumar, Ritu Kumar (O'Layla), Neeta Lulla, Gaurav Mahajan, Nida Mahmood, Manou, Rahul Mishra, Anju Modi, Pavitra Mohan, Puja Nayyar, Nazarul, Ekta Rajani, Nihal Rajan, Rajdeep Ranawat, Wendell Rodricks, Harilein Sabarwal, Priya Sachdev, Nitin Saxena, Mehul and Kaushik Shrimanker, Mandira Shukla, Sujata Assomull Sippy, Geetika Srivastava, Manasi Scott, Rajiv Takru and JJ Valaya. Additional thanks to Vineeta Nair, Savitri Ramaiah, Vinayak Razdan and Shalini Singh, and all those who generously contributed towards the book's images – as outlined in the image credits. My field research in Mumbai would not have been possible without my sister Tarana Singh's determination, endless enthusiasm and driving skills. I would also like to thank FDCI for allowing me access to attend Pearls Infrastructure Delhi Couture Week (in 2010) and Wills Lifestyle India Fashion Week (WLIFW, in 2013).

The thoughtful and thorough review notes provided by the anonymous reviewer on the initial manuscript as well as those from earlier anonymous reviews at the proposal stage helped strengthen the premise of the book. In addition, the text's edits and feedback provided by Lilian Mutsaers, Maren Nelson, Debra Parr, Shefalee Vasudev, Simon Holland and Param Sandhu—who were subject to various stages of the book's rough drafts— were an invaluable and important part of its evolution. Furthermore, this project could not have been completed without Columbia College Chicago's faculty development grants that funded various segments of field research and the supportive environment within the Fashion Studies department, chaired by Debra Parr, that allowed me the time and resources required for the preparation of the final manuscript.

Finally, I offer my deepest thanks to the publishing team at Berg and Bloomsbury, headed by Anna Wright, for supporting this project from the very beginning and providing me with the reassurance that helped bring it to fruition.

PREFACE

When I began my studies in Fashion Design in 1997 at NIFT (National Institute of Fashion Technology), New Delhi, I did so with the hope of being part of India's then emerging fashion and design culture. It was an exciting time to be a design student—interning with designers, experimenting with craft techniques, seeing fashion shows unfold—especially India's first formal fashion week in 2000, and reflecting on what personal design philosophies of an Indian designer could entail. Fashion design in those days had begun to attract significant attention that had shifted from amusement and ridicule to more serious appreciation. Since then, over the last two decades, the changes Indian fashion has undergone are remarkable; not only due to the wider availability of branded fashion and the presence of a vibrant fashion press with multiple international publications, but also in the way Indian design has evolved towards strengthening its own unique identity that is far from being one-dimensional. Many of my colleagues and peers from NIFT have since gone on to realize hugely successful careers within the field of fashion—some in the limelight as independent designers, and others through designing and managing influential Indian and international brands. Also interesting is that as new ideologies and articulations of design emerge, many within India's fashion industry are now at a point to challenge, question and reinvent the norms of what has come before.

Through its focus on contemporary fashion subsequent to India's liberalization phase, this book adds to the growing academic discourse on fashion in non-Western settings. Building upon such discourse, that unpacks the nuances of fashion in India and provides theoretical frameworks by which it can be studied, serves a crucial role of further supporting local fashion cultures, fashion systems, design and fashionability—which for established Western fashion centers happened much earlier over the last century. In this book, I attempt to (ambitiously) tackle the subject of fashion in India from various angles, and in doing so offer a broad survey ranging from fashion education, design processes and themes, the image of fashion in fashion magazines, to the influence of films, TV and fashion blogs on everyday clothing. Such wide scope that still leaves out various key topics, which could not be accommodated in the framework of a single book, may disappoint some readers. However, the need for such a broad sweep was felt due to the lack of such material and discussions housed in one current and cohesive text. The last such attempts were Meher Castelino's extremely informative *Fashion Kaleidoscope* (1994)—written outside of an academic framework, and Emma Tarlo's *Clothing Matters: Dress and Identity in India* (1996)—an invaluable account of the history of Indian dress during and after the British rule, up until the early 1990s. Other texts such as Hindol Sengupta's

Indian Fashion (2005) and Federico Rocca's *Contemporary Indian Fashion* (2009) though insightful on the subject of fashion designers, do not attempt to theorize their work in a broader context. Most recently publications and books on fashion in India have slowly begun to gain momentum, and it is heartening to note that many of these are emerging from within India. They range from designer biographies (Wendell Rodricks' *Green Room*, Suneet Verma's self-titled book) to the thought-provoking glimpse into the subtleties of the Indian fashion industry in *Powder Room* (Vasudev 2012) by noted fashion editor and columnist Shefalee Vasudev, as well as more frequent appearances about the subject in academic journals, fashion readers and books such as Wilkinson-Weber's *Fashioning Bollywood* (2013). The discussions in these texts, as well as the gaps that they inevitably leave, highlight the potential for further research within this dynamic field.

Indian Fashion is positioned to appeal to a wide audience: Primarily, as an entry level text for fashion students interested in global fashion centers as well as Indian design students interested in a consolidated account of fashion in India written from both an insider's and outsider's perspective. In addition, it is hoped that those who are more fluent with the field of fashion studies or familiar with India will also find this book engaging. The book's framework and style of writing is positioned be accessible to a broad range of readers through clearly presented ideas logically grouped in chapters and subsections that tackle various overarching themes, strategies and concepts that emerged during the book's conception and subsequent research. The research informing this book is a culmi-nation of many years (2007–13) of formal field research and a series of focused interviews (from 2010–13) with fashion professionals that represent various fields of fashion in India (design, production, styling, journalism, blogging, photography and fashionistas). Though it could be said that its process began much earlier during my years at NIFT, and would not have been possible without the networks and connections established as a result of that experience. As with any set of generalizations, there are exceptions, and not all authorities will agree with the discussion in this book. It is possible that over time some of the examples, designers, collections or scenarios mentioned in the book may become dated, be no longer as noteworthy or change significantly going forward—such is the nature of fashion. However the key ideas and concepts it builds upon should undoubtedly remain valuable points of reference.

Overall, this book is intended as an accompaniment to a pivotal moment in the trajectory of Indian fashion itself, as it reinforces its own systems, tastes, culture, termi-nology and cycles—locally and globally. Personally it has been a rewarding journey of discovery and reflection not only on various aspects pertaining to the specificity of fashion within India, but also about what it means to be a locally rooted, fashionable global-*desi*.

LIST OF ILLUSTRATIONS

Cover Off-white silk trench dress with woven silver lotus pattern and blue hem (right), alongside spiral silk dress with woven silver lotus pattern and green hem (left). Both pieces are from Rahul Mishra's Spring/Summer 2011 collection made from *Chanderi* silk woven by Hukum Koli. Image courtesy Rahul Mishra.

Plate Section

Illustrations

A NOTE ON HINDI AND INDIAN TERMS IN THIS BOOK

Italics have been used for all Hindi words in this book. The only exception is the word *sari*, which in some cases is also spelt as *saree* in keeping with quotes and excerpts. Names of cities and people have not been italicized and in some cases footnotes have been provided to give more information about the place or person. Hindi words included in the text have been written using the most common English spelling or those that are most phonetically accurate. In some cases these may differ from those the reader may be familiar with. The English letter 's' has been used to denote the plural form of Hindi words.

A glossary of clothing and general terms used regularly in the book is provided in the following section. Translations for some non-clothing related terms or those used infrequently in the book are provided in brackets within the main text or as footnotes, depending on the explanation needed.

GLOSSARY OF TERMS

Achkan   Knee length coat worn by men. Usually features a Nehru collar.

Anarkali   A knee length or longer kurta with a number of panels or godets.

Angrakha   Long-sleeved full-skirted coat of varying lengths, made of lighter fabric, often featuring a tie front flap detail.

Ari work   Chain stitch embroidery.

Badla work   Style of embellishments that uses pressed metal (gold or silver) wire (*badla*). The wire is inserted into the fabric and beaten, folded and manipulated into different shapes to create various motifs.

Bandhgala or **bandgala** [jacket]   *Bandhgala* literally means closed neck or collar, and refers to Chinese or Nehru collar style jackets.

Bandhini   Also referred to as *Bandhej.* Technique of tie-dye practiced in Rajasthan and Gujarat.

Banyan   Also referred to as a vest. Sleeveless single jersey t-shirt or singlet that is worn as an undershirt by men.

Bindi   Small [red] dot worn on the forehead. Can be applied using *sindoor* (red pigment) or an adhesive stick-on version that comes in various designs, sizes and patterns.

Buti   Small motif (flowers or dots) used as a repeat to create a print pattern or weave design.

Chaddi   Underwear

Chanderi   The name of a town in Madhya Pradesh. Here however the term is used to refer to the fine silk that is woven in this region.

Chikankari   Technique of embroidery practiced in Lucknow. Also known as *chikan* embroidery. Often done in white thread on white semi-sheer fabric. The technique resembles open work or shadow-work as the majority of the thread lies on the wrong side of the fabric.

Choli   Short fitted blouse, with short or long sleeves. Some also feature backless details with lacing.

Chooras   Traditional red and white wedding bangles worn by the bride.

Churidar [salwar]   Tight fitting salwar with extra fabric at the bottom that allows for *churis* or bangle-like folds and gathers to form at the ankles.

Darzi   Tailor

Desi   "Of the nation," which in this book's case literally means Indian.

Dhoti   Unstitched fabric draped and worn as a lower garment by men. The style of draping where the fabric is pulled between the legs and tucked at the back (like a loincloth) also allows it to function like a bifurcated garment (trouser).

Dupatta   Scarf or stole worn around the shoulder or over the head—usually worn with a *salwar kameez.* Also referred to as *chunni* or *odhni.*

Embroidery adda   Raised wooden frame on which fabric that is to be hand embroidered is stretched across.

Gamcha   Thin coarse cotton towel worn around the neck, shoulders or head by men, to wipe sweat off the body or to keep cool. Usually features a checkered weave pattern

Ghaghara   Also spelt *Ghagra*—Short or long gathered skirt.

Ghera   Usually refers to the circumference of a skirt or kurta due to the volume of fabric or number of panels (*kalis*) used.

Half Sari   A style of sari worn by young women in South India—where a *ghaghara* or long skirt is worn on the lower half of the body and a short transparent *dupatta* length of fabric is tucked into the waist of the skirt and then wrapped around the torso to resemble the *Nivi* style.

Ikat   Patterned weave that is created through dyeing the warp and/or weft yarn using a resist dye method, before the weaving process

Jamdani   A very finely woven muslin, with intricate floral patterns. *Jamdani* is woven in the region of Bengal (now Bangladesh and parts of West Bengal).

Joda   Pair or set (when referring to bridal set).

Jutti   Leather shoes, common to North India similar in shape to a ballet flat. The tops and backs often feature decorative embroidery.

Kalamkari   Hand painted or block printed cotton textiles from the state of Andhra Pradesh.

Kali or **Kalidar**   Panels or gores that add to the volume of the skirt segment. *Kalidar* literally means a garment with *kalis* or gores.

Kameez   Term for shirt or *kurta*.

Kanjeevaram Sari   Also known as Kanchipuram sari – in reference to the silk saris woven in the town of Kanchipuram in Tamil Nadu.

Kantha   Iconic embroidery style from West Bengal. Features a number of small straight stitches to fill up the ground as well as creating motifs, used for quilting as well as on saris and other textiles.

Khadi   Handspun or hand-woven cloth. Also referred to as *khaddar.*

Kota Sari   Kota is a city in Rajasthan. Kota saris are made from silk as well as cotton and tend to be of a fine and crisp weave quality, and often feature small checks in the weave.

Koti   Waistcoat

Kundan embroidery   A combination of *Zardozi* and *Kundan* work—where the embroidery comprises of both metal thread work using gold or silver wire as well as precious gemstones.

Kurta   Tunic like shirt. Length can vary from mid hip to knee length or below, depending on the fashion.

Kurti   Short form of the *kurta.* Usually waist or mid thigh length.

Lahariya   A technique of tie-dye practiced in Rajasthan that creates striped and chevron patterns in bands of colors.

Lehenga   A long paneled skirt.

Lungi   Sewn tube of fabric that is wrapped around and tied at the waist and worn as a lower garment.

Mehendi   Henna

Mojri   Similar to *jutti.*

Mundu   Draped lower garment, worn around the waist that resembles a *lungi* or *dhoti*. It is usually woven out of white or cream cotton and often features a narrow decorative strip woven in at the edge.

Nightie   Beyond being worn for bedtime, the nightie is often worn by Indian women at home during the morning or through the day as they go about doing housework and daily errands close to home (like grocery shopping, chatting with neighbors etc.). It resembles a nightgown, but is usually made of sturdier cotton (like a house coat) so that it can be worn for such casual purposes.

Nivi Style (Sari)   In this style one end of the sari is neatly tucked into the petticoat at the waist. After draping the sari fabric around the waist once more it is neatly folded into pleats, which are then tucked into the waistband of the petticoat. It is wrapped around the body one more time so that the decorative end called the *pallu* comes diagonally in front of the torso and is then draped over the left shoulder.

Odhni   See *duppata.*

Pagri   Turban

Pallu   End segment of the sari drape that hangs off the shoulder. Can also be draped over the head or wrapped around.

Parsi Gara   Sari featuring Chinese embroidery with peony, rooster and butterfly motifs on heavy borders or all over the sari that was first introduced in the second half of the 19th C within the Parsi community.

Pashmina   Fine and extremely warm wool yarn from the Pashmina goat that is reared in the Himalayan regions of North India. The term is also used to refer to the textiles made from this wool yarn, which include pure as well as blended yarns.

Patan patola   Double *Ikat* silk saris woven in Patan, Gujarat. There are only a few families in India who have the skill and know-how to weave this iconic sari. One sari can take up to a year to complete—making them extremely expensive, but also exclusive.

Patiala Salwar   Very loose style of salwar.

Pheran   Warm woolen tunic.

Pulkhari   Embroidery style that uses silk floss thread on coarse cotton cloth, done by women in Punjab. The stitches are long floated satin stitches and the motifs tend to be geometric. It is also done on finer fabrics for *dupattas*.

Purdah   Act of veiling or covering the head or entire body. *Purdah* literally means curtain.

Pyjama   Trousers or pants.

Rani   Queen

Resham   Silk or Silky.

Sadri   Sleeveless jacket (like a waistcoat) worn by men and women.

Salwar   Also spelt *Shalwar.* Loose trousers with fitted ankles and a yoke and drawstring at the waist. Usually worn with a *kurta*.

Salwar Kameez   Also spelt *Shalwar Kameez*. Pairing of *Salwar* and *Kurta.* Also know as *salwar* suit or just "suit" in some cases.

Seedha Pallu   Style of wearing the sari where the *pallu* is draped and brought over the right shoulder from the back and covers the front of the torso.

Topi   Cap

Tota   Parrot

Zardozi   Raised metal thread embroidery using gold or silver thread as well as sequins, metal wire etc.

Zari   Metal thread.

1

INTRODUCTION: INDIAN FASHION

In the summer of 2010, while conducting field research on fashion designers in New Delhi, I happened to spot a middle-aged Punjabi[1] lady shopping for vegetables in South Delhi's Kailash Colony[2] market wearing a Kota sari with bright green classic Crocs. At first, the sight was jarring, as I had by other association always considered Crocs to be distinctly ungraceful and certainly not something that I expected to see paired with a sari. However, upon further reflection and acclimatization to the rhythm of everyday life in India, this initially unusual pairing of two geographically distinct items no longer seemed odd. Instead it accurately represented the unique nature of contemporary urban fashion that features vibrant juxtapositions of local styles with global trends and traditional dress practices alongside Western influences and international brands—where designer *churidars* get accessorized with Jimmy Choo Cosma clutches, *Ikat kurtas* liven up *purani* (old) Levis jeans, leather *juttis* stay cozy with argyle socks and zip front wool cardigans can be worn to match the shades of almost any type of sari.

That same summer, much to the delight of Delhi's fashion bloggers, international store Zara was having its first seasonal sale in India. Zara had only recently opened stores in Delhi and Mumbai and the lines for the trial rooms at its City Select Mall location snaked around the store. For those who couldn't afford the marked down sale prices it was an opportunity to look and try, and then find similar styles at Sarojini Nagar's streetside export surplus stalls.

Around the same time, on yet another end of the fashion spectrum, a select group of Indian designers were showcasing their interpretation of Indian couture at the 2010 Pearls Infrastructure Delhi Couture Fashion Week. Though a formalized couture week at that time was a relatively new addition to the annual fashion event calendar, the alignment of traditional dress practices with a reinterpretation of couture to suit the Indian palette had already become a well established and profitable strategy. The platform of Indian couture had not only brought indigenous crafts and handloom textiles to the forefront, but also further ensured the continued relevance of traditional clothing styles within the arena of high fashion. The highlights from 2010's couture week included the launch of JJ Valaya's signature Alika jacket—positioned to rival the iconic Chanel suit. Gaurav Gupta's

---

[1] Hailing from or having ancestral roots in the North Indian State of Punjab.
[2] Most gated residential areas in India are referred to as "housing colonies."

Figure 1.1   Two looks from Sabyasachi Mukherjee's 2010 Couture Collection titled *Aparajito*. Showcased at the 2010 Pearls Infrastructure Delhi Couture Week. Image courtesy Sabyasachi Mukherjee.

models walked down the ramp to a remixed version of the popular Indian children's rhyme *machhli jal ki rani hai,*[3] while audiences gasped upon seeing his infamous sari and *lehenga* gowns embellished with deconstructed Swarovski crystals. Bollywood designer Manish Malhotra's exuberant *anarkalis* had a Spanish influence, while Sabyasachi Mukherjee's much anticipated catwalk show titled *Aparajito*[4] (the unvanquished) opened with the national anthem followed by scenes from the film *1947 Earth*[5] in the backdrop. Sabyasachi's collection exuded a deep nostalgia for the grandeur of India past—its textile heritage, royal ensembles and style icons (Figure 1.1).

This was emphasized through his use of rich muted colors and tarnished embellishments that made the garments appear vintage. The overall style of the garments was primarily traditiona—*lehengas*, saris, *anarkalis*, *achkans*, *angrakhas*, *cholis*, to name a few—the cuts of which were reminiscent of Mughal court ensembles. Positioned as an "epic tale in

[3] Translates to "the fish is the queen of the water."
[4] Named after Satyajit Ray's 1956 Bengali film.
[5] 1947 was also the year India got its independence from British rule.

Indian handloom, *khadi* and *Zardozi*"[6] the collection featured an impressive array of textiles and embellishments sourced from many different parts of India. These included block-prints from Rajasthan, *Kalamkari* from Andhra Pradesh, aged *Zardozi* and *badla* work, and a variety of other handloom textiles decadently layered over each other. Most notable, however, was the fact that 80 percent of the collection was comprised of *khadi*.

Mukherjee's use and transformation of *khadi* as a luxury material for creating couture was not only a thematic decision but also a strategic one—as a statement on the importance of preserving traditional dress and textiles, as well as asserting a sense of distinction for Indian design and fashion. Furthermore, the collection's promotion of Indian handloom also served to underscore his mission to "save the saree."

As indicated by the assortment of vignettes above, the past two decades have witnessed a sea change in the consumption, display, performance, composition and design of fashion in India. The catalyst for much of this can be traced back to the early 1990s and the large-scale economic reforms initiated by the Indian government at that time. Referred to as India's economic liberalization, these reforms were aimed towards making the economy more dynamic, progressive and globally competitive. This period, and the years following, witnessed a marked shift from earlier socialist policies that India had adhered to soon after it gained independence in 1947. While the older political viewpoint focused on modernization and industrial development with a protectionist approach that stressed self-reliance and social justice, India's new neo-liberal policies included an openness to international trade and investment, deregulation, tax reforms, initiation of privatization and various inflation-controlling measures.

Broadly speaking, these policies involved extensive attitudinal changes not only from an economic and political perspective, but also on a socio-cultural level across various strata of Indian society. Through generating new kinds of professional opportunities with increased financial gains, the reforms had a profound impact on the profile of the emerging elite and middle-classes in India, who were now also subject to new ideologies of progress and modernity, a new universe of material goods and new arenas of public display. Changing social roles amongst these urban classes, particularly women, combined with greater financial and social mobility, consumer confidence, and access to commodities and transnational[7] lifestyles—that were previously only within the reach of the elite or those in Western capitalist countries—also had implications on fashionable dress. Alongside an increase in choices with regard to availability of international and national clothing brands, India's fashion industry also transitioned from being largely export-oriented to focusing on local consumers, and supporting emerging indigenous designers towards establishing a strong Indian design aesthetic.

Despite such dynamism and the fact that New Delhi and Mumbai are now counted amongst the world's top fashion cities,[8] the movement and nature of "fashion" in India,

---

[6]Mentioned in the show's publicity material.

[7]I use the term *transnational*, from the concept of transnationalism originally coined by Bourne in the early twentieth century, as opposed to international, due to its reference to the global connectivity between people, beyond national boundaries.

[8]Global Language Monitor, Annual report 2011, http://www.languagemonitor.com/ (accessed August 18, 2011).

when compared to the global acclaim enjoyed by Indian traditional dress and craft practices, remains a lesser-explored subject. My initial research revealed few academic texts or discussions on the topic. Most twentieth century fashion theory regarded fashion as a Western phenomenon and categorized all other forms of non-Western dress as fixed, non- or anti-fashion (Flugel 1971[1930]; Polhemus and Proctor 1978; Hollander 1994; Lipovetsky 1994; Entwistle 2000; Wilson 2003 [1985] etc.). In addressing such inconsistencies between academic discourse and the everyday existence of fashion, combined with the general predominance of stereotypical viewpoints about Indian dress, this book offers a broad survey of contemporary fashion in India as it relates to the emerging urban classes in the decades following the country's liberalization phase. Its aim is to highlight the presence and nature of dress innovation in India, especially in the case of women's attire and its design, and demonstrate that there are other modernities and instances of fashion beyond the viewpoint of American and European fashion history.

Since the majority of the book's discussion is concerned with current dress practices in India, a key point of focus is inevitably the impact of globalization, along with an exploration of the coexistence of tradition and modernity and the resulting hybridity evident in contemporary fashion. Though such characteristics are broadly similar to the way fashion has come to be shaped in other parts of Asia, what gives Indian fashion its own distinctive nature is its specificity to the local context. This includes references to India's individual history, the continued influence of nationalist ideals, the revival and use of Indian crafts and textiles, and consideration for the vibrant and ever-evolving traditions in tandem with the socio-cultural changes taking place subsequent to liberalization. In addition to covering these aspects in depth, a central argument presented in this text is that the time period following the economic reforms brought about its own unique circumstances and identity-based anxieties as a result of which India's globalized middle-class and elite segments once again felt the need for the assertion of a distinct Indian identity, which extended to fashion and dress. Interestingly, this led to the remobilization and reinterpretation of various methods of self-fashioning that saw their roots in the colonial period and Indian nationalism, some of which also reaffirm the lasting influence of Orientalist frameworks. Various strategies of sartorial fusion practiced in response to colonial dress, the nationalist movements and the politics and symbolism of textiles and dress as part of the *Swadeshi* movement[9] continue to resonate in current day constructions of the *desi*-chic look and related design ideals, and form some of the core concepts within the book.

As its subtitle suggests, the book highlights the innovations inherent in the way women's traditional clothing has evolved to date and its continued relevance to fashion—from couture to street. The book's chapters also illustrate various instances where the perceived dichotomy between traditional dress and global fashion has instead led to some very innovative and hybrid sartorial outcomes. As evident in the case of the evolution of the sari, this phenomenon is not new to current times. To support this

---

[9]*Swadeshi* literally means "of the nation." The *Swadeshi* movement, which was part of India's nationalist movement, focused on shunning British machine-made products that had flooded the Indian market, and attempted to support the local Indian economy, Indian-made products, cloth and clothing.

point, the book highlights some key scenarios from the past century and a half that not only demonstrate this, but as indicated above, also remain central to the way fashion functions in India today.

Terms and definitions

While conducting research on the subject of fashion and dress it is not uncommon to come across significant variations in the way clothing terminology is applied and understood. Hence providing a framework of terms and definitions used throughout this book is a crucial starting point for this chapter. Outlining certain dress and fashion-related terms and their meanings, like *costume* and *traditional* [dress], is also necessary as they have frequently been employed [historically] in academic and non-academic texts to include or exclude certain societies and cultures from the phenomenon of *fashion*. Therefore making them potentially loaded terms.

Dress vs. costume

Throughout this text the term *dress* is widely used due to its ability to function as a neutral and inclusive term when referring to clothes or garments of all types and styles. This is in keeping with Eicher and Higgins' definition of *dress* as an "assemblage of body modifications and body supplements displayed by a person and worn at a particular moment in time" (Eicher and Higgins 1992, cf. Eicher, Evenson and Lutz 2000: 4). Alongside *dress,* I use the terms *clothing* and *garment/s* as they too are similarly universal terms for referring to various styles of dress, single or multiple items and outfits. In comparison, I use the term *costume* sparingly while discussing contemporary clothing. This is primarily because close attention to the term *costume* reveals it to be highly problematic due to its usage in reference to "exceptional dress, dress outside the context of everyday life: Halloween costume, masquerade costume, theatre costume" (Baizerman, Eicher and Cerny 2000: 105–6). Hence, making it largely incompatible with the majority of the discussion in this text (barring the segment on film and television). In some cases the term is also used to refer to museum collections and historic repositories of clothing from all cultures (ibid.). Bearing all of these connotations in mind, the term *costume,* when combined or associated with Indian dress, renders it incapable of being viewed as fashion.

Traditional, ethnic *and* modern

The complex nature of terms like *modern* on the one hand, and *traditional* or *ethnic* on the other becomes apparent when they are used in reference to *dress*. This is especially so in the case of most past writings on clothing practices pertaining to non-Western countries, where, for example, when the term *traditional* was applied to *dress* it was done so to denote its likeness to fixed *costume* (Baizerman et al. 2000: 106). Eicher et al. (2000: 45) have found that the term *tradition* is often used to signify practices that come from the past. Similarly, Edensor (2002) states that traditions are commonly conceived and constructed as being opposed to *modern* or modernity, and as a result become linked to notions of authenticity and continuity. In other words, *traditional dress* is regularly viewed as an authentic representation of the past or embedded in ritualized behavior that has been handed down over many generations, which in doing so has remained static or unchanged. The term *ethnic*, linked to ethnicity, signifies group cohesion, common identity, heritage and cultural background, which includes shared language, dress, manners and lifestyle (Eicher and Sumberg 1995). Through its close association with *tradition* and overarching Eurocentric frameworks that continue to impact the reception of the term as Other, *ethnic* is also commonly used in a manner that provokes a romantic, exoticized image.

Edensor challenges popular assumptions linked to such terms through highlighting the need for symbolic cultural elements like traditions and traditional dress to be flexible in order for them to remain relevant over time. Thereby, recognizing traditions as dynamic and dialogic "modern" entities that are "always in the process of being recreated and subject to evaluation in terms of what they bring to a contemporary situation" (Pikering 2001, cf. Edensor 2002: 105). When viewed in this way it is possible to see how traditional dress can and indeed does shift, change and adapt to accommodate new shapes, styles and items from other places and cultures—and in doing so it can be linked to *fashion*. Recent studies on dress and fashion have contributed to the revaluation of the terms *ethnic* and *traditional* especially when applied to non-Western dress. Tarlo (1996), Craik (1994), Cannon (1998) and Maynard (2004) all note the concept of fluidity in traditional and ethnic dress that are subject to the process of fashion change.

In this text I use both terms *ethnic* and *traditional* while discussing contemporary Indian fashion. The term *ethnic* I employ when referring to an overall style or aesthetic that draws from one or various visual elements of indigenous dress, textiles, crafts etc. However, in describing the resurgence of various Orientalist viewpoints, evident in the way fashion is designed and presented in popular visual culture, my use of the term *ethnic* in some cases is deliberately meant to evoke a romanticized or exotic image. I use the term *traditional* to refer to specific garments or styles of dress such as a *kurta* or a sari, as well as Indian textiles and craft techniques employed in making such items. I also use the term *traditional* when it is clear that the style in question is determined or is in keeping with particular social norms or traditions that have evolved over time.

In comparison to *traditional* and *ethnic*, the term *modern*, when applied to dress has commonly come to be associated with all things Western (Breindbach, Pál and Županov 2004) or the influence of Western dress in non-Western settings. Such usage of the term is easily challenged when we view traditional dress styles, like the sari and *salwar kameez*, that have continued to evolve in response to social, cultural and political changes in India *as well as* fashion trends. Bahl (2005) proposes the term *progressive* to aid the understanding of the term *modern* in the context of changing fashions and traditional Indian dress. In doing so she classifies modern clothing as those that we choose to wear according to the socio-cultural and political constraints and frameworks within which we find ourselves. She also demonstrates how the term *traditional* is highly subjective when we regard the various viewpoints by which garments like the sari and *salwar kameez* have come to be read by different wearers at different points of time. For example, the *Nivi* style of tying the sari was considered modern or progressive in the early- and mid-twentieth century, as women actively chose to wear it in favor of other existing styles of tying the sari (Singh 1966; Banerjee and Miller 2003; Bahl 2005). Yet, at the same time it was still classified as traditional dress. Today, the sari is once again being experimented with and stylized by fashion designers, and many in the younger generation choose to wear it in what are now considered "more modern" ways. In the case of the *salwar kameez,* though traditional to Northern India, it has come to be regarded as a modern or progressive garment due to its functionality and is now ubiquitously worn across India.

Local, regional, *desi,* global and Western

As in the case of any discussion on fashion in current times, many of the themes discussed in this book deal with the confluence of local and global cultural aspects towards shaping Indian fashion. I use the term *local* in reference to the style of garments, colors, patterns, crafts, meanings, ways of wearing etc. that are specific and familiar to Indians. While this may appear to be a very broad application of the term—as opposed to a smaller in scale geographical region, city or state, as is usually implied—for the context of this discussion it is appropriate as it not only mirrors its everyday use in India, but also acts as an effective format for clubbing together shared cultural symbols that are understood and valued beyond regional boundaries. However its usage is not necessary linked to the nation-state, thereby distinguishing it from the term *national*. The term *national* I use when it is clear that the style, garment or strategy of self-fashioning has some relation to the nation-state or is used to evoke a patriotic response. When the term *regional* is used, it is done so to refer to an item or style of dress that is specific to a particular region or part of India. Examples of this include the *Nauvari* sari, Kerala *mundu,* Himachali *topi*, the South Indian half-sari etc. Here it must be noted that due to the multicultural composition of urban cities and processes of fashionalization, many regional items are now worn across India.

The term *desi*, which literally means "of the nation," is also used frequently in the text to highlight instances where there is an additional assertion of pride and belonging stemming from the local. This is evident in the way the term is extensively used in India as an alternative to *local* or *indigenous*. Through its usage in mainstream cinema, songs and other forms of popular media, the term *desi* is now much more familiar globally and evokes a sense of pride and shared belonging not only amongst Indians in India, but also amongst the wider Indian Diaspora.

In comparison the term *global* is used in this text to refer to items of dress, fashion and trends that are now ubiquitously worn across the globe. While it is possible to trace the origins of some of these items or aspects of items to one particular source or origin, as is in the case of denim jeans, through the forces of globalization they are no longer anchored to any one source or territory. Instead the perceived meaning and modes of wearing of many such global items of clothing can differ from one culture to the next. Maynard attributes these changes to the way a particular group of people within a culture assigns meaning to certain items, as a result of the ways in which these items have been introduced, presented, received and adapted to local settings (Maynard 2004). Hence, despite the general uniformity of global dress, it tends to be worn in ways that are locally distinctive (ibid.: 16). This is in keeping with wider studies on globalization that highlight how contemporary forces of globalization rely heavily on local influences for wider and long-term impact (Hall 1997).

Originally when I set out to write this book, I had intended to reserve the use of the term *Western* (dress or fashion) for instances when there was evidence of a direct influence or reference to Western culture in the way the clothes or styles are worn or perceived in India. Examples of this range from the mediated flow of fashion trends from Western fashion centers like Paris and New York, that are adapted as authentically as possible (such as the "Jane Austen look"); or the appropriation of men's cowboy styles and the "Wild West" in Bollywood film sequences; or instances when Indians themselves make the differentiation between Indian and Western [clothes] especially in dealing with issues of modesty or the experience of modernity. However, through my field research and review of collected materials, I quickly realized that in India clothing items that Eicher et al. (2000) categorize as *world* or *global dress* are still referred to as *Western*. For this reason, despite the risk of appearing to perpetuate an East/West divide, I continue to use the term *Western* for most global styles and trends, as it is a more accurate portrayal of how Indians refer to them.

Fashion

Finally, *fashion* is undeniably a complicated concept to define simply, especially as there are so many interpretations of the phenomenon. Adding to the difficulty is the lack of materials prior to the start of the twenty-first century that seriously examine fashion outside of Western centers. Since the English term *fashion* itself has no direct translation in Hindi or Urdu, its earlier usage in India was also for the most part limited to the context of Westernization of men's and women's dress, or to the impact of external influences as opposed to indigenous ones especially from a critical standpoint (Nagrath 2003).[10]

While the following subsection addresses some of the issues pertaining to fashion theory's Eurocentric leanings and how the study and classification of fashion can be

---

[10]Such a viewpoint is echoed in Joshi's account on "continuity and change in Hindu women's dress," where he refers to fashion "as a word and as a concept ... [as the] deviation from the [traditional] norms of dress, and in the feminine context, generally the adoption of *alien dress* and the wearing of Western dress in the masculine context" (Joshi 1992: 220, emphasis mine) Such critiques tend to confuse *fashion* with Westernization—that is wasteful, opposed to national values of austerity and aligned with the emerging middle classes blindly mimicking the West—and fear the loss of the dignity and individualism achieved through wearing traditional dress (Varma 1998: 156).

re-evaluated in a manner that is more globally inclusive, with regard to this book's overall discussion I am in agreement with the core aspect upon which most definitions of *fashion* coincide—that is centered on the notion of style change. What causes the change in styles of dress worn at a given time is the process of fashion (Kawamura 2005). This process not only differs depending on the place and time period, it is also reliant on a system of interrelated institutions. These include groups of manufacturers, designers, retailers, journalists, promoters and consumers, all of which contribute to the making of fashion (Kawamura 2005: 43). In this way, the system of fashion is a "hybrid subject" (Leopold 1992: 102), characterized by the interrelationships between various forms of production and volatile patterns of consumption and demand (ibid.). Also relevant to this book's discussion in favor of fashion in India is Kawamura's assertion that irrespective of their size and place, *all* fashion systems have certain basic features in common—where "[t]he minimum requirement is a network of people that includes those who introduce or propose changes in dress and those who adopt at least a portion of the proposed changes … [and the] proposers and adopters … must be in communication with each other," either directly or indirectly through advertising and other forms of mass communication (Kawamura 2005: 48). And while not all clothing fits under the category of fashion, all clothing systems have the ability to possess some relationship with fashion systems and stylistic conventions linked to such systems (Craik 1994: 2).

Theorizing fashion beyond *its* traditional boundaries

Up until the start of the twenty-first century almost all writings on the subject of fashion and dress were unanimous in classifying fashion as an invention of the West. In these texts fashion was categorized under "the exclusive purview of 'civilized' nations [while] clothing systems of the colonial Other were considered to be non-fashion, or negative image: a sign of the child-like mentality of the prototypical 'primitive'"(Brydon and Niessen 1998: xi). Such claims mirror older Orientalist stereotypes that regarded those societies once associated with the Orient, as backward and resistant to change (Said 1995 [1978]) and therefore opposed to the fashion process. They also subconsciously reflect another Orientalist belief in the absolute and systematic difference between the East and West—the latter of which was rational, developed and superior, while the former was underdeveloped, inferior, irrational and effeminate (Said 1995 [1978]: 300).[11] The extent to which these assumptions remain deeply entrenched in Western thought even in recent times is evident in Lipovetsky's (1994) discussion on "Fashion and the West" where he aggressively argues against the possibility of fashion outside of the West. According to

---

[11] An example of the Western view of the Orient is evident in Garve's essay titled "On Fashion" published in 1792 which states that, "[t]he monarchy is the seat and source of fashions … [but a] single despot holding all in subjection, *like the Orientals*, is too removed from the masses, too invisible and too terrible to become an object of imitation" (Garve 1792 reproduced in Purdy 2004: 68, emphasis mine).

Lipovetsky, the social composition of non-Western civilizations, with their emphasis on ancestral legacies, social continuity, "meticulous reproduction of the past" and strict conservatism (which he terms "hyperconservative") means that "the process and the idea of fashion is completely *meaningless*" (Lipovetsky 1994: 18, emphasis mine). Lipovetsky maintains, that even in contemporary times (in the 1990s), the emergence of modern systems of state and class divisions still haven't shaken the permanence these social systems rely on, whereby "the same tastes, the same ways of doing, feeling and dressing have been perpetuated unchanged" (ibid.: 19). Other fashion theorists writing around the same time also share similar views on fashion. For example, Hollander maintains that fashionable dress is very different from ethnic and traditional dress. In her view traditional dress is more about preservation and the "confirmation of an established custom" (Hollander 1994: 17), while [Western] fashion is "relentlessly secular, at odds with the ceremonial and unifying esthetic impulses that produce garments like the *chador*[12] and *sari*" (ibid.: 15).

The firm association of fashion with the West as a result of Orientalist thought is a key reason behind the lack of materials documenting the presence of fashion in other settings, thus further limiting the possibilities of exploring its role in other cultures (Canon 1998). While clothing was meticulously studied and documented outside of the West prior to contemporary times, group and individual styles of adornment in such settings were usually linked to tradition and social roles. Tarlo (1996) finds that there was often a tendency to select styles that were classified as "traditional" for being the most "authentic" representation of local culture. This inevitably led "to a sifting out of many contemporary forms of dress, such as trousers, shirts and plastic flip-flops, all of which may still have important social significance" (ibid.: 3). Referring to this as the "museum approach to clothing" (ibid.), Tarlo notes that such systems of classification influenced the way cloth and clothing were studied by colonial ethnographers and early anthropologists (ibid.), who failed to recognize the fashion process due to the short period of time they witnessed a particular style of clothing (Niessen 2003). Thus, adding to the misconceptions surrounding Indian dress, for example, and the false impression that all traditional dress was fixed or static. When there were instances of recorded style changes, these were attributed to other events and external forces, such as acculturation and not to fashion, because of the "myth of traditional conservatism" (Cannon 1998: 24). It is most likely that if theories pertaining to the processes of fashion had been applied to the study of stylistic evolution and diversity of non-Western dress at the time, one would most certainly find greater evidence supporting the universal and global presence of fashion prior to current times.

The categories of difference created through Orientalist belief systems also played out in the way clothing and dress practices in the colonies was critiqued for being primitive when it did not meet Western levels of modesty. Yet, when presented with elaborate or sophisticated styles of dress it was common for these styles to be ridiculed and reduced to "simply bad or excessive" or effeminate style (Jones and Leshkowich 2003:

---

[12] Veil worn by Muslim women.

9). This approach, also highlighted by Tarlo (1996), was instrumental in the assertion of power, both moral and political, by the colonizer over the colonized. This continues to have a lasting impact on societies in non-Western settings, as they come to view their traditional forms of dress as less progressive when compared to Western fashion. Aside from this, the impact of Orientalist viewpoints have also in many cases led to the mobilization of traditional dress as mediums of asserting distinction in these settings. As will be discussed in following segments and chapters, this is especially the case for the growth and development of non-Western design cultures where strategies of "re-Orientalism"[13] remain popular. However, gaining global recognition for such design and the innovations inherent in traditional forms of dress remains an ongoing struggle.

In light of the imbalances that have long existed in the way fashion has been theorized up until the end of the last century, Craik (1994), Cannon (1998) and Niessen (2003) emphasize the need for a closer examination of fashion beyond its traditional borders and a re-evaluation of the definition of fashion to be more globally inclusive. In doing so they challenge the Eurocentric stereotypes that in essence helped manufacture the definition of "who had" fashion and "who didn't" (Niessen 2003), especially as we see legitimate instances of fashion beyond Western centers, that are equally dynamic and vibrant as those in the West. Critical to the discussion in this text is Niessen's (2003) reinterpretation of the Eurocentric definition of *fashion* and *anti-fashion*, coined by Polhemus and Proctor (1978), which makes it ispossible to shift from viewing non-Western systems of dress as not having fashion, to viewing them as fashion systems that evolve relative to Western fashion (ibid.: 252–3). Niessen highlights how such definitions helped preserve the boundaries between the West and the Rest. However, while the creation of an opposite in *anti-fashion* was needed in order to maintain Western fashion's position of power and act as a medium of self-definition (2003: 257), the same is true for non-Western centers for which the maintenance of the conceptual guise of traditional dress allowed for the preservation of a crucial point of difference. This, as Niessen describes, in some cases led to the intentional production of anti-Western fashion (ibid.: 257–8). The discussion in the book highlights how the creation of intentional points of difference played out in Indian clothing in historic times continues to shape contemporary design philosophies as well as methods of visual representation of Indian fashion.

Both Cannon (1998) and Craik (1994) have found that most non-Western and pre-industrial cultures do demonstrate the presence of some form of fashion-related phenomena. These include fashion comparison, emulation and differentiation. Cannon believes it all depends on how we categorize fashion—beyond its universal definition "as an agent of style change" (Cannon 1998: 23). When seen as a system of rapid and continuous style changes, made up of short-term ephemeral fads, fashion naturally

---

[13]Lau and Mendes (2011) define re-Orientalism as "the resurfacing of new manifestations of Orientalism" (Lau and Mendes 2011: 5). While Orientalism, as theorized by Said (1995 [1978]) is centered around the construction of the "Orient" by the West—devised to maintain authority over the East; "re-Orientalism is based on how cultural producers with eastern affiliations come to terms with an orientalized East" (Lau and Mendes 2011: 3). This happens either through complying and playing along with preconceived notions and expectations set by the West and the [older] rhetoric of Orientalism, "or by discarding them altogether" (ibid.).

becomes excluded from the domain of non-Western non-industrial or traditional societies prior to current times. Such a narrow way of viewing fashion tends to eliminate legitimate instances of systematic style changes and self-fashioning that occur in all cultures, which may be spurred on by circumstances that have little to do with the random style changes or planned obsolescence, for example, that are found in Western industrialized societies. In her discussion on fashion in China, Finnane (2008) reiterates the same concern, where on one hand she notes how recent [academic] work on Chinese dress shows evidence of short-term style changes but "[w]hether this amounts to 'fashion' depends on how fashion is defined ... When fashion is defined very narrowly on the basis of particular empirical detail about a 'particular sort of society,' the possibility of any other clothing culture being defined as 'fashion', is by definition excluded" (Finnane 2008: 9).

Prior to more recent times of wide-scale industrial development and globalization, it is more appropriate to separate the concept of "fashion" from "fashion industry" when attempting to explore fashion outside of non-Western settings (Finnane 2008). Finnane distinguishes the two by viewing the former in terms of its relation to taste, consumption and urbanization that entails "short-term vicissitudes in vestimentary choices, and indicates the presence in particular societies of dynamic relationships between producers and consumers" (ibid.: 43). In comparison, a fashion industry is a more recent modern phenomenon brought about through the industrial revolution. Like other non-Western countries, India did not have an established fashion industry until the later half of the last century, but it did possess thriving and extensive trade in textiles for local consumption.

In order to have a more inclusive definition of fashion, Cannon and Craik propose a basic version that still centers around style change, but avoids putting limitations on the speed or nature at which change occurs. Cannon suggests we focus on stylistic emulation and differentiation that isn't only linked to class structures and societies that have an established class system, such as that proposed by Veblen and Simmel, but also include distinctions in status, wealth and skill (Cannon 1998: 24), aspects which are common to all cultures. In this way we can see "fashion develop in all contexts as a result of self-identity and social comparison" (ibid.: 24). For Cannon the underlying common thread between fashion systems in different cultures is the ability and desire to manipulate one's appearance to "enhance or maintain a positive self image" (ibid.: 25) as well as attempting to derive some positive value from being distinctive in that appearance when faced with mandated or collective style conformity. He highlights that any significant event or extraordinary situation can create the impetus for fashion and bring about instances of elaboration, diversification and emulation in a culture (ibid.: 25). According to Craik, a "fashion system embodies the denotation of acceptable codes and conventions, sets limits to clothing behaviour, prescribes acceptable—and proscribes unacceptable—modes of clothing the body, and constantly revises the rules of the fashion game" (Craik 1994: 5). Additionally Berry defines fashion as a "system of conventions that require both constant innovation and individual decision-making" (Berry 2001: 456). Considering these definitions, it becomes possible to see "fashioning the body" as a feature that all cultures possess "although specific technologies of fashion vary between cultures" (Craik 1994: 5).

Even though Entwistle (2000) has critiqued Craik's claim of fashion existing outside of the West based on the inability to propose an alternate feasible definition or theory that can replace those that situate fashion within the framework of Western capitalism, my assertion is that the three criteria Entwistle herself sets forth that support the phenomenon of fashion are all very much in existence and thriving in India. These are namely: social mobility, production and consumption (i.e. a fashion system), and regular and systematic change (Entwistle 2000: 47–8).

Making a case for fashion in India

> To many foreigners, the saree is perceived as the only costume of Indian women. This misconception may be attributed to the fact that the majority of foreign officials who visit India do not come in contact with college students but may meet wives of the high officials. At such functions the women are attired in the saree. (Chowdhary 1984: 168)

The richness and grandeur of Indian dress and textiles have long been researched, collected, and admired, with numerous texts published on these subjects. Many of these texts offer detailed accounts on the evolution of dress and adornment in India that spans many centuries. Such accounts mention multiple style changes that have come about through various social interactions and local design ingenuity in response to the specific surroundings and new social, political, cultural and economic shifts of the time. Global trade and interaction with other societies have also played a part in this vestimentary history. Personal appearance, dress and body adornment techniques were highly valued as far back as the Indus Civilization (2500–1500BC), which is evidenced by terracotta and stone figurines found from this time period that indicate the use of stitched garments, knee-length skirts and jewelry (Pathak 2006). Miniature paintings from the Mughal period (sixteenth to the nineteenth century AD) also illustrate elaborate stitched garments embellished in gold and silver embroidery worn as court ensembles. Ghurye (1966, cf. Chowdhary 1984: 19) finds evidence of the significance of being well dressed in the literary remains from the Vedic age (1500–500 BC), where terms like *suvasna* (splendid garments), *surbhi* (well-fitted garments) and *suvasa* (well dressed) were commonly used. A more recent history of Indian dress and fashion over the past century and a half bears evidence of numerous innovative, aesthetically vibrant and sometimes politically charged instances whereby new styles of clothing have been introduced, received, selectively adopted and adapted by men and women.

Despite this, most academic texts and popular opinion on the subject of Indian dress continue to refer to it as "costume" and view fashion as a recent phenomenon. It is obvious, as noted in the quote above, that such a general misrepresentation of India's dynamic vestimentary history acts as a point of frustration for many within India, especially as Indian adornment techniques, drapes and indigenous crafts have themselves collectively acted as a rich source of inspiration in shaping fashions across the world.

If one were to apply to some of the revised theories of fashion mentioned in the previous section, then the sartorial landscape over the past century and a half along with the nature of introduction of new styles into the Indian wardrobe definitely affirm the presence of fashion in India. The development of complex and sophisticated codes of dress that reflect individual and collective identity, shaped by socially prescribed norms and conditions of the time are in line with Cannon and Craik's aforementioned characterization of fashion. In addition, the presence of sophisticated methods of local and global trade, textile production and design innovation fulfills many of the criteria required of a fashion system as set forth by Kawamura (2005)—that relies on networks of people, producers, designers, style leaders etc. who introduce and propose changes in dress, while being in contact with the larger social group who eventually come to adopt the same styles. Through dissecting some of the older Eurocentric theories on fashion, it is possible to find similarities between patterns of display, social mobility and self-fashioning in India and fashion in the West during the early part of the twentieth century—a time when fashion's presence in Western settings was actively written about. My intention here is not to say that Indian fashion was or is *like the West*, as even though fashion is a global phenomenon, its experience and meaning (like that of modernity itself) is dependent on the location of its production, as well as the interactivity between different global locations (Breckenridge and Appadurai 1995). However, through highlighting the parallels between fashion behavior in the West and India, it is possible to strengthen the argument in favor of its existence beyond the West.

To begin with, a general tenet of most social theories on fashion is that in order for fashion to exist there needs to be fluidity in a social system to allow for upward mobility; thus, making social competition, emulation and distinction through consumption key aspects of the fashion process (Veblen 1894; Simmel 1904, 1957 etc.). Historically this has been applied towards excluding dress practices in non-Western societies from the definition of and discussions about fashion. In the case of India, there was and still is the general assumption that religious beliefs and an impermeable caste system together impose clothing restrictions on people that cannot be challenged or changed. In reality, however, there is indeed evidence of the elite classes in India, even prior to independence during the early twentieth century and prior, displaying high levels of luxury consumption through local and global networks that ensured they were up to date with the latest trends within India and those emanating from the West. In addition to this, the emergence of India's middle-class during British rule as a new social entity that also showcased strong patterns of social competition further support Simmel and Veblen's theories of conspicuous consumption and social mobility through dress.

Another key aspect that has historically excluded clothing in India and similar non-Western cultures from discussions on fashion is the link to "tradition," and the assumption that traditional values combined with religious beliefs make it impossible for dress to change like fashion in the West does. Various indigenous accounts of dress in India have further perpetuated the image of Indian dress as unchanging and static, and part of an age-old system of traditional values and beliefs prescribed by generations of people who have dressed in similar styles. Such accounts present clothing in India as being completely incompatible with the mechanisms of fashion.[14] It is true that certain styles of dress, like the sari, have evolved through their close connection to tradition. In some cases the wearing of certain items, like the Sikh turban, is prescribed by a certain

---

[14]Once again, Joshi's (1992) account of Hindu women's dress outlines the way Hinduism prescribes certain codes on men's and women's dress. According to Joshi, style, color, material and method of wearing are all in theory strictly regulated by basic Hindu principles and customs (Joshi 1992: 214).

religion or caste, as a result of which they come to signify the wearer's identity and affili-ation to a specific social group. Yet closer examination of these items of dress leads to the discovery of more complex reasoning behind how and why certain groups have come to wear them, as well as the innovative trends and subtle style shifts they have undergone while simultaneously functioning within prescribed regional and cultural frameworks. In the case of the turban such trends range from the use of *lahariya* textiles, shiny polyester fabric, to pre-tied versions with the Nike logo emblazoned on them.

The sari's continued evolution over the past century and a half provides further instances of its re-fashioning. This is highlighted in Justina Singh's doctoral research from the 1960s, which focuses on the adoption of the modern style of wearing the sari[15] by educated Indian women. Her research is worth noting here, as it was undertaken at a time when no academic text equated clothing in India with fashion and sheds light on the way women's traditional dress styles were evolving and subject to fashion change during the 1960s (Singh 1966). Singh's study found a major shift amongst educated urban women towards wearing the *Nivi* style of sari, made popular in the early part of the twentieth century, in comparison to older generations (mothers and grandmothers) who mainly wore regional styles. Her research respondents were also largely unaware of the symbolism behind traditional textiles, colors,[16] patterns and motifs, and favored more so the fashions of the time while purchasing clothing. Overall Singh's findings point clearly towards the presence of fashion change that directly impacted her respondents' choices in dress, and debunks the theory that Indian women's dress strictly follows prescribed codes, or that traditions are static. Also notable is Singh's observation that "through wearing the modern Indian sari there was no longer a distinction between different regions, religions or *jati*" (ibid.).[17] This falsifies Western claims of the absence of secular clothing styles in India and provides evidence of modern fashion at play, bringing unified style to different groups. Following from Singh, Chowdhary's doctoral research in the 1980s focused on exploring fashion opinion leadership[18] amongst college-going women[19] in North India (Chowdhary 1984). Chowdhary found strong similarities between her sample in India[20] and Western research regarding the fashion adoption process—"through which a new style (an innovation) is transmitted from the point of its creation [by fashion innovators and opinion leaders and then widely diffused and adopted by fashion followers] to eventual obsolescence" (King 1963; cf. Chowdhary and Dickey 1988: 183).[21]

---

[15] This refers to the *Nivi* style of wearing the sari.

[16] "Of the 150 respondents, 130 checked that they had no restrictions regarding color... and many indicated that colors were selected according to an individual's personal liking or choice, and 125 had checked that they *purchased colors currently in fashion*" (Singh 1966: 303, emphasis mine).

[17] Term used to denote tribe, caste, clan or community.

[18] A fashion opinion leader is an individual who serves as a source of information advice for other individuals, who can be considered fashion followers (Schrank 1970, cf. Chowdhary 1984).

[19] Her reason for choosing such a sample was because the younger generation are more open to change and more likely to partake in fashion emulation—a fact that is similar across the globe.

[20] Comprising of 509 respondents.

[21] Chowdhary's study found that 35.4 percent of the respondents fitted into the category of fashion opinion leaders, which was similar to studies conducted in the West (Summer 1970, cf. Chowdhary and Dickey 1988) and is evidence of the group's openness to change—a crucial factor in the fashion process.

In addition to these two cases, various studies on adornment practices, local trade and retail networks in smaller cities (Shukla 2005, 2008) and rural centers (Tarlo 1996), combined with Meher Castelino's personal experiences of an emerging fashion industry as a model in the 1960s (Castelino 1994) are all just a few of the many examples that bear evidence to the presence of dynamic "fashion systems" that are simultaneously mindful of local expectations and Indian traditions.

The chapters that follow further illustrate instances that challenge common assumptions about traditional dress and fashion in historic settings as well as in contemporary times. In doing so they emphasize how traditions and traditional dress remain central to the process of fashion as they continue to evolve and exist within almost every nuance of personal and public life in India. When it comes to the time period that this book mainly focuses on, the emergence of a vibrant local fashion industry, Indian editions of international fashion magazines and the display of personal style and street fashion, documented through fashion blogs by "fashionistas" from large cities like Delhi to smaller cities like Kanpur—further affirm theories of modern fashion as they relate to cycles of change, style obsolescence, collective consumer selection and fashion systems, to name a few, and also demonstrate local innovation, global interaction and collaboration.

Desi-chic: An overview of fashion in India post-liberalization

> We pair fluorescent orange with electric blue, or *rani* pink with *tota* green without batting an eyelid. An Indian woman will wear a Kanjeevaram sari with a *bandhini* blouse and see nothing wrong with it. Wedding *chooras* with blue denims, *mojris* with chiffon dresses, boots with *seedha* (straight) *pallu* saris, turtle neck sweaters with Rajasthani *ghaghras*. We combine fake labels with real rubies, throw in a hippie stole from Goa with a sequined blouse from Delhi's Janpath! Sometimes, all at once. (Vasudev 2010)

Though it is apparent through my discussion in the previous section that the main theories that define fashion in the West fit seamlessly with the way fashion in India functions, what is worn in India presently, though cohesive on many levels with wider global fashion trends, is not simply a copied form of Western fashion. No matter how much Western dress may *appear* to displace traditional dress styles, clothes still need to be worn in a specific "fashion" in order to function within certain localized constructs for their meanings to be transmitted convincingly. In India, this relates as much to the past as it does to present-day pressures of modernity, and takes into consideration the evolving sense of national identity that is "not a once and for all thing" and can be "dynamic and dialogic" (Edensor 2002: 17). Hence, fears of globalization having a homogenizing impact on all aspects of indigenous societies and obliterating local cultures are easily dispelled, especially as traditional styles remain highly relevant to daily life in India and are worn as everyday dress, not costume.

Vasudev accurately sums up contemporary Indian fashion in the quote above as an eclectic mix of traditional and regional garments worn alongside global or Western styles, which include real or fake versions of popular (and luxury) international brands like Nike, Adidas, Ralph Lauren or Zara, to name a few. McGowan credits this aesthetic of "eclecticism" to the centuries of "sartorial juxtapositions" of dissimilar objects and combinations of different styles that have been introduced or developed in India (McGowan 2005: 272) and Mitra (2005) uses the term *hybrid* to describe Indian clothing that has mixed indigenous and global elements through most of its recent history. Visually and conceptually, the co-existence of numerous clothing styles that are also multifunctional in their nature remains a key characteristic of Indian fashion. This is not only visible at any and every street setting, mall or social function; even the designs showcased at fashion weeks (there are many) demonstrate a similar visual and sartorial diversity. Moreover it makes dress practices in India different when compared to some of the other non-Western countries where traditional styles like the Japanese Kimono or Korean Hanbok have undergone a linear cycle of change from everyday dress to being replaced by global styles (Slade 2009).

In order to further understand India's sartorial landscape in current times, it is important to note that the experience and meaning of fashion in India differs considerably when we consider the various social groups, religious and regional differences that co-exist within such a vast country. There are also obvious variances between large metropolitan areas and smaller cities, towns and villages in terms of consumption patterns and proliferation of global styles. Fashions become further distinguished by region—regional tastes, textile crafts and preferences pertaining to prevalent dress practices and other cultural factors. As an example, it is not uncommon to hear about the blingy flashiness of North India, compared to the cool, casual yet more fashion-forward cosmopolitanism of Mumbai, and the chic understated sophistication of the East. There are also cases where there is a greater preference for certain brands (like Ed Hardy in Amritsar) in some regions as opposed to their failure in others. Additionally the experience and meaning of fashion differs based on social demographics and class structures, the latter of which are very much prevalent in India and in some cases these have replaced older caste and religious segmentation. Various social commentators have affirmed this shift through noting a lessening impact of the caste system, but a heightened social system that is almost as rigid in urban India (Eckhardt and Mahi 2004). Bearing all of these factors in mind, it is possible to locate multiple fashion systems within India with individual fashion curves and system of trends.

Despite such variances, there also exist multiple commonalities in these systems brought about by a shared sense of culture, tradition, national pride, common nodes of collective nostalgia, exposure to national and global media, and popular culture, that this book examines in following chapters. Alongside key social and cultural factors, fashion is highly responsive to various local and global style axes that regularly converge through films, fashion magazines and related visual media, and other mediums of popular culture, which like clothing also rely on global (and local) networks for their framework and content. Bollywood, India's popular film industry, has historically been a key setter of fashion trends and continues to be influential across the nation in current times and is hence an excellent medium for brand promotion. The past few decades have also seen a growing popularity of television in influencing fashions, especially in the arena of traditional style innovation. Fashion magazines, many of which are Indian editions of international periodicals, such as *Elle* and *Vogue*, play a central role in promoting branded clothing, high fashion and couture off Indian and Western catwalks to their readers. Furthermore, these visual formats also emphasize the assertion of locally specific style identities— through the fusion of local and global cultural factors. Together these mediums not only impact the sartorial choices of individual fashion systems, but also give shape to Indian fashion and its aesthetics as a whole. While regional dress styles are still worn in rural areas, smaller towns and cities, most large metropolitan centers have witnessed a shift towards universal [Western] styles for men, and a preference for the *salwar kameez* and various iterations of the *kurti* along with a growing acceptance of Western styles for women.

Popular trends in clothing typically trickle-down from on- and off-screen fashions worn by celebrities and movie stars, as well as trickle-up from rural or tribal styles of dress into mainstream fashion. In addition we see the movement of trends trickle-across within social groups in India, as well as from similar social segments across the globe (including the widely spread out Diaspora) with whom it is now possible to find obvious commonalities in dress practices and other cultural factors brought about through shared experiences of globalization. Overall, the system of trends and fashion change responds as much to global influences and seasons (summer, brief winter) as it does to various annual festivals and rituals linked to these festivals (*Diwali, Holi* etc.), thus highlighting the local specificity of fashion change.

Also central to the nature of contemporary fashion is the emergence of "new" upwardly mobile and highly cosmopolitan[22] elite and middle-class segments in the decades following liberalization, which has led to a marked shift in the way fashion is consumed, viewed, worn and performed in urban settings. Bolstered by economic gains over the past two decades, and the overall sense of positivity experienced as a result of these gains, this time period is characterized by the sharp rise in conspicuous consumption amongst the urban classes. The eagerness to display material possessions and economic success to the rest of the world has been further encouraged through the emergence of new avenues and sites for display of fashion—such as shopping malls, clubs, luxury resorts, and online formats of fashion blogging and recording street style. The overall shift away from India's older nationalist ideals that emphasized austerity has also meant that there are now fewer stigmas attached to showing off these lifestyles. In tandem with such attitudinal changes, all forms of visual media actively promote idealized constructions of [upper] middle-class lifestyles that place importance on designer and branded items, as well as close copies, as markers of success. The influx of luxury products as well as the positioning of affordable luxury towards an ambitiously minded middle-class is evident in these visual formats. The increased emphasis on celebrity

---

[22] Here cosmopolitanism "entails an intellectual and aesthetic openness towards divergent cultural experiences, a search for contrasts rather than uniformity" (Hannerz 1996: 103) and is about "international integration" beyond the structure of the nation (ibid.: 102–3).

culture and related fashion has further led to the promotion of high-fashion and luxury brands along with Indian couture.

In charting similar shifts amongst the middle-class in Nepal, Liechty has found that fashion and adornment is a theme that links the past to the present, but its meaning is constantly changing (Liechty 2003: 125). This is similar in India, where like past instances of body adornment, contemporary fashion too is about procurement, trend consciousness and "amount." The only difference is that the kind of items this applies to continue to differ (ibid.). For example, where previously fashion may have been about gold jewelry and expensive hand-embellished saris, it is now about branded handbags and designer saris.

Fashion in the time period after liberalization is additionally characterized by a heightened interplay between local and global style factors as a result of increased globalization. Much like the cultural shifts being experienced concurrently by the urban classes, this confluence is more complex and multi-layered than a simple case of "East meets West" or Westernization of Indian clothing; especially as liberalization brought with it a renewed sense of anxiety about the preservation of Indian identity in the wake of global influences. As a result, despite the general imbalance of the flow of ideas, goods and media that trickle across from the West, there exist various (and vibrant) intersections of local and global dress practices—where both inform each other to insure their acceptance, and continued relevance to society.

This is similar to other observations in non-Western centers that demonstrate the coexistence of global homogeneity alongside vibrant and locally relevant heterogeneity in dress. In the case of India, various strategies of self-fashioning have evolved that allow Indian wearers to adapt different clothing styles to suit their lifestyles. The need to simultaneously fulfill the specificity of Indian tastes, climate, traditions, levels of modesty, morality and comfort and other cultural factors requires a significant injection of localization into Western or global styles of dress. Simultaneously, to ensure traditional styles do not appear outmoded or out of sync in current times, they too are subject to regular reinterpretations with global trends in mind. Such instances of localization, globalization and glocalization,[23] done either by the wearer or designer, take many forms that involve fusing Indian and Western aesthetics, such as color palettes, embellishments and print patterns, to wearing global or Western and Indian styles in unison, to indigenizing Western styles or Westernizing Indian styles. The resulting visual smorgasbord of colors, patterns, details and silhouettes can be overwhelming to an unfamiliar and untrained eye, and misread as bad taste or non-fashion.[24] But for India's burgeoning urban population such sartorial experimentations are logical extensions of their own construction of personal and collective identity, which involve similar negotiations between local and global culture on a daily basis.

Stylistically the resulting look is commonly referred to as Indo-Western, fusion fashion, or *desi*-chic and has led to the popularity of certain hybrid styles of clothing such as the

---

[23] My use of the term *glocalization* refers to instances where global products are adapted to local cultures and consumers.

[24] As evident in Guy Trebay's review of India Fashion Week in 2005, where he labeled Indian design as "More is more, in other words, with a dollop of too much" (Trebay 2005).

kurta for men and women, the *kurti*, the *salwar kameez*, *dhoti* pants for example, and now most recently once again the sari. Nagrath (2003) sees such fusion as a reflection of a "deep-rooted desire to move away from the limiting world of tradition to a more liberating world of global fashion" (Nagrath 2003: 366). However having a mutually beneficial framework between local culture and global influences has allowed for the preservation and maintenance of traditional values, beliefs, cloth and clothing that Indians are so fiercely proud of; alongside the possibility of enjoying highly attractive modes of experiencing modern lifestyles that are on par with the rest of the world. Therefore ensuring the compatibility of Indian and Western garments as a strategy for personal and collective styling not only acts as a medium for experiencing global modernity but also for maintaining a point of distinction (Tarlo 1996) while experiencing a sense of national pride (Mukherjee 2013 cf. Kashyap 2013a).

Beyond the indigenization of clothing and/or accessories by consumers as a result of their social conditioning, Kondo (1997), Niessen et al. (2003), amongst others, note the resurgence of Orientalist viewpoints in the conscious "auto-exoticization" of various indigenous cultural signs and symbols by designers in non-Western settings—which they regard as one of the outcomes of globalization. This can be noted in the renewed interest in historic dress and textile practices, crafts and vernacular cultural forms across various fields of design in India. The heightened importance of locality and local identity in dress is especially evident in the work of Indian fashion designers[25] like Ritu Kumar, JJ Valaya and Sabyasachi Mukherjee, who revive and incorporate historic clothing, textiles and embellishments in their garments, as well as source their design inspiration from India's rich history and style icons. Kondo (1997) applies the concept of re- or self-Orientalizing for describing such methods of design and self-fashioning, whereby fashion designers internalize the Orientalized Western gaze and begin to regard their own culture, traditions, past, dress and crafts as exotic sources of inspiration (Kondo 1997: 57). She sees this phase of design as having emerged from Western Orientalism itself, which has, as discussed earlier, shaped the way non-Western dress and fashion is viewed globally.

The strategy of re-Orientalism and self-Orientalizing fashion could be misread as a position of inferiority when read outside of the context of India as it reaffirms and recreates Western fantasies of the "Oriental Other" and related stereotypes of viewing Indian dress and textiles; and still relies on Western intervention i.e. Western styles of clothing, trends, catwalk shows and print media to legitimize it as "fashion" (Kondo 1997: 78). Within India, however, the idea that "one's own heritage and culture have become an important stepping-off point in the design process" (Teunissen 2005: 11) has led to the growth and development of locally popular design aesthetics and products. Jones and Leshkowich also observe "concrete personal, cultural and economic benefit" being derived by designers in similar non-Western centers (Jones and Leshkowich 2003: 282), and suggest viewing these examples of self-Orientalizing from the perspective of local consumers. This is because such instances of design bear different meanings when the knowledge and background the wearers and designers bring to them is taken into

---

[25] Also explored by Nagrath (2003) in the context of Lakmé India Fashion Week in 2002.

consideration. Much like the way global dress is received and worn in different ways across the globe, the perspective around the inception and reception of re- or self-Orientalizing design methods hinges on collective historic, vernacular (familiar) and ongoing social and cultural contexts within which they are practiced.

Concurrent to design strategies that reinscribe Orientalist viewpoints, there is also a resurgence in the deployment of nationalist narratives that emerged during India's fight for independence from British rule as mediums of emphasizing tactical difference in dress. Mazzarella (2003a) proposes the term "new-*Swadeshi*" for contemporary strategies of design and self-fashioning that position globalization and cultural integrity in a mutually compatible and beneficial framework. Like the original premise of the *Swadeshi* movement, these strategies share the same ultimate aim, which is the assertion of a unique Indian identity. Practiced across many design mediums, ranging from graphic, advertising, product to fashion design, these approaches mirror the wider rhetoric of modernity and globalization that holds strong in India, which like older forms of nationalism, still seeks to promote the ascendancy of the East through strategies of distinction. The difference now is that the West is no longer a space of contamination (Chatterjee 1993). Recast as new-*Swadeshi,* such approaches to design and self-fashioning can actually be subversive and empowering as they not only re-configure Western fashion for Indian tastes (and vice versa), and suit the nature of indigenous resources, but also act as powerful mediums for the maintenance of difference and the assertion of distinction—in some cases through the production of intentional "anti-Western fashion."

Introduction to the book's chapters

In the chapters that follow, the main focus remains on India's emerging middle-class and cosmopolitan elites—that constitute the beneficiaries and benefactors of India's current economic growth. Both these groups are highly visible in all forms of visual and print media, as well as actively engaged in consuming and displaying their fashions in a variety of new and established urban settings. As a result their fashion preferences are a significant feature within India's overall sartorial landscape. The evolution of modern fashion, as well as the fusion of local and global dress practices for these segments also highlights the importance they place on asserting a sense of distinction from their global counterparts—and thus forms a recurrent theme across all of the chapters in this book. Alongside a general overview on the presence and specificity of the fashion phenomena in India, concepts like *desi*-chic, new-*Swadeshi*, re-Orientalism, glocalization and the emergence of India as a fashion center in the years following its economic reforms are further explored over multiple chapters. While there is a definite emphasis on women's fashion and the evolution of traditional dress for women in this book, I have attempted to counter this imbalance where possible through an inclusion of menswear across a number of the chapters; and for the most part consider some of the wider thematic issues discussed in the book applicable to both men's and women's fashion practices.

This book draws its content from a broad range of sources, and merges primary and secondary research in response to the multidimensional, multidisciplinary, and wide scope of the subject that is Indian fashion. A review of existing literature on fashion and Indian dress, as well as existing discourses on post-colonialism, popular culture, the influence of international media, issues of class, changing tastes in luxury, the co-existence of tradition and modernity, design and national identity, and shifting body and beauty ideals shape the discussion across subsequent chapters. In dealing with sections on Indian design, designers, and production of fashion, the focus is primarily on two urban centers—Delhi and Mumbai—as they represent India's leading fashion cities and were key sites for field research. Over 50 formal and informal interviews with designers that specialize in different areas of design, as well as stylists, journalists, fashion enthusiasts, PR personnel, luxury consultants, bloggers, design professors and others involved in India's fashion industry shape a significant part of this research. Though not all included in the book's discussion, interviewees include some of India's most esteemed veteran designers and fashion professionals in tandem with newer emerging names and labels that were selected on the basis of their individual viewpoints on Indian fashion and contribution to the field. Information regarding fashion weeks, local trends, fashion education, retail strategies, means and scales of production and designer profiles gathered through first-hand experience as well as newspapers, magazines, journals and blogs over a number of years have been valuable for highlighting the ever-shifting dynamics of the Indian fashion industry. In addition to this, a review of articles, advertisements and advertorials from current fashion publications such as *Femina*, *Vogue* India, *Elle* India, *Marie Claire* India, to name a few, shape the book's discussion on the visual and textual representation of Indian fashion and the role such image-texts play in shaping local style and beauty ideals in India. As the discussion widens to include the consumption of fashion, display, fashion trends and street style, field research in local bazaars, shopping malls, as well as participant interviews and observations are included.

Since the book's key focus is on the confluence of local and global, and resulting hybridity of contemporary fashion, Chapter 2 offers a historical perspective on past instances of global interchange and sartorial fusion that continue to resonate in the way fashion is shaped in current times. In supporting the book's argument the chapter highlights various strategies of self-fashioning and dress for distinction that saw their roots in the colonial period and Indian nationalism, that have seen a resurgence in the time period following India's economic reforms. The chapter also examines how the emergence of a new middle-class and related consumption patterns influenced popular fashion in the past. The pressure of balancing tradition with expectations of modernity in men's and women's dress, and the appropriation and mobilization of certain types of cloth and clothing as symbols of resistance are also covered.

Chapter 3 examines the nature of fashion practice in urban India in current times. In the case of the middle-class, it outlines how overarching societal expectations that Saavala (2012) terms contemporary middle-class morality govern the way clothes are viewed and worn to ensure they are still in keeping with Indian values while simultaneously communicating the wearer's "modern" identity. This is especially so for women as they continue to balance their clothing in accordance with changing roles in society alongside older expectations of Indian womanhood. The chapter also examines how those in the elite segments and the upper-middle class assert their transnational identities and cosmopolitan tastes through the consumption and display of luxury fashion. Chapter 3 also serves to frame the discussion in the following chapters by offering an overview of the apparel market as well as broader consumer trends in the years following the economic liberalization.

Since fashion is an intrinsic part of popular culture through its ability to reflect the collective behaviors of mass culture (Cunningham and Lab 1991: 11), Chapter 4 highlights how the mediums of film, television, and the Internet act as crucial sites through which urban Indians can "imagine" themselves collectively—as globally connected yet locally rooted Indians. Through acting as a major point of reference for Indian culture over the past century, films in particular have come to shape how people perceive various aspects of their lives as well as changing scenarios of modernity in India. Since films also have significant impact on the material aspirations and consumption patterns of viewers themselves, the chapter illustrates not only the deep connection between fashion and films (on and off the screen—through celebrity style), but also how recent shifts towards styling onscreen wardrobes further emphasizes the need for branded goods and designer fashion. Alongside the influence of films, the chapter examines the role television has played in recent decades towards introducing new innovations in traditional dress through the extremely popular daily soap operas and reality makeover shows. The growing influence of the Internet and fashion blogs, where we see the creation of rich and vivid constructions of fashion, is also covered in this chapter.

The representation of women (and their bodies) as bearers of tradition and representatives of modernity, as well as the visual construction of the global-*desi* links the discussion in Chapter 4 to that of Chapter 5, which focuses on Indian fashion magazines. Aside from this, Chapter 5 further expands upon the idealized image of fashion and beauty that these magazines prescribe, as well as the influence of global media frameworks on creating this image. The chapter outlines contemporary fashion magazines' contribution towards the legitimization of *desi*-chic as a distinct aesthetic for Indian fashion, and their promotion of fashion that is "Made in India."

Chapter 6 shifts the focus from the representation and consumption of fashion to the design of high-fashion and couture in India. It examines design as a cultural activity and the evolution of fashion design as a legitimate field. This includes a discussion on design education and fashion as an emerging creative industry. Following from this the chapter also explores the work of key contemporary fashion designers as well as the overarching themes their work falls under. Many of these reiterate and link back to some of the key moments of self-fashioning highlighted in Chapter 2. The relationship between craft and fashion is a key point of focus in this chapter, especially as crafts play an important role in aiding Indian designers towards establishing a niche in the global market.

The book's conclusion picks up on some of the ideas presented in Chapter 6 and reflects on where the future of Indian design and fashion may be heading. In conjunction with reflection on certain themes covered in the book, it addresses the concept of developing a vernacular fashion vocabulary and examines this through the phenomenon of "saving the sari"—a concept not fully discussed in the previous chapters, but still important to mention, which hopefully will leave the reader curious to explore these possibilities further.

2
A BRIEF HISTORY OF DRESS, DIFFERENCE AND FASHION CHANGE IN INDIA

Despite this book's assertion that the overall makeup, pace, consumption and display of fashion in current times is markedly different to the decades prior to India's liberalization, it is impossible to fully understand contemporary fashion without looking back at the evolution of dress practices over the past century and a half. My intention in this chapter is not to provide a complete history of Indian clothing from this time period, but to offer some key highlights that support the following chapters and key concepts addressed in the book. The discussion will also aid readers' familiarity with certain clothing-related aspects, such as the evolution of the modern style of tying the sari, and the Westernization of men's dress. The prime reason for not going further back in time for such an historic overview of clothing is in keeping with the book's central argument that this time period—from about the end of the nineteenth century onwards—witnessed the emergence of various hybrid strategies of self-fashioning and sartorial fusion aimed at the assertion of Indian identity that continue to play out in contemporary fashion. The impact of Orientalist viewpoints and frameworks, though not discussed in this chapter, also took hold during this period—the lasting influence of which continues to be felt within India, as well as globally, with regard to the reception of non-Western fashion systems.

Since the book deals primarily with the impetus for fashion change in the form of India's recent economic reforms and the emergence of new segments of society in current times, this chapter firstly examines vestimentary history during British rule and the subsequent rise of the Indian middle-class that bear witness to similar identity-based dilemmas[1] played out in clothing. As the following segment will reveal, the need for balancing traditional dress with Western influences during the colonial rule acted as a crucial turning point for Indian men's fashions. Here the chapter also illustrates the impact shifting consumption patterns linked to class, status and evolving concepts of

---

[1] Tarlo (1996) refers to the sartorial negotiations during the late nineteenth century and throughout the twentieth century as "dilemmas of what to wear," and finds choosing what to wear in India hinged on various personal and collective factors ranging from loyalty to caste, religion, class, social roles, profession, marital status, education, location (private vs. public, urban vs. rural), perceived level of cosmopolitanism, the wearer's aims, aspirations, related projections and fashion to name a few.

modernity had on dress at the time. Following from this, the recasting of women as bearers of tradition symbolized through choice of dress as part of the Indian nationalist movements, as well as the promotion of indigenous products, clothing and *khadi* as visual and material mediums of resistance and difference are all relevant to current design practices. These instances also highlight Tarlo's interpretation of India's recent history of clothing, as being a series of "strategies of distinction" (Bourdieu 1984, cf. Tarlo 1996) aimed to create differentiation between India and the West, as well as between social groups within Indian society (ibid.: 319).

With regard to the period leading up to liberalization, the chapter explores the concept of modernity as it relates to traditional clothing and the changing status of women that impacted on their fashion choices. My aim is also to strengthen the argument presented in the previous chapter regarding the active presence of the fashion process and related systems in India. Hence, interspersed through the discussion on the key issues mentioned above, are also broader overviews of popular trends and fashion cycles. These further highlight instances of collective selection, local and global fashion networks, class competition and upward mobility, and the ability of clothing to symbolize and publicly display status as well as personal and collective identity prior to current times.

The influence of European dress on Indian clothing during British rule

The assumption that the impetus for style change only came about during the presence of the British in India is largely untrue, as is the viewpoint that global interchange and fashion did not exist prior to the influence of contemporary forces of globalization. Indian clothing already included a diverse range of stitched and unstitched garments before European dress was introduced. Many of these had been fashioned by global interactions and local adaptations, stemming from the need to cater to Indian tastes and climate and various religious and social beliefs. Such items included variations of Iranian and Chinese caps, trousers, tunics and coats (Bahl 2005: 95), that were adapted through using lighter fabrics or fabrics that matched religious requirements. Sophisticated networks of textile and clothing manufacturers, craftspeople and other style innovators also existed, as did multiple instances where the consumption of luxury items was used to bolster the status of the elite and ruling classes in India. Even during British rule local and global factors external to those from the West influenced fashions—such as the Parsi[2] *Gara* sari that was a result of trade relations between Indian Parsis and China in the 1850s, and was subsequently copied by craftspeople in Surat[3] for markets all across India (i.e. beyond the Parsi community) (Karlekar 2011).

However, it is the influence of the British and Western clothing that appears to have had the deepest impact on Indian dress, and continues to do so when we examine

[2] A *Parsi* or *Parsee* is a member of the Zoroastrian community in India.
[3] Surat is a city in the state of Gujarat renowned for its textile and silk mills.

contemporary fashion. Since the tension of choosing between Indian and Western dress is still acutely felt in India, it is important to discuss how this phenomenon has played out historically, and how clothing has acted as a material medium for experiencing change, forging new identities and shaping a new social class.

The British not only introduced new forms of education, government, language and class structure in India, they also presented new styles of clothing that closely correlated with their lifestyle and methods of social etiquette. Unlike the Mughals, who imposed their own clothing styles upon their court, the British did not force their clothing onto Indians. Instead they actively discouraged them from donning Western clothes, unless it was in the context of missionaries "civilizing" native populations who wore little or no clothing. In some cases the British tried to distance themselves further by setting elaborate dress codes for their representatives in India, which included a ban on wearing Indian clothes (i.e. going native). The symbolic value of Western products was extremely high during this time, as the British used their lifestyle and clothing to signify their racial superiority, modernity, refinement, masculinity and power over Indians. As a result, the period around the late nineteenth and early twentieth century saw elite and middle-class Indians caught in serious dilemmas with regard to their clothing choices and methods of self-presentation in public and private domains. Tarlo summarizes some of the ongoing issues by noting,

> Throughout the colonial period, when "Westernisation" was perceived by many as "civilisation", members of the Indian elite had faced the problem of how far they should Westernise their dress. At a national level, this problem revolved around a conflict between European and Indian values and tastes. At a more personal level, it touched on notions of loyalty to family, self, caste, religion, region and race. (Tarlo 1991: 134)

Here it is important to note the emergence of the Indian middle-class around the time of British rule. Unlike the rise of the middle-class in England—which was a direct result of economical and technological changes brought about by the Industrial Revolution—in India the middle-class emerged more as a consequence of changes in the system of law and public administration, and mainly consisted of those who belonged to the learned professions (Misra 1961: v). Despite the presence of various institutions considered conducive to capitalist growth, as well as the societal impetus needed for the growth of a middle-class bourgeoisie in India prior to the arrival of the British, Misra notes that the general immobility of the caste organization teamed with the nature of the bureaucracy at the time meant that "middle-class elements in society could not become a stratified order" (ibid.: 9).

The British imported and introduced their educational system into India with the aim of creating a class comparable to their own, "so that it may assist them in the administration of the country and help in the development of its internal resources" (ibid.:10) and on the whole act as a cultural mediator. This finally provided the catalyst for the emergence of the Indian middle-class. According to Misra, the middle-class in India was created to be a class of imitators and not originators of new values or methods (ibid.: 11), a viewpoint that is echoed in Thomas Babington Macaulay's much cited quote from his "Minute on

Indian Education" about the need to "form a class who may be interpreters between us and the millions whom we govern; a class of persons, Indian in blood and colour, but English in taste, in opinions, in morals, and in intellect" (Macaulay 1835, cf. Varma 1998: 2). Under these circumstances, clothing also played a crucial role in shaping the identity of the middle-class.

During this time the transition towards the wearing of European dress by Indian men offers an interesting starting point in illustrating the strategies of fusion, selective appropriation and resulting hybridity, as well as class- and identity-related tensions as they apply to Indian fashion. Although most of this book's focus is on women's fashion and pressures they face in balancing tradition with modernity, it was Indian men who were initially required to negotiate between Western and Indian [sartorial] identity during British rule (Loomba 1997). As already mentioned, the British actively used clothing as a visible means of racial segregation and exclusion against Indians. In this scenario, it became attractive, and in some cases necessary, for English-educated Indian men belonging to the elite and emerging middle-classes to don Western garb in the late nineteenth and early twentieth century. Men belonging to these groups actively chose to adopt such clothes as a way of uplifting their status in society, appealing to the ruling classes, or in many cases, to be considered equal to the British and deserving of certain professional positions that were all too often made impossible for Indians to attain. Tarlo notes that in general, Indians did not view Western clothes as beautiful or attractive. Instead, "[t]he fascination with European garments was related more to what they represented than to either their practicality or their aesthetic appeal" (Tarlo 1996: 44).

In his personal account of clothing during and after British rule, Nirad Chaudhuri[4] (1976) states that, "[the] interaction between the Indian and European costume [was] immensely more powerful" than anything prior to that point. Chaudhuri notes the influence of the West in almost all "city clothing" where either "a Western garment had been added to the Indian costume and [had] become a part of it … [or where there were] mutations of Indian garments on Western lines" (ibid.: 5).

While on the surface it is easy to mistake the adoption of Western clothes as blind mimicry, the process was far more complex and nuanced, and involved interweaving new and old styles in order to suit the specific contexts of the time. Indian men employed various strategies of sartorial fusion as they countered the dilemmas of self-fashioning and presentation in attempting to match their clothing to their social sphere, professional aspirations and personal beliefs. The simplest option for many men attempting to "modernize" their dress without giving up their traditional beliefs and identity was to have European styles tailored out of Indian fabric (Tarlo 1996: 47). Mixing Indian and European garments was another common strategy, where men wore traditional styles like the *dhoti* or *kurta pyjama* along with European garments like jackets and collared shirts with ties etc. (Figure 2.1).

Such style experimentation was popular amongst Indians working as clerks, officials and bankers under the British (referred to as *baboos*), but were ridiculed by conservative

---

[4] b. November 23, 1897–d. August 1, 1999.

Figure 2.1 "Our Music Master." Photograph of author's grandmother's *sitar* teacher—who is seen wearing a turban along with a European-style coat over a *kurta* and trousers. Circa 1920s. Image courtesy Amrita Sandhu.

Indians as well as the British at the time. Often Hindu men would wear European clothes in public, but on entering their homes (i.e. the inner sanctum) would remove these "polluted" clothes and don indigenous garments that were in keeping with their religious beliefs (Chaudhuri 1976; Tarlo 1996).

Chaudhuri describes his own personal experiences and observations from that time, and notes the ubiquitous presence of tailored shirts, worn with almost every style of "lower garment" including the *dhoti* (Chaudhuri 1976). In painting a vivid picture of the evolving tastes of the Indian elite classes he recounts that during his childhood the European dress shirt was favored for formal occasions and was "much admired and respected" (ibid.: 6). During this time, "[w]ealthy people went to visit and even to parties in these shirts, looking very imposing with their starched fronts, gold or diamond studs and links, sometimes a gold chain, and a very fine crinkled *dhoti* as diaphanous as the finest Muslin, and also patent leather pumps with bows" (ibid.: 6). The European coat was popular in the cities and was regularly worn with a *dhoti*, and sometimes styled with an embroidered shawl placed on top. A style that Chaudhuri mentions as his personal favorite was of wearing a coat without any shirt underneath (for informal outings) over a *dhoti*—the end of which was pulled up and wrapped around the neck like a cravat (ibid.: 7). Towards the end of the nineteenth

Figure 2.2 Photograph of author's great-grand parents in the 1920s. Author's great-grandmother is wearing the *Nivi* style of sari in what appears to be an imported fabric. Author's great-grandfather, who served as a doctor in the British army and was stationed in Europe during the First World War, is wearing full Western dress. Image courtesy Amrita Sandhu.

and beginning of the twentieth century, a growing segment of men began to adopt full European dress, especially those Indians who had travelled abroad and donned European clothes in the process, and found it easy to continue wearing these styles once they returned to India (Figure 2.2).

Though this came at the cost of being ridiculed, many men who wore full European dress continued to wear some sort of Indian headgear such as a cap or turban, perhaps as a mark of distinction and loyalty to their culture (Tarlo 1996: 57). Interestingly, for those who attempted to avoid wearing European clothes, the dilemmas were even further heightened, as there was no single style of Indian dress prior to the arrival of the British that they could adopt as an alternative, and with changing fashions many educated Indians had begun to look upon regional styles as old-fashioned (ibid.: 58).

Women, on the other hand, did not wear Western clothes outright during this time. With the exception of some in elite circles, especially those belonging to families with transnational connections with opportunities to travel abroad (Figure 2.3), women from families who had converted to Christianity and Anglo-Indians, most Indian women did not find European women's dress attractive or appealing. Instead they saw such clothes as being impractical, cumbersome and unsuitable for the Indian climate. There was also the issue of exposing the body through wearing clothing such as the evening gowns that

Figure 2.3 Author's grandmother (extreme left) pictured alongside her parents and siblings in the early 1920s. All are wearing European style of dress. Author's great-grandmother in particular is seen wearing a dress, stockings and fashionable shoes. Image courtesy Amrita Sandhu.

were fashionable in Europe at the time (Borthwick 1984). However, as Chaudhari notes, the influence of European dress and fashions on traditional styles though initially subtle was also "penetrating" (Chaudhuri 1976: 8). Many of these influences centered on shifting fabric preferences and in the detailing of clothing. This included switching to lighter mill-made cloth, imported satins, velvets and artificial silks, which occurred alongside a growing preference for finer Indian silks and handlooms. Bayly (2005) dismisses the claim that the switch from handloom to imported mill-made cloth happened mainly due to the latter being cheaper—instead he sees this as a reflection of the changing culture and political economy. The vivid colors from aniline dyes and vibrant prints of British mill-made fabrics designed to suit Indian tastes were immensely popular and desirable when compared to the duller shades of Indian textiles. In addition such fabrics were finer and lightweight, and on the whole had a much more "exotic" allure to Indian women who were accustomed to the traditional handloom fabrics. McGowan notes that women belonging to well-to-do agricultural communities in Poona,[5] who would probably be considered upper middle-class at the time, also began to favor finer silk saris instead of

---

[5] Now referred to as Pune, in the state of Maharashtra.

Figure 2.4   Author's great-grandmother wearing the *Nivi* style of sari holding a parasol. Circa late 1920s. Image courtesy Amrita Sandhu

their traditional cotton ones—a sign of changing consumption patterns linked to "local categories of value and desire, associated with texture, color, caste and class" and upward mobility (McGowan 2005: 272).

Other noticeable changes in women's fashions included new trends in sari blouses that clearly mirrored European fashions and levels of modesty. Details such as lace sleeves, high collars with ribbons, frills and jabots and leg-o-mutton sleeves were popular (Castelino 1997; McGowan 2006; Karlekar 2011). Chaudhuri notes that *kameez* styles exhibited "continual fluctuations," where at times it resembled a corset, or in some cases was cut like a frock or a dressing gown (Chaudhuri 1976: 9). Methods of styling hair and makeup also paralleled Western trends, which was evident in ladies' magazines and related visual culture of the time. European accessories such as gloves, parasols, shawls, brooches, fur muffs, stockings, and closed shoes also became popular (Figures 2.3 and also 2.4). Though not all attributed to Western influences, other changes that were occurring within women's styles reflected greater emphasis on functionality and mobility linked to evolving tastes and social roles—as women's saris were becoming lighter (due to shorter length of fabric as well as finer fabrics) and *salwars* were becoming less voluminous with a lot less *ghera*.

Politics of women's dress during British rule: The "new" Indian woman and the "modern" sari

Towards the end of the nineteenth and beginning of the twentieth century the status of women came under close scrutiny from both British and Indian reformers. Bhatia (2003) maintains that women's bodies during the colonial period presented a highly contested terrain between tradition and Westernization, and their clothing came to visually represent the tension between these two factors. The British viewed the treatment of women in Hindu society to be proof of India's backwardness, and felt the need to uplift and reform the status of women as being of central importance to their role (and assertion of their masculinity) in India. Subsequently, Indian nationalists also initiated their own set of reforms to ensure the colonizers did not interfere too much in this space, which, as I will discuss shortly, was central to the nation's spiritual domain and its distinction from the West. To begin with, the emphasis was on the emancipation of women from the "cruelties" of Indian society and certain Hindu customs—which included practices such as *sati*,[6] the poor treatment of widows, and the age of consent.[7] The focus of reform later shifted to women's education, with the intention of further modernizing and emancipating women, albeit within the framework of Indian morality and respectability.

Changing levels of modesty for elite and middle-class women also affected women's dress at the time. Shifting social roles and expectations meant that it became "essential to 'dress' appropriately" (Karlekar 2011). The dilemma of presenting educated women and girls in public wearing respectable attire was a concern for reformists, particularly in Bengal, as the regional style of sari was often made of transparent fabric and worn without a blouse or petticoat.[8] The solution to the dilemma of finding an appropriate style of dress is credited to Rabindranath Tagore's sister-in-law—Jnanadanandini Devi,[9] who also found herself in a similar predicament (Banerjee and Miller 2003: 254; Karlekar 2011). Jnanadanandini experimented with a number of sari styles to counter this issue, and in doing so was influenced by the way Parsi women in Bombay wore their *Garas* along with a blouse and petticoat. She further adapted the Gujarati style of tying the sari by bringing the *pallu* around her body and throwing it over her left shoulder for the sake of convenience. The petticoat was initially a Western influence, but the covering and "respectability" that it offered to the sari "molded subtly with the wider issues of reform and progress" underway in India at the time (Karlekar 2011). This resulting combination of indigenous styles, Western influences and local ingenuity, which one women's magazine referred to as "a new mode of dress that took from English, Muslim and Bengali traditions

---

[6]The Hindu ritual of self-immolation by a widow at her husband's funeral pyre.

[7]The age of consent was ten for women prior to 1891.

[8]In describing this Bengali style of sari Chaudhuri quotes Fanney Parkes, an Englishwoman who visited India and noted: "[t]he dress consisted of one long strip of Bengali gauze of thin texture, with a gold border, passing twice round the limbs, with the end thrown over the shoulder. The dress was rather transparent, almost useless as a veil" (Parkes, cf. Chaudhuri 1976: 62).

[9]Satyendranath Tagore's wife.

yet retained a Bengali essence" (mentioned in Karlekar 2011),[10] was soon adopted by families involved in the reform movement in Bengal, and subsequently became fashionable across India amongst women from urban middle-class and elite families. It also suited women who were active in the public sphere, especially those who participated in anti-colonial demonstrations as part of the nationalist movements.

Indian nationalism and the *Swadeshi* movement

The transition from "traditional" to "modern" clothing by women in India is as much visually vibrant as it is socially and politically charged, especially due to the fact that "it is very often the responsibility of women to carry national culture on their bodies by wearing national or 'traditional' clothing" (Edensor 2002: 108). The Indian nationalist movements and freedom struggle in the early twentieth century reinforced this notion by recasting women and their clothing as idealized symbols of the "nation" and "tradition."

It is important to note that the emerging nationalist ideals at the time did not necessarily regard modernity and tradition in opposition to each other. Instead, they "separated the domain of culture into two spheres—the material and the spiritual" (Chatterjee 1993: 119)—as a way of coming to terms with the need to select and incorporate certain aspects of Western civilization, such as "rational forms of economic organization and modern forms of statecraft" (ibid.: 120) in order to progress and develop, while still maintaining a sense of distinction between the East and West—where the East was far more superior to the West in the spiritual domain. "What was necessary was to cultivate material techniques of modern Western civilization, while retaining and strengthening the distinctive spiritual essence of the national culture" (ibid.: 120). Chatterjee maintains that in this process material and spiritual distinction became condensed into the opposing poles of "inner" and "outer," where the home came to represent one of the strongholds of the inner sphere—the representation of which was the Indian woman (ibid.: 120). In keeping with this, the role of a woman was to look after the home as a perfect wife and mother, and through this protect and nurture the spiritual quality of national culture. Despite being educated, they were not allowed to become *too* Westernized. The "new" Indian woman of the time was different from older traditional versions of womanhood as well as her Western counterparts. Much like Indian nationalism itself, which selectively incorporated both Indian and Western elements, the construction of the ideal Indian "gentlewomen" (known as the *bhadramahila* in Bengal) fused together "older brahminical[11] notions of female self-sacrifice and devotion with the Victorian ideal of enlightened wife and mother" (Loomba 1997: 282).

In terms of clothing, this translated into shunning Western garments *as well as* regional styles, and donning the modified version of the sari, in the aforementioned *Nivi*

---

[10] This description was rumored to have been penned by Jnanadanandini Devi herself, writing under a pseudonym (Karlekar 2011).

[11] Relating to *Brahmins*—who form the scholar (most superior) class in the traditional Hindu society.

style, which was worn along with a blouse, petticoat and shoes. Also referred to as the *brāhmikā* sari, this style had become fashionable in middle-class Bengali homes (refer to Figure 2.2) (ibid.: 130). Loomba states that the *Nivi* style of sari was "extremely decorous" when compared to other sari styles and "more conducive to certain kinds of movements than others, easier to combine with shoes and coats, easier for walking fast" (ibid.: 284). Much like Indian nationalism, it too emerged out of the dialogue between tradition and modernity where the addition of the blouse and petticoat acted as a "mark of an emancipated modern woman" (Bhatia 2003: 336). Featured in numerous iconic and nationalist propaganda images of the time (Banerjee and Miller 2003: 219), the *Nivi* sari gained symbolic status as a national garment, and the "modest sari-clad middle-class woman, symbol of 'Hindu Indian national identity,' became the everyday face of 'tradition'" (Bahl 2005: 101).

The role of clothing in narrating national heritage and thereby differentiating the colonized from the colonizers, took on added significance during the struggle for freedom as part of the *Swadeshi* movement. The term *Swadeshi* comes from the word *swadesh,* which is a combination of *swa* meaning "self" or "own" and *desh* meaning "country." Hence meaning "of one's country," which is also taken to mean self-sufficiency. The *Swadeshi* movement was an economic strategy aimed at encouraging the use of Indian-made goods, which included cloth and clothing, and shunning all Western and imported goods. In addition, Mahatma Gandhi understood the highly valued semiotic properties of cloth in India. When faced with the dilemma of unifying a nation during India's struggle for Independence without the benefit of a common written language, he saw merit in the symbolic value of material and visual culture in creating a common platform for instilling national pride (Bean 1989; Tarlo 1996; Trivedi 2003, 2007). Alongside *Swadeshi* demands of shunning imported fabrics and Western clothing, Gandhi championed spinning, weaving and the use of unbleached plain *khadi* as the primary fabric for Indian clothes. Portrayed as a "material artifact of the nation" (Trivedi 2003: 13–14), *khadi* subsequently became a "visual symbol in that it marked individual bodies as distinctly Indian" (ibid.: 14), and was officially incorporated into the nationalist program as part of the *Swadeshi* movement by the Indian national congress. Trivedi notes the key role visual culture played during this time to firstly communicate messages of nationalism and promote *khadi*, and secondly to inspire "new modes of consumption," again in the aim of securing a sense of shared identity through material items, such as *khadi* clothing (Trivedi 2003: 13). Through the medium of *khadi* exhibitions, for example, Indian visitors were able to experience the "contours of the nation" through a "wide range of products [and images] drawn from different regions" (ibid.: 15).

Tarlo has argued that despite some success, on the whole, the principles and material medium of *khadi* were not universally adopted. In a number of cases this time period also heightened the dilemma of choosing "what to wear" for many Indians (Tarlo 1991). She substantiates this claim through highlighting how the elite classes used high quality, expensive "luxury" *khadi,* which was much finer in comparison to the coarse version prescribed by Gandhi, as a way of maintaining their status and distinction from the lower classes. She also notes that those who had become accustomed to wearing Western styles of dress now preferred to wear those styles but had them tailored in *khadi* (ibid.).

Much like when Indian men would change out of their Western clothes upon reaching their homes, during the *khadi* movement many men would shed their *khadi* clothes upon returning home and don clothing made of luxurious or comfortable fabrics. In addition, the use of *khadi* posed a problem for women who wanted to continue wearing their traditional fabrics and colors. As a result, many tried to counter this issue by dyeing or applying embellishments to realign their clothing with fashion.

However, while not entirely successful, the concept of *Swadeshi* and the preservation and promotion of indigenous goods as being superior to others and crucial for maintaining a unique identity has had a deep influence on emerging design viewpoints as well as representations of Indian fashion in print—which will be elaborated upon in following chapters.

Fashions following India's independence

After gaining independence from the British in 1947, the rhetoric of patriotism and nationalism in India remained closely linked to earlier aforementioned themes. However, despite the continued representation of symbols, images and ideas related to patriotism within various forms of popular culture, the subsequent course of modernization brought about gradual changes in public opinion with regard to fashion. This included the return to mill-made fabrics, use of synthetics, and greater tolerance for Western clothing for women, through availability in the Indian market as well as increasing visibility in print media and films. With advances in communication and the growing influence of popular visual media in a newly independent and unified country, Altekar (1956, cf. Singh 1966) notes that more and more women were in a better position to observe and learn about the various regional styles prevalent in India, which they may not have known about before.[12] This also encouraged the spread of the *Nivi* style across wider segments and sections of Indian society, and led as well to the growing popularity of the *salwar kameez* (beyond Northern States) and greater awareness of current fashions across India.

Meher Castelino's account of fashion in the decades following India's independence[13] bears witness to the vibrant fashion scene enjoyed by those in the elite and upper middle-classes. This includes numerous fashion shows, such as those organized by the Spencer sisters,[14] an emerging professional modeling scene, new magazines like *Femina, Eve's Weekly* and *Trends*, a growing apparel industry with emerging brands, fabric mills and

---

[12] Through her research on Indian women's wardrobes during the 1960s, Singh (1966) notes a greater use of textiles and saris from different regions, which she credits to wider availability through craft emporiums.

[13] Meher Castelino was winner of the Miss India title in 1964. She subsequently worked as a commercial and catwalk model, and is currently a fashion columnist in India. Castelino's book (1994) records key milestones in the story of Indian fashion from the last century up till the 1990s and highlights the entrepreneurial spirit of India's fashion industry pioneers as well as the ongoing local and global interchange that ensured fashion in India was in step with the rest of the world.

[14] The Spencer sisters—Sylla and Nergish Spencer—organized a number of fashion shows and related events from the early 1960s onwards in India, as well as abroad. They also trained and managed the first batch of professional models in India (Castelino 1994: 12).

Figure 2.5   "How to look stunning in mid-air!" Advertisement from 1972 for Bombay Dyeing's 100 percent Terene, anti-crease cotton and Swiss voile saris. Image courtesy Bombay Dyeing.

fashion designers, and the general experimentation with fashion and beauty by women in urban centers (Castelino 1994). In describing some key fashion trends during the time, she notes that imported synthetics and printed saris (Figure 2.5) were extremely popular amongst urban women and the sari blouse or *choli* saw frequent style changes. These included the *katori* (rounded) cut, the no-bra *choli* and fluctuations of necklines. Other stylistic experimentations included the popularity of the Kashmiri *phiran, kalidar kurtas, lungis* and the Patiala *salwar* alongside the introduction of Western styles—pant suits, maxi dresses, bell-bottom pants (worn with *kurtas* for a "hippie" look) and denim jeans— which were popular amongst young college-going women, especially in larger cities like Bombay and Delhi (Khan 1992; Castelino 1994). All of which highlight evolving clothing styles that were in step with changing lifestyles and indicate an openness to new trends and experimentation with global fashion.

This is further evident in early issues of magazines like *Eve's Weekly* and *Femina* (first started in 1959), as well as in Mrs. Cora Pal's *Dictionary of Fashion and Beauty for Indian Women* (published in 1968), for example, that offers advice to Indian women on numerous items related to fashion and beauty—ranging from A for acne, B for brassiere, C for chiffon, D for dancing, E for elegance … through to Z for *zari* (Pal 1968). In it we see a unique blend of Western and Indian techniques of beauty and self-fashioning with instructions that actively promote experimentation with current fashion trends. This is evident in the book's advice on picking the right brassiere, gloves (preferably "kid gloves"), cut of jeans and French chiffon, contrasted with segments on matching sari blouses to different kinds of saris, preparing face packs using indigenous ingredients and yoga exercises to tone muscles and shed weight.[15] With instructional segments on ways of wearing Indian and Western garments it is assumed that the reader may not be familiar with one or the other, and so lessons on tying a sari as well as how to pick the right color of slacks are both equally stressed upon. In the book, Mrs. Pal strongly recommends readers to selectively negotiate between Indian and Western styles of clothing and adornment, and choose the right mix for themselves. An example of this is emphasized in the segment on sweaters where she suggests that, "[s]weaters that are over-influenced by Western fashions look completely wrong with saris … [However, for] wear with slacks and skirts chunky, Western sweater is best" (Pal 1968: 160).

The absence of discussion on menswear in this segment is deliberate—as one could say that stylistically the changes were not as dynamic, and politically or socially charged when compared to women's fashions. However, it is important to highlight that men's clothing in India saw a surge in ready-to-wear brands entering the market, many of which were international brand tie-ups. Arrow, Van Heusen, Louis Philippe and a number of Indian apparel brands like Chirag Din (CD), Vimal and Raymonds began to offer casual and professional ready-made and ready-to-stitch clothes for men.[16] In comparison to the popularity of branded goods and organized retail in menswear, a phenomenon that still persists, womenswear did not see similar brand innovation or retail presence till recently. The majority of women preferred to wear traditional clothes at home and for work, and as a result the design and retail of womenswear continued to rely heavily on personal interactions and creative negotiations between tailors and individual clients. Trends and fashion advice were actively sourced from popular movie stars and their costumes in films, magazines and clothing design catalogues[17] made especially for tailoring purposes. The ubiquitous presence and affordability of tailoring services was a key factor within the Indian fashion system that made it a more feasible alternative to ready-made clothes in comparison to Western countries. In addition, women were wary of ready-made traditional clothes in the early years of their introduction into the market, due to being accustomed to getting personalized, one-off designs as well as a good fit through getting their clothes tailored (Bahl 2005; Khaire 2011). Women were also not ready to pay the extra cost for "designer" ready-made clothing as they felt they could get a similar look for less through their own tailor (Castelino 1994). There was also a concern that ready-made clothes may lead to a loss of individuality for women who rarely had to worry about owning the *same* clothes as their friends and neighbors, due to the

---

[15] The emphasis on trends is further highlighted in the section on "Magazines" where she advises readers to try buying or borrowing Western magazines when possible (Pal 1968: 92), or avoiding piercing their noses as this was no longer trendy and only suited women with "classic features" (ibid.: 106). She also cautions readers from following fashion trends too slavishly or blindly as this could lead to a loss of individuality.

[16] Castelino also notes a "revolution" in shirt design during the 1980s and 1990s with apparel brands experimenting with new fabrics, colors and even embellishments for men (Castelino 1994: 35).

[17] Such catalogues featured various sari blouse and *salwar kameez* styles copied or modified from popular film costumes. They continue to be published even today, and remain popular in smaller towns and cities.

variety of fabric choices available to them from which they could have their individual styles created.

A popular concept that bridged ready-made and tailoring was the pre-matched suit set,[18] which consisted of pre-cut fabric lengths (mostly synthetic) for the *salwar*, *kurta* and *dupatta*, mixed and matched, and ready for tailoring. Here the customer had the flexibility of choosing the cut and design details they desired, without the hassle of matching fabrics, colors, and prints. However, the growing popularity of Western styles like shirts, trouser-suits, t-shirts and jeans also gave a boost to ready-made clothing for women as tailors found it hard to achieve the fit and finish required of such clothes. Export surplus garments and second-hand branded clothes, the latter of which were shipped from Western countries, purchased in bulk and sold by street-side vendors in local markets in urban centers, were extremely popular among the younger generation who wanted to be trendy on a budget. Both sources offered consumers a choice of well-known Western brands in current or recent styles, sometimes at throwaway prices—almost as a sort of "fast" disposable fashion much before that term or model of fashion retail was originally coined.

Another "new" woman

Women are taking their places in many vocations of the nation both in the urban and rural areas—in education; in the arts; in aviation; in politics; in journalism; in literature; in business—at the local, state, national, and international levels. Yet women's task is importantly still that of homemaking. (Singh 1966: 247)

Justine Singh's research on the growing popularity and suitability of the "modern" style of sari amongst educated Indian women[19] provides a snapshot of evolving clothing styles in the 1960s in conjunction with modernizing lifestyles. Singh praises Home Science colleges in India for training women in two careers—"as intelligent homemakers and as professional women" (Singh 1966: 247). Thus highlighting how the construction of modernity with regard to Indian women continued to hinge on earlier nationalist constructs, despite the change in their outward appearance.

In describing this appearance, Singh credits "modern means of travel" (Thapar 1963, cf. in Singh 1966: 248) for having a liberating influence upon women, and states, "[t]oday a woman drives a car herself, plays the role of housewife, mother, professional educationist. Modern transport is a kind of enabling measure making new roles possible and forcing the reinterpretation of old ones through the freedom which it confers" (ibid.). To this Singh adds, "[t]raditional customs [such as *purdah* and certain kinds of regional clothes] are not always easy to maintain on modern vehicles. Distance from

---

[18] Here the use of the term *suit* refers to the *salwar kameez*.
[19] "Modern Draped Sari Replaces Traditional Costumes of Educated Indian Women and the Relation of this Change to the Development of Education and Communication in India" (Singh 1966).

familiar social environment makes some customs seem unnecessary, even ridiculous" (ibid.: 248). As already mentioned in the last chapter, one of Singh's key findings shows that in comparison to previous generations, the preference amongst urban educated women in India towards wearing the *Nivi* style of sari and *salwar kameez* along with some Western styles, also meant that regional, religious and caste differences were less obvious. Hence clothing was becoming more unified and secular in the time period following India's independence. This correlates with the earlier aim of the Indian nationalist movements and Gandhi's use of *khadi* as a unifying force; only this shift can be credited more so to changing fashions linked to education, class and modernizing lifestyles.

In charting the alteration of the modern woman's outward appearance, Lakshmi states that even after Indian independence the need to "associate femininity and good qualities with certain kinds of dress" prevailed, where "[p]rinted sarees, georgettes and chiffons were considered, at the time, symbols of the educated woman."[20] However by the 1980s this was no longer the case, and in the decades prior to economic liberalization Loomba (1997) notes a shift in the representation of women in all forms of print and popular media, where modern women were increasingly shown wearing Western clothes leading socially and publicly active lives, smoking cigarettes, choosing birth control and exercising for example. Such portrayals did not seem to be at odds with the national paradigm at the time that focused on economic development and modernization of the nation, nor did it offend Hindu beliefs—due to the strong assumption that women would still retain their traditional beliefs and morals on the inside despite appearing Western or modern on the outside (Loomba 1997). The common belief being that a "'really educated' [modern] woman—one who uses her education to nurture traditional culture"—did not require such literal symbols of dress and traditional outward appearance (Lakshmi 1988: 275). Once again, much like Indian nationalism, the separation of inner and outer spheres allowed for a transition to Western clothes for many urban women without jeopardizing Indian traditions and traditional values.

The "modern" [youthful, casual, and trendy] *salwar kameez*

If the story of women's dress in India during the Indian nationalist movements is about the evolution of a new sari style that captured the essence of the political and social climate of the time, the later part of the twentieth century could be discussed in terms of the *salwar kameez* as the material medium for the experience of modern roles and new fashions for women.

Typically consisting of a long shirt or tunic called the *kurta* worn over loose pants the *salwar kameez* suited the needs of women who were looking to modernize their

---

[20]Singh also found a direct relationship between the education level of her respondents and the modern style of draping the sari (Singh 1966: 282).

Figure 2.6 Author's mother Amrita Sandhu wearing a *salwar kameez* in the fashionable *churidar* style during the 1970s. Image courtesy Amrita Sandhu.

clothes, yet be traditional. Due to resembling a shirt and trouser ensemble, where the fit and proportions of both could be adjusted, the *salwar kameez* was able to take on a greater number of trends and was a more practical and accommodating choice for active lifestyles and as everyday casual wear. As an example of its stylistic versatility, Castelino recounts that during the rising popularity of the mini skirt in the West, while most Indian women were not so "daring" as to try this style themselves the *salwar kameez* echoed the trend through a severe shortening of the *kameez* worn with a tight *churidar salwar* that closely mimicked the overall look (Castelino 1994: 7) (Figure 2.6). Made popular through films by actresses like Sharmila Tagore, Sadhana and Waheeda Rahman (Figure 2.7), the *salwar kameez* offered the perfect foil for mirroring global trends through traditional garments. Clothing in Indian films through the 1960s and 1970s communicated the character of the heroine and other female roles through dress; and marked the distinction between Indian and Western values, which were often reduced to "good" and "bad." In these films Western clothes were commonly associated with being too "foreign" or were used to portray women with wayward characteristics or in many cases "vamps." The *salwar kameez* on the other hand "could finally be Western without being immodest" (Castelino 1994: 7) and portrayed a young modern woman as opposed to an older married [old-fashioned] woman.

Part of this representation, in films as well as in print in magazines, stemmed from the fact that the *salwar kameez* was slowly evolving into a bridging outfit for adolescent

Figure 2.7 Film actress
Waheeda Rehman wearing the
churidar style of *salwar kameez*
in 1972. Photographed by
Dhiraj Chawda. Image courtesy
Manjula Chawda.

Figure 2.8 *Salwar kameez* from Ritu Kumar's *Khadi* collection modeled by choreographer Anu Ahuja, on the seaside at Mahabalipuram, near Chennai. Circa early 1990s. Image courtesy Ritu Kumar.

women prior to marriage.[21] With the exception of the maxi style dress (i.e. the nightie), which Indian women commonly wore as nightwear and during the day around the home, Western clothes became inappropriate to wear with age for young, unmarried women as they were seen to emphasize the body. There was also the issue of Western clothes indicating that the wearer was "sexually available" (Loomba 1997: 291), which was further heightened by the way they were portrayed in films. As the sari was becoming a less viable option for this age group, the *salwar kameez* was the perfect hybrid choice. The *salwar kameez* was further popularized through its inclusion as school uniforms for (older) girls in schools, such as at the government-run Kendriya Vidyalayas (schools) across India.[22] This added to its wider acceptance from being originally a regional

[21] It was common for girls to wear Western dresses and skirts at a younger age especially at home and through their early school years as uniforms. Tarlo (1996) notes that girls in smaller cities, towns and rural areas were seen wearing skirts and frocks and Singh (1966), in her categorization of Indian women's clothes labels such clothes as being for children and young girls (hence could be read as childish).

[22] The *salwar kameez* countered issues of inappropriate skirt lengths (a frequent issue with Western-style uniforms) and was "an asexual grown-up garment" (Banerjee and Miller 2003: 238–9) that hid the body while still allowing young women to take part in sports, cycle to school, and appeared more "modern" and freeing than the sari (ibid.). Singh's survey of modern educated Indian women's clothing also highlights a shift in school uniforms where in comparison to her survey of respondents' grandmothers, who mainly wore regional clothes as school uniforms, the respondents and their mothers mostly worn the *Nivi* style of sari and *salwar kameez* (Singh 1966).

garment worn mainly in Northern India by Punjabis as well as Muslims across India, into modern women's professional as well as casual wear wardrobes across the country.

As a result of becoming associated with youth culture and modernity along with its stylistic resemblance to Western clothes, the *salwar kameez* presented an excellent canvas for India's emerging fashion designers (Figure 2.8), who were keen to incorporate their ideas and awareness of global trends into Indian clothing. This is especially evident in the fashions popular in the 1980s and 1990s, where the *salwar kameez* was cut to resemble Western dresses with shoulder pads, puff sleeves and floral prints. In addition there were numerous experimentations with embroidery details, faux layers, shape and silhouette, and the *dupatta* kept changing size and placement on the body. It is also important to note that while this particular garment received wider acceptance in India, it was also gaining popularity amongst the Indian Diaspora, especially in England, for similar reasons.[23]

Ethnic-chic

In countering the transitions taking place in women's fashions towards greater Westernization, along with the preference for synthetic materials over handloom textiles, a small segment of Indian elites began "pushing the concept of indigenism and 'authenticity' through [wearing] ethnic dresses" (Bahl 2005: 88). This culminated in the ethnic-chic trend during the 1980s, which Tarlo also notes during her visit to Hauz Khas village in New Delhi, where a cluster of fashion boutiques had opened up to deliberately use the village's "rural" setting to promote peasant-inspired clothes (Tarlo 1996). Concurrent to the surge of interest in Indian textiles and dress on Western catwalks, ethnic-chic fashion in India in its purest form involved donning embellished tribal dress and jewelry by an elite minority at a time that the majority of Indian villagers were shunning such styles in favor of synthetics (Tarlo 1996: 324). Tarlo viewed this trend as a direct response (and opposition) to the Westernization of middle-class dress and a strategy of distinction from those who were following the earlier styles set by the Indian elite, much like the cycle of fashion behavior proposed by Simmel.[24]

While ethnic-chic may appear to bear some resemblance to Gandhi's promotion of *khadi* and the *Swadeshi* movement, for most wearers it did not go beyond a trend of visual identification. It was, however, an interesting twist whereby elite women were

---

[23]Bhachu (2004) describes the transnational design and manufacturing networks pioneered by Indian women in England—as they would design their own (and subsequently their clients' outfits), have them tailored in India and shipped to England, which became a starting point for lucrative business ventures.

[24]Simmel's (1904, 1957) theory linking fashion change to class distinction and competition has been one of the most influential in attempting to explain fashionable behavior in nineteenth century Europe. He saw fashion as an endless sequence of change that came about with those in the elite classes distinguishing themselves through their dress styles, leading those in the classes subjacent to them to copy these styles as a way of satisfying their aspirations and desires for a more superior status, which then leads the elite classes to further distinguish themselves again by changing their styles of dress, thereby changing the stakes for those below them and causing the cycle to continue.

wearing styles of indigenous clothing that would once have been associated with being backward and lower class a century ago by the same strata. These were now a means of distinction, at a time when the very people who were associated with such clothing viewed them as backward. The trend did, however, mirror one key aspect of an older nationalist perspective—that of the promotion of the ascendancy of the East over the West—in this case in the aesthetic realm, as a strategy for the Indian elite to distinguish themselves not only from other classes but also from the West (Tarlo 1996). While in its truest form it was a short-lived trend and only worn by those who could afford such clothes financially and practically, it did set into motion a key strategy for Indian design and designers towards reviving textile crafts and traditional clothing styles. Many also found a niche for themselves in the local and global fashion scene, and further went on to shape popular trends and terminology in Indian fashion.

Tarlo (1996) is cautious against celebrating the resurgence of Orientalist stereotypes that such design strategies create in the wake of globalization and developing sense of cultural and sartorial distinction. But as already mentioned, the hybridity that these strategies involve can also be empowering. Khan (1992) highlights this outcome through crediting the popularity of ethnic-chic for not only encouraging India's emerging fashion industry and reviving an interest in regional styles and forgotten textile crafts, but also enfranchising urban women across India, who began to set up small fashion boutiques of their own or took part in travelling trade shows selling *salwar* suits and other designer traditional clothing in the wake of this trend. As mentioned already, women were accustomed to dealing with tailors in crafting their personal wardrobes, and so the prospect of them extending these networks towards setting up their own boutique selling *salwar* suits, *kurtas* etc. was not seen as a threat to women's commitments at home or their role in Indian society. In explaining this Khan states:

> A boutique, or a modest line of clothes, has proved a gentle, uncontroversial entry into the male world of work. After all, people argued, what was entailed? Little more than what respectable women had always done—conferring with their tailor at home over clothes and designs. And the little shops started by some women would not deal with the *hoi polloi* and certainly not with men, but with women, and women of a similar social background. A respectable and safe step, in short, to liberation. (Khan 1992: 64–5)

Conclusion

Many of the instances mentioned in this chapter highlight the hybridity and multifunctional nature of clothing in India—as forms of resistance, group association, political symbolism, embodiment of modernity, changing lifestyles and evolving social roles, which occur both as a result of and in tandem with the forces of fashion (Figure 2.9).

Women's refusal to adopt Western dress in the early part of the nineteenth century in favor of the new style of tying the sari, or the later preference for the *salwar kameez* are both instances of style experimentations that were simultaneously modern and traditional.

Figure 2.9 Portrait of a fashionable couple—friends of author's grandparents. Circa 1940s. The man is wearing a turban as part of his military uniform. The woman is wearing the *Nivi* style of sari over a fashionably cut blouse with puff-sleeves. Image courtesy Amrita Sandhu.

They are also in keeping with Bahl's (2005) definition of "modern" or "progressive" clothes as being those that we *choose* to wear according to the environment within which we find ourselves. In this way, the shifting image of the modern Indian woman, and her clothing, represents the ability of tradition and modernity to be evolutionary processes that are not in opposition to each other. Additionally, the mobilization of dress as a material medium of negotiating various shifting cultural contexts involved a constant reevaluation of dress practices and an interweaving of past and present styles, which included Indian, Western and global elements. This was apparent in the transition witnessed in men's clothing during the late nineteenth and early twentieth century, that went beyond a simple case of Westernization. The mimicry of British clothing by Indian men was not a complete re-inscription of their clothes but instead a means of instilling distinction through a highly selective appropriation of dress as strategies of resistance, subversion and empowerment.

As the following chapters will reveal, the strategies of dress and distinction, as Tarlo refers to them, discussed in this chapter, continue to be relevant to shaping popular fashion in current times. This includes various levels of sartorial fusion between local and global dress and cultural factors. Since the increased influence of global forces following

India's liberalization once again led to concerns about the preservation of dress and a distinctive Indian identity—such concerns teamed with various identity-based anxieties have led to a renewed interest in and reinvigoration of *Swadeshi* ideals. Recast in more globally receptive formats they are now a key part of creating locally centered design, for which Mazzarella (2003a) proposes the term new-*Swadeshi*. This was evident in the scenario presented in the beginning of the book about Sabyasachi's 2010 couture show *Aparajito,* where he not only promoted the use of *khadi* as a luxury fabric but also emphasized the preservation of traditional techniques of weaving [therefore wearing] of the sari.

Beyond asserting a sense of distinction through the way fashion is created and represented in India, the use of clothing as a form of political symbolism also persists—for which the Indian nationalist movements are a key visual reference as well as recurring themes. This was apparent most recently during New Delhi's local elections in December 2013, where the *Aam Aadmi* Party (party of the common man), led by Arvind Kejriwal, wore white Gandhi *topis*[25] to differentiate themselves from other political parties. The wearing of the *topi* additionally symbolized the party's key mission, which was to rid India of its widespread corruption and other political vices. The politics of women's dress as it links to evolving social roles, also remains an ongoing issue in India. One of the many instances that highlight this fact occurred in January 2009, when a group of women were attacked in Mangalore by religious activists from the right-wing Hindu group *Sri Ram Sena*, while they were at a pub with some male friends. Nirmala Venkatesh, a spokesperson for the National Commission for Women (NSW), who surveyed the scene after the crime, stated that it was partially the fault of the women who were wearing provocative [Western] clothes and dancing to a live band (Balakrishnan 2009). In response to this and similar events at the time,[26] Nisha Susan, Mihira Sood, Jasmine Patheja and Isha Manchanda launched a nonviolent protest titled the "Pink *Chaddi* Campaign." Calling themselves the "Consortium of Pub-Going, Loose and Forward Women," the campaign initiated on Facebook involved drumming up public support against the attacks and sending pink *chaddis* (underwear) as a sign of protest to the chief of the *Sri Ram Sena* —Pramod Muthalik's office. The use of pink underwear deliberately touched upon many symbolic local and global factors—where pink denoted Valentine's Day (which the Ram Sena opposes, and had threatened to conduct further attacks on celebrating couples on that day, in 2009), *chaddi* in Hindi is a childish word for underwear, as well as a derogatory term for the short pants commonly worn as uniform by the right-wing Hindu nationalist group *Rashtriya Swayamsevak Sangh* (RSS) across India.[27] Invariably there was also the connection to lingerie*,* which, like Valentine's Day, is deemed a Western import. The Pink *Chaddi* campaign received considerable attention through its promotion via social media networks and the wider media, and as a result many (mainly) middle-class Indians,

---

[25] Iconic style of cap as worn by Mahatma Gandhi and his supporters during the Indian nationalist movements.
[26] Following this, there were reports of other attacks on women wearing Western attire in Bangalore that appeared to be inspired by the one in Mangalore. One of the women even noted that her attackers said she "'deserved' it for wearing jeans and sleeveless kurta…" (Arwind 2009)
[27] Also referred to as "right wingers" (Susan 2009a).

as well as people across the world, were aware of it and showed their support through sending over 2,000 *chaddis* towards the protest.[28] The campaign, which ultimately led to a short-lived truce with the *Sri Ram Sena*, is yet another example of how Gandhian values continue to resonate with the current generation, as they employ the visual and material symbolism vested in clothing along with newer global modes and mediums, that become localized, as effective methods of peaceful resistance.

[28] Susan (2009b).

3
CONTEMPORARY FASHION PRACTICE IN URBAN INDIA

Last Sunday I visited a nearby water theme park with my family and a family in the neighbourhood. We thoroughly enjoyed the day playing in water and going on scary rides... But always I am confused what dress I should wear in such places. My husband told me to put on a cotton three-fourth pants and tee shirt. I felt very comfortable in the water in that dress... Some orthodox Muslim women were in Burqa *and I was wondering how they will enjoy in water. But what struck me is the sight of a lady wearing an ankle length nightie!!!! Yes you heard me right, a nightie. There were lot of women wearing saree and* salwar kameez *etc but I didn't feel anything odd about it. But how nightie will give comfort to a lady in a theme park!!! ... Another funny fusion dress that I see is pairing up a* kameez *with jeans and wearing a matching* dupatta *with it. I always wonder what mistake would have the poor* salwar *committed so that the lady kept it out of her outfit. Some females even enhance their looks with jeans and* kurta *by wearing a* bindi *and lot of gold jewellery. I am not telling that it's wrong to dress up like this but to me it looks funny. Friday is the best day to find such people who dress up weirdly since most of the companies and offices consider Friday as a casual wear day.* [1]

Introduction

Clothing and fashion provide the perfect material medium through which cultural and conceptual shifts, and evolving identities can be negotiated, fine-tuned and [re]shaped to suit individual and collective needs. The excerpt included above, from a blog entry titled "Yuck" by Neeta (an Indian fashion and beauty blogger), offers a first-hand account and response to clothing-related issues that have only recently come about as a result of the

---

[1] Excerpt reproduced from blog entry dated from June 2012, with minor spelling changes and name changed (at the request of the blogger).

introduction of new kinds of public spaces in India. It emphasizes the role clothing and fashion play in charting new territories, expressing new identities as well as challenging older ones. It also captures the dilemmas that many Indians currently face as they attempt to make fashionable choices, that are in keeping with the nation's approach to further modernization, economic development and globalization, as well as, mindful of traditions vested in indigenous styles of dress.

Typically most fashion and dress historians have overlooked the clothing choices of the urban classes in India described in the blog excerpt above in favor of richly embellished tribal garments, rural styles or the clothes worn by [past] royal elites. More recently the focus has expanded to include high-fashion designer wear, whereas instances of everyday dress like the nightie or mixing of Crocs with saris, preference for Western clothes, Louis Vuitton bags (real and fake) and brands like Puma or Levi's, for example, in tandem with the exuberant layering of both Indian and Western garments commonplace in what Vasudev (2010) refers to as a "free-to-wear-anything" country, continue to be excluded from more serious examinations of dress and fashion. This is largely due to the lasting influence of Orientalist frameworks and patterns of past ethnographic and anthropological research, mentioned in the first chapter, as a result of which casual and everyday styles have been disregarded due to their apparent lack of "authenticity" (Tarlo 1996). Yet, despite the perceived lack of respect for "centuries of tradition" and stylistic constraint, that are in stark contrast to the kinds of clothes documented in coffee table books on Indian costumes and textiles, everyday clothing and the fashion tastes of urban Indians are equally deserving of attention. This is not only because they have significant impact on apparel manufacturing and the retail sector, but also because they form an integral part of India's sartorial landscape—seen in malls, markets, bazaars, in films, on reality TV and online on blogs. Closer inspection of these clothing preferences highlights how they "substantiate and give concrete cultural meanings" about class, status, gender, age, beauty, and modernity as well as various value systems and beliefs to individuals and social groups (Cunningham and Lab 1991: 5), which this chapter's discussion on contemporary fashion practice in urban India will examine. Through offering an overview of dress practices as they relate to social class, modernization, influence of globalization, ongoing issues of morality and the consumption of branded goods, as well as the apparel market it supports the following chapters that address various aspects of Indian fashion from a more thematic standpoint.

Living life kingsize:[2] India's "new" urban classes

Introducing the reader to the nature and makeup of India's prominent urban classes that have prospered in the years subsequent to its transition towards a capitalist system

---

[2] The phrase "Live Life Kingsize" was made popular by the cigarette brand Four Square Kings through their Western styled advertisements in the 1970s and 1980s that featured famous personalities like film actor Suresh Oberoi and cricketer Kapil Dev.

of economy is a crucial starting point for this chapter. These include the "new" Indian middle-class that has witnessed unprecedented growth in recent decades and the cosmopolitan elite "global Indian." Both of these groups are highly visible in various urban settings and attract significant [positive] media attention. Together they also constitute a large consumer base for a variety of fashion brands and products, as a result of which their tastes and preferences have significant impact on Indian design aesthetics and popular fashion. Alongside an increased emphasis on commodity consumption, India's emerging middle-class, in particular, is also most impacted by the social pressures of balancing Indian and Western elements in their clothing choices. The ongoing tension and dilemmas of "what to wear" as experienced by this group as it negotiates between co-existing, often conflicting, discourses of high and low, local and global, old and new, and tradition and modernity, become reflected in numerous ways in the fashions worn.

McKinsey Global Institute (MGI) estimates that while the middle-class made up for only 5 percent of the total population in 2007 (roughly 50 million people), it is projected to grow to 41 percent (583 million people) by the year 2025 (MGI 2007: 10).[3] This estimation is in line with most other case studies and publications that propose India will eventually become a middle-class country within the next few decades. As in the case of any such class in a society, there is an engaging mix of generations within the Indian middle-class, where each is rooted in its beliefs and practices that stem from various factors that have shaped India's recent history. In contrast to older generations that still tend to follow a socialist pattern in their thinking, the current generation of young professionals and entrepreneurs (that media accounts on the "new" middle-class and youth culture generally focus on) has experienced an entirely different time due to economic liberalization. Globally connected via the internet as well as through being exposed to a far wider array of Western and global media—films, cable television networks, MTV etc.—combined with a strong preference for speaking in English, acceptance of Western clothes and an overall sense of greater global awareness and confidence are characteristic of this generation. However, it is the overall mix of generations that allows for various viewpoints and beliefs within middle-class society to co-exist and ultimately helps maintain equilibrium amongst them (Mathur 2010),[4] while also contributing to the diversity of dress practices prevalent in India.

Due to the size and complexity evident in its composition, the nature and status of

---

[3]"The 'Bird of Gold': The Rise of India's Consumer Market," McKinsey Global Institute, 2007.

In this report MGI classifies Indian households into five segments based on income per annum. These are: the deprived (earning less than Rupees 90,000 per year—approx US$1,624, which currently dominate the Indian population; the aspirers—a class that the former poor will slowly move into (households earning between Rupees 90,000–200,000 per year—approx US$3,611); the seekers (Rupees 200,000 to 500,000 per year—approx US$ 9,027); the strivers (Rupees 500,000 to 10,00,00 or 10 lakh a year, US$ 18,055) and the global Indians (earning more than Rupees 10 lakh a year). MGI classifies the Indian middle-class as being within the Rupees 200,000 to 10 lakh income per year, i.e. the seekers and the strivers. This definition is in keeping with India's National Council of Applied Economic Research (NCAER). The members of these groups range from young college graduates, mid to senior level government officials, traders, business people and well-to-do farmers.

[4]Another notable shift is in the caste composition of this segment of society, which was originally comprised mostly of the traditional, upper castes; but is now increasingly constituted by non-traditional caste groups (Sridharan 2004: 421).

the middle-class in post-liberalization India has attracted significant academic interest—where the class as a whole, and its segments and regional distinctions have been studied from various sociological, anthropological and cultural perspectives (Fernandes 2000, 2006; Liechty 2003; Donner 2008; Ganguly-Scrase and Scarase 2009; Lukose 2009; Saavala 2012, etc.). Most of these studies invariably deal with two recurring themes—namely: a) the shifting balance and ongoing negotiations between old and new, traditional and modern (often read as Indian and Western), and local and global towards pioneering new standards of national identity; and b) the role contemporary consumption practices play in class and identity management.

It is essential to highlight that the use of the word "new," commonly employed when referring to India's growing middle-class, for the most part, is a constructed entity (Fernandes 2000, 2006; Saavala 2012). That is, it is not a new social class but it is "novel" in the way it differs from the old middle-class. Firstly, in terms of the new segments of society and professions that now comprise this class, and secondly, due to the shared experience of changing lifestyles and social status achieved as a result of their own or their parents' generation's experience of upward mobility following India's economic reforms (Saavala 2012: 11). According to Fernandes, another distinctive feature of the new middle-class lies in its construction as a "new class" of entrepreneurs "who are potential leaders of the Indian nation with a new global outlook" (Fernandes 2000: 92), which is ultimately a sign of the positive outcomes of liberalization and a new model of national and economic development that hinges on India's integration with the global economy. In this way it is possible to see links between the rise of the current middle-class with the rise of the Indian middle-class in colonial times, the latter of which was also charged with the role of mediation and cultural leadership. However, now the process of mediation is about being "able to negotiate India's new relationship with the global economy in both cultural and economic terms; in cultural terms by defining a new cultural standard that rests on the socio symbolic practices of commodity consumption, and in economic terms as the beneficiaries of the material benefits of jobs in India's 'new economy'" (ibid.: 91).

The shift in its overall image from that of austerity to being much more globally aware and immersed in consumption also defines the Indian middle-class's newness. Fernandes notes a surge of idealized representations in print media and on-screen (films, television) portraying the urban middle-class as "an affluent consumer, who has finally achieved the ability to exercise choice through consumption" (Fernandes 2000: 88). Concurrent to the opening up of the Indian market to international brands along with more relaxed rules for foreign direct investment (FDI) that have transformed the face of Indian retail, such image-texts[5] emphasizing upper-class trendy globalized lifestyles are now commonplace even in local publications based in Tier-II cities.[6] Here the idealized middle-class are often

---

[5] A term I borrow from Reddy (2006) while referring to the combination of image and texts in magazine articles, advertisements and advertorials.

[6] Indian cities are typically classified using a ranking system developed by the Indian government on the basis of their population. Under this system cities are referred to as Tier-I, Tier-II and Tier-III cities, where Delhi, Mumbai, Chennai, Kolkata, Ahmedabad and Hyderabad comprise the first Tier.

portrayed wearing branded jeans, "bodycon" evening dresses, designer suits or Indian couture; carrying branded handbags and accessories; driving luxury cars; attending wine tastings, movie premieres or hanging out at clubs. Through depicting such products and lifestyles as new symbols of progress, these image-texts further fuel the desire of the newly prosperous urban classes to actively partake and be seen partaking in the public display of consumption. Despite being out of reach for most within the actual middle-class bracket, the constant promotion of such material items and lavish lifestyles in all forms of current print and televisual media, where they are classified as crucial markers of modernity and urban lifestyles, means that they have come to shape the collective aims and aspirations of the Indian middle-class.

While projections of India's economic growth and global position are currently mixed, and not as strong as they were when the MGI report was published, most research and media reports continue to paint a positive picture of what lies ahead for the elite and middle-classes. The former of which MGI's report projects will account for 2 percent of India's total population by the year 2025.[7] While it may appear to be a small percentage, this elite segment, which the report classifies as "global Indians," in actual numbers is greater than the entire population of Australia. Also worth noting is Forbes magazine's estimation of the net worth of India's 100 richest people in 2012—at approximately US$250 billion (Karmali 2012)—thus emphasizing the importance of this growing elite segment as an extremely attractive market for Indian and international designer and luxury brands and services. Beinhocker and Farrell further affirm such projections by noting the existence of a new breed of fiercely competitive and "ferociously upwardly mobile" Indians whose tastes are indistinguishable from similar groups of "prosperous young Westerners" (Beinhocker and Farrell 2007). Many from this emerging group already own "high-end luxury cars and wear designer clothes, employ maids and full-time cooks, and regularly vacation abroad" (ibid.). These reports serve as reminders that those belonging to the upper crust of the global Indian segment have the means to experience lifestyles that are easily on par with their global counterparts; and in some cases surpass global markers through various cultural and social aspects that are unique to India—such as the relative affordability of housekeeping and related services, as well as cost of living.

Unlike other countries, India also has a growing younger population that is a lucrative market for branded consumer goods and services. According to Gopal and Srinivasan, Indians constituted a fifth of the world's citizens below the age of 20 in 2006—which they categorize as "a youthful exuberant generation weaned on success [that] is joining the ranks of Indian consumers" (Gopal and Srinivasan 2006: 22). MGI's study in 2007 suggested that if India managed to maintain high levels of economic growth (7–8 percent at the time of the report), average household incomes would triple, making it the world's fifth largest consumer economy by 2025.[8] It also projected that as incomes rise, the

---

[7] McKinsey Global Institute, 2007.

[8] While these numbers have been significantly dampened in the wake of India's most recent economic downturn (2013), projections for the market still remain bright, despite being lower than those cited in 2007 by MGI.

shape of India's income pyramid would also shift dramatically and spending patterns would begin to shift in favor of discretionary purchases.

The apparel market and current consumer trends

Following from such reports, India's domestic apparel market is currently tipped as being "the" destination for emerging and established luxury, high-fashion, mid-market and mass-market brands, the success of which is contingent on understanding and catering to the specific tastes and needs of the urban elite and the middle-class.

In 2012 the clothing and apparel sector accounted for 33 percent of organized retail in India, making it the largest segment in the market.[9] Technopak's apparel report states that India's domestic apparel market was worth Rupees 1,90,300 crore[10] (US $40 billion) in 2012, and is expected to grow by 9 percent per year to reach Rupees 4,62,250 crore (US $98 billion) by 2021 (Technopak 2012).[11] Within this market there exist a number of large Indian brands, such as Wills Lifestyle, Pantaloons, Westside (Figure 3.1), and store-in-store department stores like Shoppers Stop that have national presence. These brands offer a mix of products—Western, fusion, Indian, men's, women's, and youth fashions. Alongside these are a plethora of international brands (some of which are local to India, but have gained popularity through being positioned as global brands) that have entered the market since liberalization. While the years following further heightened the cultural and symbolic value of Western labels through constant promotion in magazines and other forms of popular media, not all incoming brands have been successful. In the absence of large-scale investments and brand tie-ups, most locally based high-fashion designers have preferred to focus on an elite clientele and the occasion-wear market, where Indian aesthetics and textiles still hold an edge. While a growing number of Indian designers have begun to design and produce Western wear as well, most tend to create a mix of lines—comprising of fusion wear, bridal couture and *prêt* (ready-to-wear) to maintain a balance of products that can be locally and globally marketed. Competing with these designers are numerous global luxury and Western designer brands that are now a prominent feature in Indian retail. Encouraged by further relaxation of India's FDI rules, as well as availability of retail sites beyond five-star hotels for exclusive outlets, they made up for a quarter of all the international brands that entered the market in 2011—a boom that has only been witnessed over the past decade (Dutta 2013). With the increasing desire to own luxury items on the one hand and the reality of the modest means of the middle-class on the other, the gap in affordable luxury when comparing mid-market brands (where items range from an average of Rupees 900 to Rupees

---

[9] Images India Retail Report 2013, www.indiaretailing.com (accessed October 12, 2012).

[10] A *crore* (abbreviated cr) equals ten million or 100 lakhs and is written as 1,00,00,000.

[11] "Textile & Apparel Compendium 2012," report prepared by Technopak (2012), www.technopak.com (accessed December 15, 2012).

Figure 3.1 "Endless Possibilities." Advertising campaign for Westside featuring Giselli Monteiro, a Brazilian actress who acted in the Bollywood film *Love Aaj Kal* (Love Nowadays, 2009) opposite Saif Ali Khan. In these ads Monteiro represents the many avatars of the Indian woman that Westside caters to. Image courtesy Westside.

3,000, approx US$15–50) to the average price point of a designer item (at approximately Rupees 25,000 or US$400) has also opened up a lucrative space for affordable luxury (Tewari 2012). This gap is slowly being addressed by brands like Karmik (which features Indian designer wear at affordable prices), Manish Arora's tie up with BIBA for a new label "Indian", as well as designer collaborations by mid-market brands like Westside (Rahul Mishra, Wendell Rodricks, Narendra Kumar) and Levi's (Tarun Tahiliani).

Menswear constitutes the biggest segment of organized retail in India, with a variety of clearly demarcated garment segments—jeanswear, smart casuals, tailored formals, lifestyle wear and sportswear. The prominence of menswear is even greater in smaller cities, where branded stores for men outweigh those that cater to women. There is also a significant presence of global brands in this arena, some of which have been present even prior to liberalization. Due to its dominance in organized apparel retail, the design and styling of men's fashion are emerging lucrative fields. Categories like "Casual Fridays," popular in the 1990s, have expanded greatly in the men's market—as witnessed by the growth of luxury professional clothing labels and the transition of basic sportswear brands into "lifestyle brands." The latter is a reflection of the growing interest in fitness and sporting activities in urban areas, as a result of which brands like Nike,

Puma, and Adidas have expanded their traditional sportswear categories into a wider "sports-inspired casual wear" that offer more casual clothing that can be worn for everything "outside the office" (Dhir, Sachdev, and Jain 2010: 39).

My conversations with mid-market focused fashion designers and buyers working for Indian and international brands, all highlighted a difference in tastes between Indian male consumers from their global counterparts. While Indian men actively seek out fashionable clothing that is in keeping with international trends, their preference for vibrant colors, prints and visible detailing sets them apart. Here it is important to note that despite the adoption of Western styles into the Indian male wardrobe at the turn of the last century, men maintained many prevailing aspects of indigenous color and aesthetic sensibilities as part of their clothing tastes. This made Indian menswear distinct when compared to the visual gendering that took place during similar transitions in other cultures. Tastes for color and pattern were further encouraged and cemented through popular films, especially in the 1980s, and many of these influences still hold strong. Rajesh,[12] a product developer for a jeanswear brand, notes how design teams cater to the specific tastes of Indian men by consciously experimenting with interesting design details, new denim washes, contrast trims and hand finishes, as men look for "greater visual impact" in their clothes. According to some of the designers interviewed for this book, Indian menswear has moved beyond the kitschy version popularized by actors like Govinda and Jeetendra in Bollywood films, and is slowly becoming much more sophisticated. However, despite this shift, the preference for bold graphics, logos, and chest prints is still one that retail stores feel most confident selling.

In comparison to men's apparel, womenswear, which comprises of Western wear, ethnic wear and fusion styles, remains largely in the hands of the fragmented sector. Despite being witness to more obvious design innovation showcased at various fashion weeks and greater prominence in print media, there are few large-scale brands across the country that cater to womenswear. This is mainly due to the fact that women still rely on local tailoring services or unbranded apparel stores. Within the organized sector saris and ethnic wear (that includes items like *salwar kameez* and other fashionable traditional or fusion styles) are most prominent. However, Roy and Saha (2007) have found a 15–20 percent annual growth in the women's trendy Western wear segment. This is further confirmed by Zara's runaway success since launching in India in 2010,[13] which was followed by the entry of Forever 21 and now H&M (forthcoming[14]), to name a few. Technopak's report also notes a higher growth rate over recent years in denim, innerwear and t-shirts in the womenswear market, which can be attributed to a growing desire to experiment with global trends.[15] Shifting consumer tastes point to the fact that while a few decades ago it was the younger generation which felt more comfortable in Western

---

[12] Name changed at the request of the interviewee (interview with the author in 2012).

[13] See Vasudev (2013).

[14] Projected to open in 2014.

[15] The increase in wearing of Western clothes, in tandem with the popularity of dresses as occasion wear has had direct impact on demand for innerwear (intimate apparel and lingerie) that supports the shape and silhouette of such clothing (Technopak 2012).

wear, now even older, middle-aged women are more open to wearing Western styles or at least "Westernizing" their wardrobes—through adopting trendier *kurti* styles or Lycra *salwars* that resemble tights, for example.

Despite these factors, fashionable ethnic wear[16] continues to be a dominant segment across the womenswear market and constitutes almost 30 percent of its total share (Chakrabarti and Baisya 2009). This resilience is largely due to the fact that a majority of women still feel most comfortable in traditional clothes, and a significant number of India's female workforce prefer to wear styles like the *salwar kameez* for work. Ethnic wear also remains the main preference for traditional occasions linked to religious festivals and weddings. Most importantly, traditional or ethnic fashions have remained in step with contemporary global and local trends, thus allowing for their continued relevance in current times.

My discussion in this chapter purposely avoids a more detailed survey of the Indian apparel market and itemized listing of labels and brands etc., as firstly such data was felt outside of the book's immediate discussion. And secondly the exclusion was made in favor of highlighting emerging tastes in fashion demonstrated by the urban classes. As already mentioned in this book's introduction and further discussed in the following chapter, fashion consciousness and the awareness of popular trends, for the most part, continue to be derived from Bollywood. Contemporary films in particular mirror the shifts being experienced in urban lifestyles through featuring aspirational scenarios that heavily emphasize the consumption of branded fashion and related products—which in turn further impinge upon consumers' tastes. As the format of costuming shifts from tailoring to styling, films further enforce the message of materialism in relation to fashion labels and luxury brands. Recent years have also witnessed a growth in the importance of reality television, celebrity culture, fashion magazines and the Internet as sources of local and global fashion. Besides these popular mediums, fashions continue to be influenced by local market forces that rely on regional events and auspicious seasons.

Various consumer studies show that design and style are essential factors for Indians. Following from which, brands are extremely important, especially in the case of men's clothing (Mohan and Gupta 2007; Jin, Park, and Ryu 2010[17] etc.). Technopak's apparel report further states that the Indian wardrobe has undergone a transformation from primarily comprising of need-based clothing (like shirts, trousers, jackets, saris, *salwar kameez*) that centered around function, comfort and affordability—to now being more about occasion-specific dressing (which includes working out at the gym, career wear for the office, ethnic wear, night and party wear for example) where the key requirements are trend consciousness and the overall look (Technopak 2012). This mirrors the changes

---

[16]Chakrabarti and Baisya describe this segment as "clothing where Indian aesthetics have been married with a sensitivity to Western design" (Chakrabarti and Baisya 2009: 706).

[17]The results of a comparative study between Indian and Chinese customers and their evaluative criteria when selecting denim jeans by Jin, Park, and Ryu (2010) highlights the importance Indians place on fit, brand and its country of origin, and design—in that respective order. In comparison, a similar survey of Chinese tastes shows a preference for affordability (price), then fit and brand (Jin, Park, and Ryu 2010).

in lifestyle experienced by the middle-classes—who work harder, focus more on their appearance and have a wider variety of options for recreation and entertainment.

Adding to this, Gallup International's surveys on the habits, hopes, plans and preferences of the Indian consumer in 2006, led to three key findings: a) Indians are getting more materialistic, i.e. more and more Indians are motivated by personal ambition, material gains and financial success; b) consumerism is becoming a way of life, not only for the younger generation but across the board; and c) "foreign is passé; Indian is paramount" (Gopal and Srinivasan 2006: 23). The last of the three insights is particularly crucial to highlight, as it points to how the Indian consumer mindset has undergone another shift in recent years, where before international brands were crucial for showing status and global acumen, now it is more about creating a sense of uniqueness. Hence, the assertion of class and status increasingly relies on the ability to discerningly select from numerous Indian *and* international products in building this distinction. In terms of fashion, this can be achieved through creative combinations and juxtapositions of local and global cultural elements, which make it possible to be locally rooted yet globally stylish.

Fusion fashion

Further affirming the aforementioned observation is the way in which the widespread influence of global forces in India is concurrent with an increased interest amongst the urban classes in all things local—vernacular culture, cuisine, travel destinations, textiles, dress practices etc. In terms of fashion, there exists an unproblematic enshrining of Western labels, logos, brands and clothing on one hand, alongside an equally vibrant and in many cases conscious indigenization of dress. This coexistence is emphasized by all forms of fashion print media that further promote the mutual compatibility of Indian and global garments and brands—with an emphasis on creating a uniquely Indian aesthetic that can be fine-tuned to match personal and collective tastes and expectations, and respond to local sensibilities. Style experimentations by leading Indian designers and fashionistas combining traditional clothing and ethnic elements with global trends and Western cuts have led to the popularity of the Indo-Western or *desi*-chic look. Such fusion not only helps Indian women and men to fashion themselves in ways that are in keeping with societal pressures, it also allows them to be part of the larger network of global fashion, yet simultaneously maintain a sense of distinction.

Seeing the potential in this genre of design and Indo-Western mix and match—brands like Anokhi (Figure 3.2), FabIndia[18] and "W" focus on styles of *salwar kameez*, *kurtis* and other traditionally inspired garments that combine global trends with Indian textiles, colors and embellishments. In doing so they also cater to corporate and casual clothing niches.

---

[18]Fabindia's employment of India's mix and match mentality as part of their retail framework (where for example— buyers can match their *kurta* to any color, pattern or cut of *salwar* and then choose whether or not they would like to do the same with the *dupatta*) is yet another way the confluence of local and global leads to unique outcomes in Indian fashion [retail].

Figure 3.2 "Melon and Mint." Ensemble featuring block-printed sleeveless blouse worn with low crotch *salwar* style bottoms. From the Anokhi photo archives, May 2013. Image courtesy Anokhi.

Beyond designer high-fashion, which is discussed in Chapter 6, Anokhi and Fabindia in particular, can be credited with the establishment of a casual ethnic fusion niche[19] that also allows consumers to mix and match various types of garments (Indian and Western) while making their purchase. Following from this, other Indian retailers like Shoppers Stop, Westside (see outfit on the left in Figure 3.1), Globus and Pantaloons have also begun to offer their own in-house labels that cater to this segment of fashionable and casual ethnic wear. The *salwar kameez,* in this context, remains a popular fusion and fashion-friendly garment due to its similarity to the Western shirt and trouser combination. As already discussed in the last chapter, it lends itself to numerous design experimentations and further allows for its components to be individually styled. Dhir et al. (2010) cite a popular trend amongst younger women of wearing t-shirts along with *salwars*, much like Kareena Kapoor's look in the popular film *Jab We Met* (*When We Met* 2007) (Refer to

[19]In addition Anokhi and Fabindia have centered their design strategies on preservation of Indian crafts and design that has heightened their popularity amongst a growing generation of Indian fashionistas that are looking for ethically produced and sustainable fashion.

Figure 4.1 on p. 78). Equivalent to a simple jeans and t-shirt look, such experimentations allow women to pare back ostentation and formal fabrication of more embellished traditional styles, so that they appear basic and comfortable. Similarly, shortening the *kameez* into a *kurti*—another very popular garment—allows it to be worn with jeans or trousers and jackets. The *kurti* embodies many attributes that make it attractive to women, as through resembling a Western blouse or even T-shirt it can be fashionable and hip, but with its Indian cut and traditional tag it stays within acceptable norms.[20] As a result the *kurti* has been subject to numerous style innovations, further popularized once again through stores like Anokhi, Fabindia, Global Indian[21] and scores of unbranded shops and stalls. Recent years have also seen design experimentation with various other traditional garments such as the *dhoti* and even the sari, all of which has added to a renewed sense of excitement amongst urban fashionistas towards trying out these styles.

Contemporary fashion practice: Keeping up with the Kapoors, the Joneses, *and* the Kardashians

> ... fashion practice—as a communicative mode—is class practice; it is a new performance medium through which people attempt to synchronize their lives with those of others. In this way fashion integrates the new middle class, less around a set of agreed-upon goods or styles than around a shared practice or mode of consumption. (Liechty 2003: 139)

In the current context, fashion for the growing elite and middle-classes forms an important part of public practice in India. This is especially so because in India class struggle is centered around social belonging and acceptance (Liechty 2003; Saavala 2012: 8).[22] As a result, certain goods and practices become key social markers towards achieving acceptance and maintaining status, thereby making consumption itself a highly visible and key social practice. The role of branded and designer clothing as markers of displaying wealth and distinction through conspicuous consumption is re-emphasized through the presence of global fashion and luxury brands, as well as new forms of local and globalized media that promote them. Since the domestic fashion industry is itself also experiencing a boom in popularity (as more and more designers emerge and fashion weeks multiply manifold), the visibility of fashion in print media has further increased.

---

[20] During a number of interviews in my fieldwork, people would comment on the versatility of the *kurti*. Men also commented on how if women wore jeans and T-shirts in less affluent neighborhoods they could appear too Western and provocatively dressed, but a *kurti* made wearing jeans more Indian and acceptable.

[21] Mumbai-based designer Anita Dongre's fusion brand that caters to the middle-class Indian woman (Anita Dongre in an interview with the author in 2010).

[22] According to Saavala class struggle for the Indian middle-classes is neither about economic or political struggle between classes, and nor is it purely a struggle over distinction and taste within classes, as theorized by Bourdieu (Saavala 2010).

The ability to partake and be seen partaking in acquiring and wearing the "latest" styles and labels that are on par with the rest of the world are crucial for the image of the "new" middle-class as well as the nouveau riche, who are charged with forging new and meaningful relationships with the global economy. Ultimately "fashion" for India's emerging middle- and new elite classes is also a crucial medium of individual expression and the lived experience of modernity—that not only helps them to keep up with the Kapoors but also with the Joneses, *and* the Kardashians.

Indians generally demonstrate a keen awareness towards their dress and demeanor in public settings. Historically speaking there are numerous venues and cultural events that go beyond class and regional boundaries for which the purchase, performance and appreciation of new fashions is central. Examples of these include festivals like *Diwali*— where gifting and wearing of new clothes is part of tradition; weddings—where clothes act as markers of status; and street markets, fairs and local bazaars—that often feature open stalls where the latest trends in clothing are on prominent display. The importance of clothing choices, not only for proper presentation but in terms of being aware of current fashions is evident in texts on past and present adornment practices in India (Castelino 1994; Tarlo 1996, Banerjee and Miller 2003; Shukla 2005, 2008) and confirmed through my field research as well as in my own experience of growing up in India.

Since shopping is a crucial aspect in the public practice of fashion, it is important to highlight here that Indian shopping habits are distinct from other countries'. Research indicates that Indians see shopping as a family pastime (Sheth and Vittal 2007).[23] This not only impacts the way shopping centers, retail stores and fashion collections are designed and planned, but also the way purchases are made and the kinds of purchases made. Key shopping seasons tend to revolve around annual religious festivals, as well as the auspicious wedding season (ibid.), which means the cycles of fashion are highly responsive to their timing. A survey of India's traditional retail landscape with bustling bazaars and market streets, such as those found in Lajpat Nagar, Sarojini Nagar (Figure 3.3), Janpath and Khan Market (Delhi); Brigade Road (Bangalore); Fashion Street and Colaba Causeway (Mumbai) bears evidence to how shopping is a cultural pastime in India. Here street vendors, illegal hawkers, small shops, larger branded showrooms, fruit juice stalls and snack-*wallahs*[24] are all layered together and offer a diverse, visually rich and something-for-everyone experience. These spaces act as semiotic neighborhoods[25] in that they are "historical creations in which the streets belong to people, property ownership is decentralized, and passersby are exposed to a full scale of life rather than to a managed version of it" (Koskinen 2005: 14). Through their structure and environment these markets provide consumers with the necessary atmosphere for shopping to be enjoyed collectively; where seeing and being seen are all part of the experience. The

---

[23] A McKinsey research survey in India found that 74 percent of the respondents across various age groups, income segments as well as different regions (more than twice the average of Russia, Brazil and China) viewed shopping as a great way to spend time with the family (Sheth and Vittal 2007).

[24] *Wallah* is a commonly used term (used as a suffix) to refer to a person who is involved in a specific business or trade, or a seller of goods that can range from vegetables, clothing to magazines etc.

[25] See Koskinen (2005) for his explanation of a "semiotic neighborhood" with particular reference to such neighborhoods in Helsinki.

hours of operation reflect how these institutions accommodate Indian lifestyles and climate—as they open later in the mornings but stay open till late in the evening to allow for cool, family outings. The need to appear modern is heightened in the presence of others, who are similarly placed in an arena of conspicuous consumption. Here, buying, or choosing clothing, and other products, becomes dependent on the choices being made simultaneously by others who are also participants in this collective social activity.

Till a few years ago, the success of shopping malls was an uncertainty, as most Indians preferred the familiar open atmosphere of local shopping streets and markets, as well as appreciated the personalized attention they received from retailers in such settings (Mohan and Gupta 2007). However, as cities become more congested and traffic makes travelling stressful (a common complaint amongst all urban dwellers), studies show that more and more customers have begun favoring the newer malls with parking facilities, food courts and controlled shopping atmospheres. With established local and global chains, select eateries, and branded fashion stores adding to the exclusivity of malls, the overall mall experience itself has also adjusted to the way Indians like to shop (for example by including smaller stalls and street food) (Figure 3.3). As a result, malls are now convenient and "fun" venues to shop. They are also popular family hangouts, and safe places to meet with college friends or potential suitors. In the case of Delhi, a city noted for its love of "bling" and flashy fashions, the last few years have seen several malls spring up ranging from the extremely popular City Select mall and adjoining DLF Place frequented by middle-class shoppers—where one encounters a plethora of brands which

Figure 3.3 A comparison of a street stall selling export surplus clothing in Sarojini Nagar market, New Delhi (left) and a clothing stall within City Select Mall, New Delhi (right). Both images by author.

Figure 3.4 International luxury and high-fashion brands at DLF Emporio Mall, New Delhi. Image by author.

include Zara, Hidesign, Fabindia, Vero Moda, the Body Shop, Forever 21, and Aldo, to name a few; to the most exclusive DLF Emporio mall—crammed with international luxury brands, which include Jimmy Choo, Dior, Burberry and Fendi (Figure 3.4) etc., and all the well-known Indian designer boutiques.

Following the emergence of mall culture in the Tier-I cities, now even smaller cities like Chandigarh and Gwalior boast of new malls opening on a regular basis. Furthermore, the establishment of popular theme parks, bowling alleys, multiplexes, sports bars, multi-cuisine restaurants, salsa dance clubs, as well as numerous fashion weeks and fashion-related events also act as new venues for the public display of fashionable clothing. To these India's elite and upper middle-class have added and re-contextualized a number of other exclusive locations—such as farmhouse parties, lavish five-star-hotel-weddings, nightclubs etc.—for the performance of their material achievements that cater to both traditional and modern lifestyle needs. Dressing appropriately for each of these settings can be a new, exciting and stressful experience, as Indians come to enjoy new kinds of recreational activities, evidenced in the blog excerpt at the start of this chapter. In these settings, "the body" is both the carrier of culture and identity, as well as, "the primary locus of consumption, with adornment its primary focus" (Beng-Huat 2000). The problem of what to wear in such sites of exhibition is acutely felt by women who are aware of their ambivalent identities—as bearers of tradition as well as symbols of modernity in a fiercely competitive class-based arena.

Without sounding clichéd, a simple survey of the styles of clothing worn by middle-class Indians in various public settings outlined above, draws attention to the widespread presence of Western styles of dress, especially when one singles out the younger school- and college-going generation for whom jeans, t-shirts, dresses etc. are almost the given norm.[26] Such an image is mirrored in films and fashion magazines, where Western clothes are showcased as being more modern, fun, "sexy" (Dwyer 2000b) and crucial for modern lifestyles. Seeing as men's clothing in India underwent a complete transition in the last century, fashion for men in these settings tends to be centered on shifting lifestyle markers and conspicuous consumption. This translates into an importance of branded goods, prominent logos and labels, eye-catching design detailing, emphasis on quality, and an adherence to globally trendy styles. The emphasis on fitness and ideals of masculinity—projected through popular films and reality TV—feeds into a preference for clothing that highlights the wearer's physical attributes.

In the case of women's fashions, the increasing visibility of Western styles has meant that once again there is speculation in relation to preservation of Indianness, the longevity of the sari and the sense of distinction Indian clothing has upheld to this point. Accounts of Indian women being unfamiliar with wearing the sari, as well as negative stereotypes of being labeled a *"behenji"*[27] from wearing traditional clothes in certain Westernized settings are common. Indeed, the sari does appear to be outmoded for some within modern urban settings, where it has been deemed cumbersome and impractical; and discarded and replaced by Western clothes amongst the younger generations. However, looking beyond instances of youth fashion and elite or celebrity style worn at select venues, a wider survey of urban dressing reveals how women's clothing choices continue to be about achieving the right balance of tradition and modernity as they make their selection from a vast variety of clothing styles to negotiate their day-to-day lives.[28] While women wearing Western clothes are more visible in popular print and visual media as well as out and about in larger cities, their choices, for the most part, continue to remain in keeping with Indian expectations of modesty and morality (Saavala 2012).

Saavala (2012) highlights the demarcation between the domestic and public sphere when it comes to women's clothes in India—where at home or more private social

---

[26] In 2011 ASSOCHAM (the Associated Chambers of Commerce and Industry of India) surveyed 2000 "youngsters" (13–21 year olds) to evaluate their apparel purchase and spending habits. The sample included an equal number of male and female respondents from a combination of Tier-I and Tier-II cities—belonging primarily to the middle-class segment. Published in 2012, ASSOCHAM's report on this survey states that teenagers show a preference for wearing "new and racy," "modern" clothes, which translates to Western styles. Teenagers also favor buying branded items such as sportswear brands like Nike, Adidas and Reebok and casual wear brands like Levi's (most popular), Lee, Wrangler, Diesel, Spykar, and Numero Uno to name a few. www.assocham.org (accessed July 24, 2012).

[27] While the term literally means sister, it is often used as a derogatory term to refer to someone who is unfashionable, unaware of modern trends and/or appears to be from a small town or village.

[28] In a recent article about fashion in India for returning "repats," the *New York Times* notes Poornima Vardhan's (India returned expat from NYC, investment banker) experience of having to expand her wardrobe by 50 percent upon returning to India—in order to cope with diversity of clothes "needed" in India. Stylistically, the article also notes Ms. Vardhan's attempt to reacquaint herself with the brighter more vibrant colors preferred in India, as well as the need for versatile clothes like the *kurta pyjama* or *salwar kameez* that can be "modest and cool" both in terms of climate as well as in its style quotient (Harris 2012).

settings women may be comfortable wearing shorts, mini-skirts and dresses, they are more conservative in wider open settings. This is a reflection of the fact that despite the past few decades of economic development, in tandem with social and cultural changes, women continue to be unsafe leading professionally, socially and publicly active lives. As a result, Delhi-based fashion designer Anju Modi observes that Indian women are very conscious of how clothing fits and moves on their body when out in public.[29] She offers the example of if a boat neck slips off a shoulder—this would not be an issue in the West, as the Western woman would wear it as if "it was part of the look." However, in India barring a few avid fashion followers this would be a point of discomfort.[30] Since modesty is a crucial factor for women when it comes to the selection of clothes, being able to match clothing to one's whereabouts relies on knowing the difference between what is accepted and what is not. This can involve complex calculations based on place, mode of transportation, climate etc. For example—wearing jeans and t-shirts (through their familiarity) may not be frowned upon but exposing legs and thighs in public places by wearing short skirts, dresses or shorts is still a "no-no" (Bannerjee, cf. Harris 2012).[31] In some cases a fashionable sleeveless *kurta* worn over a tight *churidar* goes unnoticed, as it is still within the realm of traditional clothing, but a low-cut spaghetti top worn may attract too much unwanted attention. Assisting women in making appropriate but simultaneously stylish and fashion forward transitions and transactions in this arena are numerous style agencies in the shape of bloggers, magazines and stylists. Jasleen Kaur Gupta, and Sonu Bohra (Figure 3.5), who run the popular style blog titled Fashion Bombay,[32] not only post regularly about their style dilemmas and solutions, but also offer personal and group styling consultancy. In both these cases, Jasleen and Sonu focus on fashionable strategies for personalizing professional and casual outfits that stay within acceptable boundaries of modesty and morality, often by being inclusive of Indian design sensibilities.

　　Despite the image presented in visual and print media, as well as the flamboyance exhibited at weddings and special occasions, prominent Mumbai-based fashion stylist, Ekta Rajani, maintains that most Indian women [and men] are at heart still very simple dressers.[33] Rajani describes Indian style for everyday dressing as "simple and convenient," and puts this down to the nature of India's climate and the lack of public infrastructure—such as clean and safe roads, footpaths, trains and buses, for example, that inhibit fashion experimentation. "Try getting into a train in Bombay (Mumbai)," she states, "you can't wear heels and catch a train. In such a scenario 'fashion' is not on the top of your mind."[34] However, both she and bloggers Jasleen and Sonu,[35] note that more and more Indians have come to realize that they can have fun and be individualistic, and as a result want to experiment with new trends, labels and styles of clothing. This is especially heightened amongst the younger generation where fashion is a key part of

---

[29] Anju Modi, in an interview with the author in 2010.

[30] Ibid.

[31] Ibid.

[32] www.fashion-bombay.com.

[33] Ekta Rajani, in a phone interview with the author in 2010.

[34] Ibid.

[35] Jasleen Kaur Gupta and Sonu Bohra, in an interview via email with the author in 2012.

Figure 3.5 Fashion bloggers Jasleen Kaur Gupta (left) and Sonu Bohra (right) from Fashion-Bombay.com. Images courtesy Jasleen Kaur Gupta and Sonu Bohra.

identity management, competing with one's peers, and becoming part of or belonging to popular groups.[36] The virtual medium of fashion blogging and developing interest in displaying street style have further impacted fashion behavior in urban environments—as once more both these formats emphasize the importance of brands as well as local and global style acumen as essential cultural capital.

Luxury's tryst with India

Crucial to the discussion on contemporary fashion practice in India is the growth in importance of luxury goods and their display amongst the urban classes. Following the nation's economic reforms and the growth and prosperity witnessed by many segments of society, India is now a lucrative market for luxury goods and services, following from China. India's emerging luxury market also highlights the ways in which current forces of globalization, with their focus on localization, give the local consumer in emerging markets greater agency as an active participant and not just a "chooser" of goods (Appadurai 1990). While the initial influx of global luxury brands and retail appeared less

---

[36] The aforementioned report by ASSOCHAM (footnote #26) highlights the importance of fashionable clothing to the younger generation (13–21 year olds) who see it as a crucial part of self-expression and asserting their individuality due to which they spend a large chunk of their allowance on clothes. In the larger cities this amounted to an average spending in upwards of Rs 5,000 (US$ 82) a month. www.assocham.org (accessed July 24, 2012).

responsive to Indian consumers, the current environment shows greater consideration of their outlook towards appraising and owning luxury items.

Emphasizing this fact was the limited edition collection of saris launched for the Indian market by French luxury brand Hermès, to mark the opening of their new boutique at Mumbai's architecturally iconic Horniman circle in 2011 (Plate 1). Though the brand had launched a collection of saris earlier,[37] this collection of four designs—in a total of 27 pieces—was unique to its Indian store. It was also a way of bridging the traditions associated with Hermès—fine craftsmanship, exclusivity of design and the highest quality of materials—with the traditional Indian sari that had in turn also been an inspiration to the brand. Through referencing India in their design, such as the close-up of Indian textiles "seen on a fabric stand in a marketplace"[38] or painted Indian cotton from the sixteenth century; and the choice of fabrics, which included mousseline,[39] double-mousseline,[40] cashmere, and silk; along with the extension of Hermès' highly revered methods of designing and printing scarves to accommodate longer lengths required of the sari—it was evident that every effort had been made to express a deep desire to connect with and celebrate the Indian consumer.[41]

It is important to note here that the demand for and showcase of luxury in India is not necessarily new. India's royal past boasts of rich and elaborate sartorial extravagances in the shape of bejeweled wardrobes and accessories to match, that have captivated the rest of the world and served as inspiration for numerous contemporary fashion and accessory designers. In addition, Western luxury brands like Louis Vuitton, Hermès, and Dior—to name a few—have all enjoyed personal ties with India for their design, raw materials and inspiration, as well as patronage from royal families who had a penchant for the likes of Cartier jewelry, personalized Louis Vuitton trunks, and Ferragamo shoes (Bagchi 2012). The need to compete through conspicuous consumption has historical roots in the way priceless shawls, *lehengas* and saris (such as the Patan *patola*) were collected and worn amongst select circles in the past. In addition, Indians have for generations considered gold and ostentatious gold jewelry as wise long-term investments, and categorized them as necessary luxuries. However, contemporary markers of fashion and status, especially amongst the growing elite class, have now shifted in favor of branded handbags, shoes, gowns and designer saris. Page 3 parties,[42] black-tie events, art exhibition openings, couture weeks, and celebrity red carpet appearances all bear witness to the fact that a familiarity with Western brands or being a patron of local emerging or established couture designers is the current benchmark for elite dressing. The growing desire and ability to purchase and experience *luxury* has also meant that it

---

[37] Launched in 2000, in London.

[38] Hermès press release dated September 19, 2011.

[39] Very fine quality sheer muslin.

[40] Two layers of muslin, which in this case are rolled together by hand and take roughly nine hours to handwork (as outlined in the Hermès press release).

[41] The exclusivity of this experience was further emphasized by the way buyers of the Hermès sari had the option of ordering a made-to-measure *choli* and would ultimately receive the entire ensemble in a specially created box.

[42] Page 3 (culture/parties/lifestyles) refers to instances of high society parties and other upper-class events that tend to be featured on page three of tabloid newspaper segments in India.

is now a much-used buzzword in India, and the demand for luxury (fashion, accessories and lifestyle products) has grown significantly in cities beyond the large metros [*sic*] into satellite cities like Ludhiana,[43] Chandigarh and Kanpur.[44]

Brands such as Louis Vuitton, Dior, Gucci, Burberry, Hermès, and Ferragamo—amongst others—currently wield significant visual presence in India through celebrity endorsements, brand placement in films, advertising, and editorial material in fashion and lifestyle magazines, as well as through numerous luxury-related events. Yet, in spite of this prominence on the surface, international luxury is still not as successful in India as it has been in China. This is in part due to the market regulations to-date alongside numerous infrastructural challenges within the retail environment, as well as recent fears of economic downturn; but more so due to the specificities of local tastes, consumer mentalities and various cultural factors that have shaped the reception to these brands.[45]

In highlighting some of these issues, retail consultant and former executive director of FDCI,[46] Vinod Kaul, believes that some of the apparel sensibilities of foreign luxury brands are just "too Western" and "too niche" for a wider clientele who shops solely in India. According to Kaul,

> Indians are not willing to pay massive amounts of money for a dress that to our sensibilities looks like a "plain Jane," and there is no big label in front. You have to keep telling people it's a label. But they will spend that kind of money on a [designer] sari. (Kaul 2010)[47]

Luxury accessories, especially handbags and shoes, on the other hand, have been far more successful as they tend to be much easier to team with a variety of outfits—Indian, Western or fusion. Handbags, for example, can be worn more often than clothes, repeated with multiple outfits, and through obvious logos or recognizable and well-respected designs their quality and exclusivity can also be easily gauged. Initially, there was a time when the glass windows and facades of luxury retail stores discouraged some clients from openly purchasing expensive luxury products in full view of others, since such items were often purchased in cash (using "black" money).[48] But now, despite there being discerning clients in India, a key challenge remains the absence of fun shopping environments (like a "high street") and high import duties that increase the price in India. This has led to a continued preference for purchasing luxury fashion and accessories overseas; where many Indian customers still believe the selection is more varied and up-to-date.[49] Those who do make their purchases in India, are more likely to expect greater visible

---

[43] See Vasudev (2012) for a vivid discussion on the "Ludhiana Ladies"—women from well-to-do industrial families in Ludhiana (Punjab) who have a fierce desire to own and flaunt the latest luxury labels, skinny belts and equally skinny waistlines.

[44] See Tewari (2012).

[45] See Amed (2013).

[46] Fashion Design Council of India.

[47] Vinod Kaul, in an interview with the author in 2010.

[48] Commonly used to refer to undeclared earnings in cash, on which income tax has not been paid.

[49] Indians are known for liking to shop while on holiday.

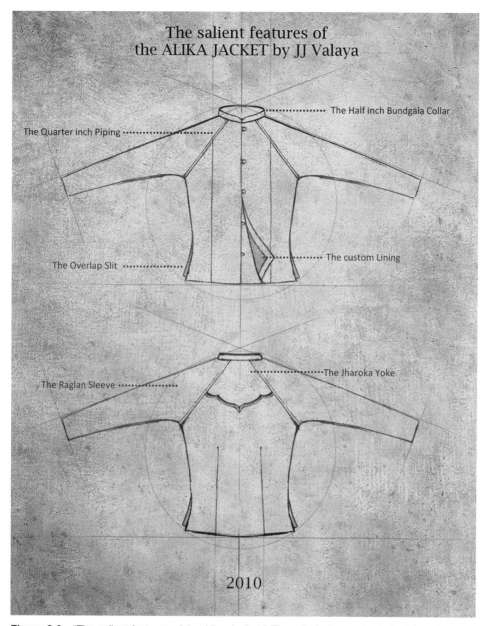

The salient features of
the ALIKA JACKET by JJ Valaya

The Half inch Bundgala Collar

The Quarter inch Piping

The custom Lining

The Overlap Slit

The Jharoka Yoke

The Raglan Sleeve

2010

Figure 3.6 "The salient features of the Alika Jacket." These include quarter inch piping at seams, half inch *bandgala* collar, custom lining, overlap slit at side seam, raglan sleeves and *jharoka* (window, typically part of an enclosed balcony traditional to Rajasthani architecture) yoke. Digital illustration of the Alika Jacket, 2010. Courtesy JJ Valaya.

returns for their money, or a better deal, pushing luxury brands to consider lower price points, or introducing limited or special edition items with the Indian customer in mind. As a vast majority of India's new luxury consumers continue to have modest means,[50] companies and brands aiming to sell to this group need to be innovative "to square the difference between the rising aspirations of consumers and their still modest pocket-books" (Beinhocker et al. 2007).

In many cases, India's own luxury fashion designers understand more intimately the trends and triggers of the domestic market—especially the need for personalized services, popular design aesthetics and value for traditional occasion wear. As the chapter on design will highlight, the linking of the term *couture* to Indian bridal wear, in tandem with creating branded wedding experiences, has been a winning combination for designers like Tarun Tahiliani, JJ Valaya and retail stores like AZA.[51] Furthermore, Indian designers have successfully created indigenous versions of luxury fashion through tapping into traditional crafts, regional dress styles, past patterns of elite consumption and urban Indians' nostalgia for such items, as evident in the success of Sabyasachi saris. An interesting example of locally specific luxury fashion is the Alika jacket (Figure 3.6), designed by Indian couturier JJ Valaya. Named after a fictitious character, the garment is a mix between a jacket and a shirt, and resembles a *sadri*. Bearing visually recognizable detailing, such as its cut, inclusion of a back yoke and use of piping at the seams, the garment can easily be worn with traditional garments (paired with a *lehenga* or even worn as a sari blouse) as well as with jeans or Western designer items. Each month the House of Valaya creates a limited edition design of the Alika that an avid Valaya follower can collect and flaunt—much like the iconic Birkin bag or Chanel suit.

Retail consultants like Kaul (2010)[52] and Dutta (2013) suggest that such locally specific products and services are the key to accessing the Indian buyer—and a number of inter-national brands have considered this route. In 2010 Louis Vuitton created a special *Diwali* collection, Gucci released a special edition of bags for India for the festive shopping season in 2012, Canali has created a modernized "Nawab Jacket" in the Nehru or *bandhgala* style, and Ferragamo has commissioned personalized designs for Bollywood actresses and fashion icons Priyanka Chopra and Sonam Kapoor (see Plate 5). In spite of these gestures and the desire for urban Indians to flaunt their fashions, the Indian market is still largely untapped for its global luxury buying potential. The success of some global brands over others underscores the fact that it is not possible to categorize all luxury markets as the same—and in the case of India, cultural factors play a significant role in determining the future of this lucrative segment (Boroian and Poix 2010), which cannot simply be done on the basis of appealing to traditions, nor the assumption that all luxury is aspirational.

---

[50] Unlike consumers in China, few middle-class Indians are open to saving up a year's salary to purchase a luxury item (Dutta 2012).

[51] AZA is a multi-brand luxury fashion store that offers Indian designer occasion and wedding wear.

[52] Vinod Kaul, 2010.

Epilogue: Ongoing fashion dilemmas

It is clear through this chapter's discussion that contemporary fashion practice amongst India's urban classes offers numerous examples of shifting tastes that respond directly or indirectly to ongoing economic changes within the Indian market. Clothing, like identity, responds to the way the pressures of modernity push and pull it into adapting and adopting new material forms and non-material attributes that, in turn, further shape the lived experience of modernity. In this way, clothing plays a central role in being both the means and the end towards experiencing change (fashion). Alongside the empowering sartorial choices available to Indians in recent times also come new challenges, due to which Tarlo's (1996) coinage of the phrase "dilemmas of what to wear," in reference to the sartorial negotiations during the late nineteenth century and throughout the twentieth century, remains an accurate description for the way fashion continues to evolve for urban Indians. In an environment where the public display of fashion is more common-place and urban Indian men and women actively aspire to lead transnational lifestyles that are on par with Western nations through commodity consumption that is emphasized in all forms of visual media—choosing what to wear continues to hinge on various personal and collective factors. These range from class-related pressures, shifting social roles and the need to balance local with global, tradition with modernity, and older values with new ones. The uneven structure of Indian society—with a rapidly modernizing, upwardly mobile elite and middle-class, but a relatively unchanged lower class in terms of material gains, alongside continued observance of rigid religious beliefs—also means that certain instances of modernity in the public sphere continue to have explosive consequences or are met with mixed responses. The circumstances that led to the Pink *Chaddi* Campaign, mentioned in the previous chapter's conclusion, is one such example where changing lifestyles and the emphasis on materialism have complicated the way women's clothing is received by the wider social milieu.

Beyond these factors, it is perplexing to note the heightening polarity between India's rich and poor, with widespread consumption and display of fashion products by the elite and middle-classes on one hand and the extreme poverty that exists alongside. Furthermore, the emphasis on commodity consumption as a means of maintaining social standing and class have also increased the anxiety felt by those who are at the fringes of the middle-class bracket to live up to such expectations. Yet, while critics of emerging elite and middle-class lifestyles blame India's market reforms for the negative traits of increasing materialism and decreasing social altruism,[53] links to economic progress and the role of these classes as benefactors of liberalization and arbitrators of national progress (Fernandes 2000; Liechty 2003) casts consumerism in a positive light. In addition, there is increasing acceptance of the notion that consumption of cultural goods performs another important role—the construction of personal identity within the premise of a "modern" lifestyle that is not entirely based on a Western model—and is ultimately an egalitarian activity (Miller 1990, cited in Dwyer 2000b).

---

[53] For example, see Varma (1998).

4

REEL TO REAL LIFE: RE-FASHIONING INDIA FROM BOLLYWOOD TO STREET

When Disha, Season 3 Bride on NDTV's *Band Baajaa Bride*[1] is asked about her ideal wedding look by celebrity designer Sabyasachi Mukherjee, she responds by saying that she has always dreamt of looking like a "Rajputana Princess"[2]—in particular like Jodha Bai.

While there is no clear written record or visual proof of Jodha Bai's existence—some suggest she was the Hindu wife of Mughal emperor Akbar in the sixteenth century, whereas others say she was Jahangir's (Akbar's son) wife—Indian cinema has created its own version of history through cinematic license and immortalized Jodha Bai's romance with Akbar in films such as *Mughal-e-Azam* (1960, played by Durga Khote) and once again in *Jodhaa Akbar* (2008) starring Aishwarya Rai Bachchan and Hrithik Roshan.[3]

Disha was referring more specifically to the "*Jodhaa Akbar* look"—a modernized interpretation comprising of ornate and heavily embroidered *lehengas* in rich warm colors, featuring expensive silks, brocades, *Zardozi* and *Kundan* embroidery designed by Neeta Lulla (with jewelry by Tanishq) and popularized in the film *Jodhaa Akbar* by former model and Miss World (1994) Aishwarya Rai Bachchan (Plate 2). Following the success of the film, Neeta Lulla has designed and sold numerous *lehengas* inspired by the look, the style of which have also been copied by designers and tailors across India, as well as abroad, within the Diaspora.

And now Disha, a bride-to-be from Jaipur, was about to receive her own wedding makeover and *Jodhaa Akbar* look on reality TV.

---

[1] NDTV India's bridal makeover show that features designer Sabyasachi Mukherjee and television anchor Ambika Anand.

[2] Term used by the British to refer to the general area and its then kingdoms that now comprise present-day Rajasthan.

[3] I have maintained the two different spellings *Jodha* and *Jodhaa* in keeping with the usage in the film titles.

Introduction

Cinema in India is an extremely influential cultural medium. India has the world's largest film industry with over 1,000 films produced every year in more than 20 languages[4] and over 14 million Indians go to the movies on a daily basis.[5] Many more watch them at home—on television and on the Internet, in India, and abroad. Television on the other hand has undergone a radical transformation since the 1990s, after the arrival of cable networks and satellite television. From its humble beginnings in 1959, with one government-run national channel—*Doordarshan*—there are now more than 600 channels (in 2012) for the Indian viewer to choose from. Through its inclusion of multi-network programming sourced from across the world, television now makes for a truly globalized medium in India. The local content is equally, if not more, vibrant and diverse as various channels offer programs targeted towards national as well as regional audiences. In addition, reality shows and drama series regularly draw inspiration for their content from films, which in turn has helped further the influence and popularity of Bollywood as well as its projected ideals of masculinity, romance, family relations, women's roles and modern fashion. More recently, access to the Internet and its inherent nature of "globality" has led to the emergence of new virtual spaces of fashion blogging, shopping and display of celebrity styles and street fashion that have come to play a key role in influencing fashion in India.

Despite their different mediums and outreach, a common factor these fields share is the way each presents an image of fashion and style of and for India that is actively shaped by viewers', participants' and fans' imaginations, hopes and desires, which in turn comes to shape their clothing choices as well. Popular films and television programs tend to employ clothing strategically towards creating and asserting desirable stereo-types through the process of image making, connotation and repetition. This makes them effective and familiar mediums to convey key ideas about culture, society, identity, modernity and fashion. Through transmitting clothing innovations and emerging trends to a wider audience they also ensure their success in becoming fashion, and collectively offer lucrative venues for product placement and promotion that target various segments of society. In these mediums not only are the clothes an essential part of viewership and consumption, but the bodies on display also become commodified, as do related ideals of gender, beauty, fitness and youth.

What these fields also share in common is the way they have come to be shaped and reshaped as a result of the policies of liberalization, ongoing shifts in the Indian market and forces of globalization, while simultaneously retaining older ideologies inherited from the past. As discussed in the previous chapter, India's growing urban elite and middle-classes play an active part in the nation's economic progress. They also represent a class of globally savvy entrepreneurs and consumers, vested with pioneering new standards

---

[4]Ibid.

[5]In 2008 the industry was valued at approximately US$2.2 billion, and expected to grow by 9 percent p.a. till 2015 (Deloitte 2011 report: "Media & Entertainment in India Digital Road Ahead." www.deloitte.com/in [accessed June 4, 2013])

of national identity that hinges on their successful mediation between local and global. An exploration of idealized and trendy representations of fashion and clothing in popular mediums like Bollywood films, television and the Internet—the last two of which many urban Indians see themselves more accurately represented in (when compared to the ideals presented in films, on catwalks and in high-fashion magazines)—reveals how clothing acts as a material medium for this mediation. Furthermore, each of these "sites" provides rich evidence of active experimentation of self-fashioning fuelled by a sense of optimism as a result of India's booming economic success and its growing importance in the global marketplace as a potential consumer of various luxury and non-luxury cultural goods and services.

Alongside a review of literature on contemporary Indian popular culture and the design and reception of Bollywood film costumes, the research and discussion for this chapter is shaped by my own critical analysis through viewing a selection of contemporary popular films, television serials and reality shows; combined with actively following Indian fashion blogs over a period of three years,[6] as well as through interviews with designers, stylists and fashion bloggers. The need to discuss such a cross-section of domains, beyond fashion magazines, is crucial to get an understanding of how they interact and communicate together towards the production of style and the discourse of fashion in India.

Global, local, global-*desi*

Appadurai consoles those who feared large-scale cultural homogenization as an outcome of globalization by highlighting the fact that as soon as the various "forces from various metropolises are brought into new societies they tend to become indigenized in one or other way …" (Appadurai 1990: 295). In other words they become glocalized. Global cultural flows have the ability to facilitate the expansion of national identities by providing cultural resources that can be integrated into popular and everyday national cultures (Edensor 2002: 29). In the case of India, Dasgupta et al. (2012) find that today's globalized media acts as a go-between home and the world, and has the dual potential of encouraging homogenization of regional cultures on one hand, and at the same time ensuring the maintenance of distinctive heterogeneity of local cultures on the other (Dasgupta et al. 2012: 2). In this way the content in films, television and the Internet are representative "image-texts" of change *and* continuity in a technologically enabled and globally positioned India (ibid.).

This becomes evident as we see how television in India currently offers a hybrid mix of programming that fuses together global formats with Indian content, stars and storylines. This has been an extremely successful strategy in India, as even though viewers are aware of the global counterparts, they express a preference for indigenized versions. Examples of these include *Kaun Banega Crorepati* (*Who Wants to be a Millionaire?*, hosted by film icon Amitabh Bachchan), *Nach Baliye* (loosely based on *Dancing with the*

---

[6]From 2010 to 2013.

Stars), *Indian Idol* (*American Idol*), *Big Boss* (*Big Brother*), and numerous other reality-based shows that tap into viewers' love of and familiarity with Bollywood music, films, film stars, family and fashion. As mentioned in previous chapters, in such mediums the West is no longer a negative influence as it is possible to take what is best from the rest of the world, and still retain a sense of Indianness. This ethos transfers into the design and styling of clothing on television, in Indian films and other visual media that show this fusion with great clarity and creativity.

A central character that emerges in all these mediums is that of the confident, modern, global Indian citizen or global-*desi*—as an idealized representation of cosmopolitan Indianness that many urban Indians can relate and aspire to. Mazzarella locates the origin of this idealized construction during the time period following India's economic liberalization as a result of the heightened anxiety felt by those within the media and advertising industries about the meaning and value of local identity in the wake of globalization (Mazzarella 2003b). Many Indian firms believed that in order to compete with the international brands and companies entering India, the key to success lay in the invention and projection of a "world class Indianness" (Mazzarella 2003b: 36), which could be positively positioned within a globalized field (ibid.). Also during this time, Cullity notes that the introduction of satellite television led to the appearance of a "new form of cultural nationalism based on *active and self conscious indigenization*" imposed upon various media channels (like MTV) by a globally connected or wired-in middle-class—who, despite liking pizzas, burgers, branded Western clothes and music still liked Indian things such as Hindi films and film music, and valued their traditional family networks (Cullity 2002: 408–12, emphasis mine).[7] MTV and its competitors focused heavily on the creation of "*desi* cool"[8] by featuring hip Indian and NRI[9] VJs, like Ruby Bhatia, who were comfortable speaking *Hinglish,*[10] wore trendy clothes and played Hindi film clips. These channels also developed new programs as well as refocused their global programming to suit Indian tastes. Cullity believes that the global-*desi* emerged as "MTV's version of the Indian citizen [who] is an irreducible and unashamed cultural hybrid" (ibid.: 420) within which "global and local, cosmopolitan and traditional, modernity and tradition are all inextricably bound together" (ibid.: 409).

A review of popular box-office oriented Bollywood[11] films following India's liberalization also highlights the emergence of such characters through plots that seamlessly navigate between local and global sites and scenarios. In these films we see a celebration of transnational, globally positioned Indians who are equally comfortable dancing at a

---

[7] Film music accounted for 70–80 percent of music sales in the 1990s (Cullity 2002).

[8] Nair (2009).

[9] NRI—Non Resident Indian.

[10] *Hinglish* is a hybrid mix of Hindi and English.

[11] Term commonly used to refer to popular *masala* films originating from Bombay (Mumbai), where *Masala* refers to a "mix of spices." *Masala* films are of multi-genre style, that follow fairly formulaic plots, with a little bit of everything (romance, comedy, action) thrown in (Kabir 2001). Despite their formulaic framework Indian audiences are highly discerning when it comes to watching these films. Out of the hundreds of films released each year, only an average of eight or so end up being box office hits (Shahrukh Khan, cf. Kabir 2001: 217, also noted by Thomas 2008).

wedding in a village in Punjab, as they are travelling across Europe (*Dilwale Dulhania Le Jayenge* [The Brave Hearted Will Take Away the Bride] 1995), or for whom studying in Oxford and wearing mini-skirts does not mean they can't sing Hindu *bhajans* (devotional songs) like "*Om Jai Jagdish Hare*" (*Kuch Kuch Hota Hai* [Some Things Happen],1998), and living in New York doesn't mean the redundancy of the sari (*English Vinglish*, 2012). Much like their ability to shift seamlessly through such scenarios, fashion for global-*desis* is similarly hybrid, in that it functions across national borders, while retaining a distinctly Indian identity.

It is interesting to note here that much like the evolution of the global-*desi* and related fashions, the term Bollywood itself is a recent construction that has acted as a conceptual aide for promoting national identity and Indian culture—that extends into filmmaking, costumes, music, performance and acting acumen—on a global platform, especially amongst the Diaspora. Conceptually it refers to a "reasonably specific narrative and mode of presentation" (Rajadhyaksha 2008: 1994) and "a way of producing culture within a national and global context that is inextricably linked to the Indian nation-state and postcolonial economy of liberalization" (Dudrah and Desai 2008: 2). Such "box-office oriented cinema is not only concerned with profit but also critically shaped by concerns about prestige, symbolic capital and global distinction" (Ganti 2012: 358).

Films and fashion: Styling dreams

> The T-shirt and *salwar* combination [in *Jab We Met*] happened by chance ... Nobody knew that would become the talking point of the film. Next thing I know, young girls everywhere were wearing the same combination to college. Street stores around India were flooded with printed *salwars*, harem pants and casual tees [*sic*], because suddenly it had become the hottest selling item, and the look is copied even today. (Kapoor and Pinto 2012: 91)[12]

Films have acted as a major point of reference for Indian culture over the past century. In doing so, not only have they come to shape how people perceive various aspects of their lives and changing scenarios of modernity in India, but the props, products and costumes featured in films also have significant impact on the material aspirations, tastes and consumption patterns of viewers themselves (Dwyer 2000a; Dwyer and Patel 2002; Wilkinson-Weber 2005a, 2010, 2011).

In terms of influencing fashion, the costumes worn in popular Hindi films have long been a key part of viewers' enjoyment of these films as audiences (men and women) have paid keen attention to the heroine or hero's clothing choices (ibid.). Women have for decades designed their personal wardrobes based on close scrutiny of these costumes, the discussions of which have formed an integral part of design negotiations with tailors; and most tailoring establishments have kept close tabs on film-related trends. Despite

---

[12] Excerpt from Kareena Kapoor's "The Style Diary of a Bollywood Diva."

Figure 4.1　Film still from *Jab We Met* (When We Met, 2007) where film actress Kareena Kapoor is seen wearing the infamous T-shirt with Patiala *salwar* look.

the presence of flamboyant costumes in some films, it is usually the simpler outfits that have had real influence on viewers' clothing choices. Rather than copying the entire outfit exactly, women have tended to combine different features from different looks and films to create their own individual interpretation—through a mix of color, fabric, cut, neckline, embellishment details (Wilkinson-Weber 2005a). Men on the other hand have relied mostly on ready-made clothing (branded as well as from local shops and street stalls) to replicate their favorite film heroes' looks.

To this day, costumes of leading heroes and heroines have the ability to spark an instant style craze, as seen by the popularity of Superman T-shirts in 2010 (worn by Salman Khan in the film *Wanted*, 2009), or the pared down T-shirt with Patiala *salwar* look (worn by Kareena Kapoor in *Jab We Met* [When We Met], 2007) (Figure 4.1), and Sabyasachi's designer saris and *lehengas* (made popular through his design for films like *Black*, 2005 and *Guzaarish* [Request] 2010). It is not uncommon for certain fashions to be referred to by the names of the films or stars that made them a "hit"— such as "Kareena *wallah* red" in reference to the color of the sari she wore in the title song *"Chammak Challo"* in the film *Ra.One* (2011). Alongside contemporary trends, iconic looks that have captured audiences in the past continue to be remembered fondly. These include Sadhana's tight *churidar salwar kurtas* from *Waqt* [Time] (1965), Sridevi's yellow sari in *Chandni* [Moonlight] (1989) and Madhuri's purple sari and peek-a-boo back blouse in *Hum Aapke Hain Kaun..!* [Who am I to You..!] (1994), to name but a few.

After India's liberalization phase, the shift witnessed in the overall lifestyles and related types of clothing featured in films closely mirror broader socio-cultural shifts occurring amongst the Indian middle-class. There is a growing preference for realism in films (within the limits of Bollywood) and Kabir notes that inspiration for most Bollywood films now comes from global culture (Kabir 2001). The latter of which often translates to storylines that emphasize overseas settings or transnational lifestyles, and scenarios that center on various iterations of the aforementioned global-*desi*. Western clothes, namely jeans and tees [*sic*], dresses, skirts, and even swimsuits are fairly common for young female and male characters. Despite this, Rao (2010) maintains that the Indian audience "does not passively succumb to complete Westernization, but rather successfully demands a compromise between Westernization and India" (Rao 2010: 1). In terms of fashion, this translates to a balance between traditional and Western styles, and consideration for social expectations when it comes to women's dress.

Currently, the emphasis on realism in clothing sets and scenarios exists alongside a healthy dose of spectacle and fantasy in these films; witnessed in "item number" song and dance sequences,[13] foreign locales [*sic*] and flamboyant wedding ceremonies—where clothes are central to selling the dream. From a visual perspective, films like *Barfi!* (2012), *Aisha* (2010) and *3 Idiots* (2009), to name a few, collectively portray a neat well-presented image in the way clothes and overall look is styled. Men are usually clean-shaven, well-built and neatly dressed in jeans and t-shirts or Western suits, and tend to wear bright colors. Women are always well presented wearing a myriad of styles—Indian, Western and fusion. This is rarely sacrificed in favor of gritty realism or authenticity in the kind of feel-good films that mainstream Bollywood epitomizes.[14] In general, the prominence of bright colors, youthful styles and crispness of the clothing matches the carefully curated spaces in which they are presented—where much of India is airbrushed out. Through this visual style, films actively project a sense of split public (Rajagopal 1997 cf. Kumar 2010) where Indian society is demarcated; with the well-presented, well-networked ideal representation on one side, and the rest as "Other." When there are instances of crossover they seldom impact the clothing worn.[15]

Within the ideal landscapes presented in films, clothes rarely appear aged through wear, and the connection between financial ability of the character and the quality or quantity of clothes is rarely a concern. In this way, despite the income disparity experienced by Indians in real terms, films match the rising aims and aspirations of the urban classes and stress commodity consumption as a way of establishing and maintaining status. An extreme example of this is *Heroine* (2012) starring Kareena Kapoor, who is styled by Manish Malhotra. The film featured close to 120 outfits budgeted at Rupees 1.65 crore (approx US$ 290,000)—amounting to roughly three changes per scene. There is also a heightened presence of foreign brands like Abercrombie and Fitch, Gap, American Eagle, Ralph Lauren Polo Sport etc. that are linked to modern lifestyles. This makes them

---

[13] An "item number" is a stand-alone song sequence within a Bollywood film that has little to do with the film's plot. The nature and style of the song, which includes its cinematic style, is usually provocative, and features a cameo performance from an actress who is not part of the film's main cast. Item numbers have historically been used as platforms for launching as well as re-launching film careers, and have often created clothing-related controversies in India.

[14] While there are other genres within Indian cinema that differ stylistically—I would argue they are not as influential from a fashion perspective hence not included in my discussion.

[15] In *Barfi!*, where despite hailing from a poor family and not having a clear occupation or job throughout much of the movie, the key character Barfi (played by Ranbir Kapoor)'s clothes appear fresh, trendy and change frequently.

familiar, fashionable and desirable to the wider public. Additionally, this past decade has seen greater strategic harnessing of the powerful influence of films with companies like Pantaloon (*Krrish* 2006; *Ta Ra Rum Pum* 2007), Shoppers Stop (*Om Shanti Om* 2007) and Pepe Jeans (*Dhoom* [Blast] 2004) that cater to the middle-class, teaming up with films for product development and placement, and creating themed merchandise (Ingale and Chandorkar 2010). International luxury brands also make their presence felt as brands like Hermès (*Zindagi Na Milegi Dobara* [This Life Won't Come Again] 2011, which featured the Kelly bag), Dior (*Aisha* 2010) and Burberry (*Rockstar* 2011*)* appear regularly as part of on-screen costumes and off-screen celebrity endorsements.

As evident from the discussion above, the approach to designing film costumes is markedly different from earlier times, when costumes were a result of creative negotiations between the art director, costume designer and dressmen,[16] and garments were mostly tailored from scratch (Wilkinson-Weber 2006b, 2010). Now fashion designers and stylists play a key role in putting together the look for a film, or a single key star, and rely heavily on the sourcing of garments from domestic markets, designers, brand endorsements and overseas shopping trips, and combine them with a selection of specially designed and tailored pieces. The emphasis on branded goods and such styling (i.e. buying clothes off the rack to put a an outfit together) also impacts the way viewers must now tailor their own looks to follow fashion trends, which translates to greater reliance on ready-made clothing. Wilkinson-Weber (2010) links the emergence of styling for films to the rise of consumer culture and class-based consumption patterns, highlighted in the previous chapter. She states, that for contemporary designers working on films, "characters are globally situated, part of a commodity-rich fashion world that has tangible existence outside Bollywood's environs. It is eminently logical, then, that the achievement of 'real' costumes must rely to a large degree upon 'shopping' for costumes in the 'real' world of commoditized clothing" (Wilkinson-Weber 2010: 14). As an example, for the film *Kambakkht Ishq* ([Damned Love] 2009) designer and stylist Aki Narula sourced a number of outfits from various boutiques in Milan to complement Kareena Kapoor's role as an international supermodel. The film featured designer labels like Dolce and Gabbana, and Roberto Cavalli, with a total of 63 outfits and 47 pairs of shoes (Kapoor and Pinto 2012). According to Narula he consciously chose pieces that he knew would be trendy for when the film was due to release and brought in new shapes, pastels and color blocking for the film's styling. Through emphasizing on-trend styling and lack of "bling" elements Aki wanted to "keep the look as if it was actually worn in real life" (Narula, cf. Amin-Shinde 2009). Similarly Manish Malhotra states that his key goal when designing and styling for films is to make costumes more relatable (and fashionable) to the Indian viewers. He does this through paying close attention to the changes occurring in Indian women's wardrobes in real life, which he finds to be women's acceptance of Western clothes, men and women's familiarity with brands, and their openness to trying new cuts and silhouettes.[17]

---

[16] Term used for those who staff the wardrobe department (Wilkinson-Weber 2005b).

[17] Cited from various interviews about his work and on films—featured on television channels as well as posted on YouTube.

Such examples highlight how important it is for film stylists nowadays to be fluent in brands and global fashion trends. Alongside these criteria, the credentials and transnational networks of the stylists are equally important as that of the clothes they source. A notable film from this perspective and that of global-*desi* aspirational styling is *Aisha,*[18] starring Sonam Kapoor, styled by New York returned "re-pat" Pernia Qureshi.[19] (Plate 3) In putting together *Aisha's* female characters' looks Qureshi sourced numerous Western designer garments (including Chanel and Dior) as well as vintage pieces from New York, which she paired with Indian designer labels (such as Manish Arora) and garments especially made by Dubai-based designer Ayesha Depala. In this way the film not only fetishizes Western high street, luxury, and high-fashion brands that are now accessible to urban, elite consumers within India, it also visually constructs an ideal image of Indian cosmopolitanism that is capable of making discerning choices from a plethora of brands and is able to mix and match Indian with Western, and new trends with vintage finds to create a unique look.

Women's bodies as sites of contention between modernity and tradition

A well-documented aspect of film costume prior to contemporary times has been the clear demarcation of Indian traditional and Western clothing styles worn by female characters, which sartorially communicated films' assertion of gender roles and stereotypes that actively marginalized women. Up until the 1980s, the wearing of Western styles by women more often than not was linked to perceived negative Western traits—such as sexual promiscuity, smoking, drinking and disrespecting tradition. The "vamp" was a central character in Indian cinema through the 1960s and 1970s, and was seen wearing risqué Western clothes while dancing at cabarets, parties and bars. In comparison, the heroine and other *sati-savitri*[20] typecast female characters portrayed Indian beliefs and good character through the wearing of fashionable traditional dress. The change from Western to Indian clothing, that takes place in many a film like *Purab Aur Paschim* [East and West] (1970),[21] was meant to denote the transition from brash Western modernity to good Indian morals, traditions and spirituality. Through these films women's bodies performed the dual role of bearers of Indian tradition, as well as markers of national pride

---

[18] While the film *Aisha* itself did not do well at the box-office, Indian fashionistas found the film very inspiring.

[19] Pernia Qureshi returned from New York after studying law and interning with fashion publications. She is now a very successful stylist and designer in India, and also owns the online store Pernia's Pop Up Shop.

[20] *Sati-Savitri*—pure, un-adulterous, and religious wife like characteristics.

[21] In the film, Preeti (played by Saira Banu), is a British born and brought up Indian who sports long blonde hair and mini-skirts. She smokes and drinks, grooves to Western music and regularly ridicules Indian traditions. Through Bharat (played by Manoj Kumar), the hero of the film and her love interest, she learns to appreciate Indian values and traditions and eventually gives up smoking and transitions to a more demure persona and traditional clothes.

and superiority in comparison to the West—much like the ideal promoted by the Indian nationalist movement.[22]

Towards the late 1980s and 1990s, the advent of the modern Westernized woman as a central character led to a diminishing demarcation between East and West [read: good and bad], even in terms of costumes. The sartorial representation of these roles were in step with wider socio-cultural changes that were in keeping with the national paradigm at the time as well as religious beliefs, which assumed that women could still retain their traditional values on the inside despite wearing Western clothes on the outside. Contemporary cinema continues to witness this shift, as more and more female characters wear Western and globally trendy clothes, and are increasingly cast in lead or active roles. Films like *Aisha, Fashion* (2008)*,* and *Heroine*, for example, depict women as liberated and globally aware, leading transnational lifestyles. However, despite gaining more "reel space," their roles also continue to follow older idioms that place emphasis on women as representations of traditional and national identity, and continue to portray them in passive roles, as the object of male gaze (emphasized through popular "item number" song and dance sequences), in need of protection (Derné 2008) and deserving of the fallout that occurs due to over-ambitiousness (reiterated in the plots of *Fashion* and *Heroine*).

Alongside the emphasis on women's fitness and related body and beauty ideals and greater prevalence of revealing clothes that feature toned bodies, actresses are keenly aware of the demarcating line between "sultry" and "slutty." Kareena Kapoor stresses on wanting to do "clean" films and wearing clothes that don't look "cheap" in her style diary (Kapoor and Pinto 2012: 84). Such expectations are also voiced by other female stars as they continue to show their commitment to family values and traditions and are uncomfortable with kissing scenes for example, especially after marriage. These instances point to the ongoing contradictions and ambivalence presented in films that affirm the continued influence of older nationalist ideals as they relate to women's bodies, where on one hand there is the expectation of wearing certain kinds of global fashions to symbolize a modern identity. These include items like bodycon dresses and swimsuits that enforce rigid body image and beauty ideals on to female stars.[23] However, when needed, women must also be able to fill out their curves to look good in traditional roles and clothes.

Locally rooted ideals of masculinity

The idealized depiction of masculinity in Bollywood is worth noting briefly, especially as it emphasizes once again distinctive locally specific constructions of global ideals. Derné (2000, 2008) highlights the influence films have had on the understanding of masculinity in India. Popular *masala* films typically emphasize violent masculinity and further impinge

[22]Evident in a film clip from *Yeh Zindagi Kitni Haseen Hai* [This Life is Beautiful]] (1966) where Sarita (played by Saira Banu), upholds her Indian morals and modesty by refusing to wear a swimsuit at the Miss Universe contest in Paris and dons a sari instead.
[23]Watch *Tashan* (2008) for Kareena Kapoor's size zero transformation and infamous swimsuit scene.

Figure 4.2 Film poster for *Dhoom 2* (Blast 2, 2006). Image courtesy Yash Raj Films.

upon the sexualization of women as subjects of the male gaze. However, there is a definite shift from the "angry young man" persona of the 1970s and 1980s, to the emergence of a new "consuming hero" post liberalization, "for whom transnational movement is a distinctive feature" (Derné 2008: 180). Gehlawat makes a similar observation by noting the recent popularity of the "metrosexual male protagonist—one largely defined by his physical fitness, grooming and cosmopolitanism" (Gehlawat 2012: 61) in mainstream Bollywood films. This macho stereotype is affirmed by the idealization of muscular male bodies in tight fitting clothing, that more often than not feature bold logos, bright colors and identifiable fashion labels in films like *Dhoom 2* [Blast 2] (2006) (Figure 4.2), *Salaam Namaste* (2005), *Desi Boyz* [Indian Boys] (2011) and *Zindagi Na Milegi Dobara* [This Life

Won't Come Again] (2011). The prominence of fashion brands and designer labels that emphasize commodity consumption is in sync with the dominance of menswear within organized retail in India. Additionally, the focus on physical fitness parallels the growing popularity of gyms, as well as the use of cosmetic products for fairness and hair removal by men as part of a broader shift that has been classified as the "'liberalization' of urban Indian masculinity" (Deckha 2007, cf. Gehlawat 2012: 62).

Much like film stars' bodies in Hollywood, recent Bollywood films require heroes to re-sculpt themselves according to the demands of the role. As a result men's bodies are increasingly presented as a work in progress—an on-going project in achieving physical goals, maintaining or transforming physiques for the purpose of exhibition, and fashion, which can be a full-time occupation or "timepass."[24] Here we see multiple examples such as Aamir Khan's fitness regime to achieve a "ripped" look for *Ghajini* (2008) contrasted with his leaner look for *3 Idiots*, and Shahrukh Khan's six-pack-ab transformation for *Om Shanti Om* that are glamorized by all forms of popular media. Since film stars are also active brand ambassadors—in the case of male stars this ranges from fashion brands like Hugo Boss, Zegna to fitness and lifestyle brands like Puma and Reebok—through special appearances and features in advertisements, fashion shows, reality TV programs and special events they not only promote these ideal physiques, but also the fashions.

Most notable, however, is Bollywood's version of Indian metrosexuality, which in comparison to its global counterparts, easily oscillates between macho-muscular violent characteristics and the ability to sing and dance in step to catchy tunes while wearing a fusion of trendy clothing styles. The latter of which is not considered effeminate or gay. This is evident in the way Bollywood heartthrob Hrithik Roshan is comfortable doing action scenes as much as he is undulating to the songs in his films, as well as Shahrukh Khan's pairing of *Bharatanatyam* dance moves while wearing a tuxedo, dancing to *"Chammak Challo"* (sung by Akon, in Hindi) in the film *Ra.One*, where he is cast as a shape-shifting superhero—a reflection of how Bollywood's version of globalized masculinity remains rooted in local culture much like the case of fashion in India.

Re-Branding tradition: *Saas-Bahu*[25] soaps and *Band Baajaa Bride*

In comparison to the costumes and lifestyles presented in films, Mr. RK Deora, husband and business partner of noted costume designer Ritu Deora, believes television is gradually becoming more influential in terms of setting fashion trends in India.[26] While films tend to be more individualistic through storylines that center on the hero and heroine, television serials' plots tend to focus on the "Indian family" and have the added flexibility of maintaining regional specificity. This is of great importance to the middle-class

---

[24] Timepass—popular Indian colloquialism for killing time.
[25] *Saas-Bahu*—mother-in-law and daughter-in-law.
[26] RK Deora, in a phone interview with the author in 2010.

audience. Even though both films and television attempt to create aspirational fashion within the framework of realism, television offers just a little more gloss than reality— "reality with a twist" Deora calls it.[27] And while Western-styled clothing is fairly ubiquitous across most reality-based and fiction shows on television, especially for men, it is also on television where Indian heritage is often turned into a spectacle (Breckenridge and Appadurai 1995: 8). The following two instances sourced from contemporary television shows are examples of where traditional clothing and related rituals in tandem with commodity consumption have received a significant boost in recent years.

The first of these are the infamous *saas-bahu* soap opera style daily serials that have garnered enormous viewership within India and abroad. The typical target market of these serials is the middle-class housewife and their families.[28] As in the case of any program, the success of a daily serial is determined by its longevity—for example *Yeh Rishta Kya Kehlata Hai* [What Is This Relationship Called] (STAR Plus) and *Balika Vadhu* [Child Bride] (Colors) both completed 1,000 episodes in 2012, and were amongst the top ranking serials of the year (Sarkar 2013). A few of these have also been successful overseas, and in some cases their popularity goes beyond the Diaspora. *Balika Vadhu,* for instance, is telecast in 16 languages across 18 countries (Raghavendra 2013). The makers of television serials use a number of standard ploys to prolong the life of a story, such as focussing on conflict and separation, and family drama set in grand homes with sweeping staircases much like the sets of the iconic family film *Hum Aapke Hain Kaun..!* (1994). Female protagonists play lead roles in these serials, and are often portrayed as overbearing, scheming and even downright evil characters within joint family settings.[29] Popular fiction writer Shobha Dé maintains that such characters are very popular amongst Indian audiences, even if they are not accurate reflections of real roles in society (Dé cf. Bajpai 1997).

When a soap runs for an extended length of time, it is mainly because people have fallen in love with the characters of that show and it is this affection, teamed with regular, repetitive viewing, that encourages a loyal fashion following. In turn, the costumes worn on-screen also play a key part in capturing the audience of *saas-bahu* shows by helping them connect with the characters. To ensure viewers remain tuned in, Deora's design team constantly try to experiment and innovate with the costumes within given regional and character-specific boundaries. For example, if the plot outlines that the show's lead families are based in rural Rajasthan—as in the case of *Balika Vadhu*[30]—then the strategy is to feature a mix of women's regional Rajasthani styles. In *Balika Vadhu*, this translates to either a *ghaghra choli* with a *ghunghat* for some characters and the sari where the *pallu* covers the shoulders for others (Figure 4.3).[31] By doing a "spin" on these regional

---

[27] Ibid.

[28] RK Deora, 2010.

[29] Bajpai (1997) charts a shift in the character of women's role in Indian television series before and after liberalization, and points to an increase in dominant, ambitious [read manipulative] and power hungry female characters. She refers to this "new woman" on television as the "urban elite outspoken female" who acts like a man, but dons a petticoat (i.e. traditional dress) (Bajpai 1997: 305).

[30] Costumes designed by Winnie Malhotra.

[31] Younger characters may also be styled in Western clothes or *salwar kameez*.

Figure 4.3 Screen still of *Diwali* celebrations and the *puja* ceremony in *Balika Vadhu*. Episode date November 2, 2013.

styles, through introducing an unusual detail, textile or embellishment techniques the overall aim is that even if viewers from that state recognize the style, they too should feel the urge to try and copy it. According to Deora, "no one wants a look that is too authentic and rustic—this is just not interesting enough." What works is being able to offer a fresh approach on relatable clothing.[32] This kind of design experimentation is evident in all the popular serials on television and includes numerous versions of tying the sari, creatively placed embellishments and emphasis on key details like embroidered sleeves (an important focal point for a blouse and kameez), necklines and borders of saris and *kameez* hems. New and hybrid versions of the tying sari that have come about as a result of these shows include a twist on the Gujarati style (that introduces a different way of folding the *pallu*), the semi-Bengali style, mermaid style and *lehenga* style, to name a few. Since the storylines are usually based around joint families, whose backgrounds are mapped out in great detail in terms of geographic location and other demographics,[33] the majority of the costumes are designed keeping in mind the look of an entire family. This is done to maintain clear sartorial distinction for each character, as it is common for scenes to feature the entire family in one shot (Figure 4.3).[34] Additionally, Deora explains that once a character's look is fixed they try to stay within those boundaries to maintain cohesion and continuity of the character. If the character wears printed saris in reel-life,

[32] RK Deora, 2010.
[33] Ibid.
[34] Ibid.

for example, she will not wear a plain one all of a sudden, as one would in real life. Such "sartorial branding" of characters has been extremely successful and viewers can easily distinguish between a Kumkum look (*Kumkum*, STAR Plus), Akshara look (*Yeh Rishta Kya Kehlata Hai*, STAR Plus) (Plate 4) or a Pammi look (*Des Mein Nikla Hoga Chand*, STAR Plus) and fashion a similar outfit for themselves from local tailors or sari shops.[35] The ability for viewers to copy these styles adds to their vested interest in the show and the overall TRPs[36]—which is the eventual goal.

Over the years, television serials have helped popularize various fashion trends—such as layered looks, colors like pink and purple, and *chikankari kurtas* for men; and cut and join saris, net sleeves, various dyeing techniques for saris, and velvets for women. The popularity of these styles is evident in the numerous copies available at sari mills,[37] fabric shops and small designer boutiques. Viewers' fascination and investment in these fashions is also evident from the multiple web forums, websites and YouTube clips that have sprung up dedicated to popular looks. Also worth noting is that a lot of costumes for these serials are designed around festivals or occasion-related scenes,[38] such as *Diwali, Holi, Karwa Chauth*,[39] weddings, *Godh Bharaai*[40] and funerals. The emphasis on such occasions and rituals has meant that many middle-class Indians have begun to reintroduce and celebrate a greater number of religious events, as well as new imports like bachelor- and hen-parties—not to be confused with the *Mehndi* (henna) ceremony and ladies' *Sangeet* (songs)—which continue to be celebrated alongside. In other words through their portrayal in reel life, television has come to influence the value of traditional dress and rituals in real life.

Besides *saas-bahu* serials, NDTV's hit show *Band Baajaa Bride* (BBB), which I mention in the beginning of this chapter, is worth highlighting here, as it too idealizes tradition and traditional clothing through its bridal makeovers (Figure 4.4). The show bridges India's design fraternity (via Sabyasachi Mukherjee, and other fashion designers in its first season) with the popular mainstream format of a makeover type reality show, and acts as a platform for product placement for fashion and accessory brands (TBZ jewelry, Rado, Nine West, etc.), stores (AZA) and various cosmetic and dental surgeons. By labeling "gold bangles as a quintessential part of an Indian wedding," "the *chandan* process[41] in Bengali weddings as being equivalent to going to a Spa" and "mother daughter bonding through shopping," BBB emphasizes commodity consumption but links it to tradition within the framework of India's most loved and treasured establishment—the big fat Indian wedding. The ambivalence of women's roles is evident once again as we see an awkward contradiction, where on one hand it is the bride who is the star of the show and perfect in each way, while simultaneously presented as a "project" for the show's hosts

---

[35] RK Deora, 2010.

[36] Target rating point.

[37] RK Deora, 2010.

[38] Ibid.

[39] An annual one-day festival celebrated by married Hindu women, which involves fasting from sunrise to moonrise for the health and longevity of their husbands.

[40] Baby shower.

[41] Application of Sandalwood paste.

Figure 4.4 *Band Baajaa Bride* bride Soumi Chakrabarty featured in the show's first Christian wedding (Season 4). The wedding ceremonies emphasized a fusion of Christian and Bengali nuptial traditions, which included a white wedding that takes place in Kolkata. Soumi's gown, designed by Sabyasachi Mukherjee, is an example of this fusion—as it is a cross between a white wedding dress and a traditional *lehenga*. Image courtesy *Band Baajaa Bride*, NDTV Good Times—"India's leading lifestyle channel."

that *needs* to be improved upon (body, beauty, hair, teeth, facial hair, *and* sometimes personality)—all of which ultimately casts her in an imperfect light.

Through its focus on romance and various family-related negotiations across religious, class, caste, regional and international boundaries, as well as modern and traditional ideals, the scenarios featured on the show mimic wider socio-cultural shifts occurring in India. Most interestingly, the team at BBB attempt to resolve any disparities between couples' families through the medium of clothing and the creative mobilization of familiar symbols vested in Indian dress and textiles—such as mixing Gujarati with Bengali by using a white Kota sari with gold *butis*, with a customized embroidered red border;[42] or Bengali with Telugu-Christian through a *lehenga* inspired wedding gown illustrated in Figure 4.4.[43] As Sabyasachi says in one episode, "Don't worry at *Band Baajaa Bride* the value of your parents are as important as your independence. We'll find a way to bridge both of them."[44]

Who are you wearing?: Off-screen celebrity style

Viewers' enjoyment and following of their favorite celebrity's fashions in current times goes much beyond what is presented on-screen. Alongside established film magazines like *Filmfare* and *Stardust*, that have featured Indian stars and their fashions for readers to enjoy since the 1960s and 1970s, there are now multiple formats in the form of celebrity magazines, websites, blogs and other forms of social media that document the latest celebrity styles. Concurrent with this is the increased visibility of film and television stars at various red carpet events, brand endorsements, live entertainment shows etc., where the display of fashion and individual style statements have gained greater significance than earlier times. In highlighting this, Vasudev notes how in 2010, when veteran actress Hema Malini attended an awards function wearing a *Kanjeevaram* silk sari she was asked by a reporter, "[Whose sari] are you wearing, *Hemaji*?" (Vasudev 2012: 277).[45] Expecting her to reply with the name of a designer or brand, the reporter's question was indicative of the distinct shift that has occurred in the exhibition and reception of celebrity style, where there is a consideration of not only what is worn, but also "who" is being worn. This is in line with the growth of consumer culture and related media that prescribes branded labels for appearance and status management in India. Increased public scrutiny of the clothes worn by stars off-screen via the medium of websites like www.missmalini.com and www.highheelconfidential.com, and gossip magazines like *Hello!*, makes what they wear to these events as important as their on-screen style statements, and in turn also influences the clothing choices of their fans.

In harnessing this potential, film and television stars act as brand representatives, endorsing a variety of fashion, accessories, health, fitness and small electronic products, to name a few. The key reason also being that fashion in India, for the most part, still gets categorized as entertainment by mainstream media channels, and so who better to represent it than the entertainment industry? As a result, much like in the West, Bollywood stars actively promote their favorite designers by making front row appearances or featuring as "show stoppers" on Indian catwalks to bring glamour and publicity

---

[42] BBB, Season 3, final episode, 2013.
[43] BBB, Season 4, episode on "the first ever Christian wedding on the show," 2014.
[44] Sabyasachi Mukherjee, quoted from BBB, Season 3 episode featuring Dr. Chytra V. Anand.
[45] To which Hema Malini responded, "Mine of course…" (Vasudev 2012: 277)

to these events.[46] Global luxury brands increasingly look towards building relationships with stars "who compliment their own heritage and values" (Ahluwalia 2012: 171) as seen in the teaming up of Ferragamo with style icons Sonam Kapoor (Plate 5) and Priyanka Chopra—both of whom present impeccable fashion sense in their style choices that has been further legitimized by India's fashion print media.

In keeping with these endorsements, a survey of popular red carpet looks points to the importance of current local and global trends, luxury brands and designer labels. However, there is also a heightened need for celebrities to distinguish themselves from their Western counterparts on a more global platform. This has led to a second and more interesting shift witnessed within Indian celebrity style, where alongside the enshrining of Western fashion brands there is now a renewed confidence and pride in wearing Indian designer labels—ranging from Sabyasachi Mukherjee, Manish Malhotra, Masaba to Raw Mango. Bollywood stars in particular are also vested with promoting Indian culture globally. Nowhere was this more pronounced than at the 2013 Annual Cannes Film Festival. As Indian cinema completed 100 years, all eyes were on the film stars who went to represent India at the festival. While their presence was of importance from the perspective of gaining global recognition for Indian cinema, their choice of clothing was perhaps even more important, as it acted as a key visual medium (beyond the films being showcased) for the assertion of Indian distinction in what have historically been Western-dominated fields (films, fashion and red carpet style). In 2013 Indian actress Vidya Balan served on the prestigious Cannes jury, alongside Nicole Kidman and Steven Spielberg, among others. Amitabh Bachchan (*The Great Gatsby* 2013), Aishwarya Rai Bachchan and Sonam Kapoor also made appearances at the festival. All, but Vidya, wore an impressive mix of Indian and Western designer labels. Aishwarya, who was the only celebrity to receive regular coverage for her outfits in U.S. mainstream press for her red carpet looks, was seen wearing a dress by Elie Saab (Figure 4.5), a gown by Gucci, a black sari by Sabyasachi Mukherjee, a gold sari by Tarun Tahiliani, and an *anarkali* gown by Abu Jani and Sandeep Khosla. Sonam was seen wearing a sari ensemble by Anamika Khanna and a dress by Dolce Gabbana.

Vidya's wardrobe on the other hand was entirely conceptually curated by Sabyasachi Mukherjee, who positioned her (body and clothing) as a symbol for asserting his design philosophy for and of India—i.e. empowerment through local design, textiles, handloom and traditional dress—as well as imposed upon her his expectations of what fashionable modern *Indian* women should wear. As a result Vidya was seen wearing traditional Sabyasachi styles, which included *khadi* saris and *lehengas* that ranged from being well balanced and chic, to appearing a little heavy handed for her body type and choice of venue. Based on the daily comment thread unfolding on Sabyasachi's official Facebook page, as well as the media outcry over the following weeks, the response to this strategy was mixed. Many of Sabyasachi's followers were proud to see Indian clothing showcased at the Cannes, and as a result felt inspired to wear traditional clothes themselves. Others

---

[46]In my own experience while attending such fashion shows, a number of the press photographers were more interested in who would be the show stopper than the designs, and the reviews of the collections in the mainstream press, the day after, reflected the same.

Figure 4.5 Film actress Aishwarya Rai Bachchan wearing an Elie Saab Dress at the 2013 Cannes Film Festival. (Shutterstock) Copyright: Jaguar PS.

felt embarrassed by the repetitious outfits, "heavy styling," and lack of competition in what has typically been the arena of Western designer brands. Sabyasachi's design statement and focus on texture, fine detail and craft appeared to be lost on such a large platform, and critics felt that he had presented a regressive version of Indian womanhood and fashion through channeling historic costume and nationalist agendas, as opposed to a more progressive stance. Some dismissed it as "costume," and others felt he had recreated the subservient positioning of Indian men and women during the Colonial rule—in particular by making Vidya cover her head (Plate 6) (Tewari 2013).

Addressing this concern in an open letter to Sabyasachi, Malika V. Kashyap, founder of the web-based fashion journal *Border&Fall* writes,

By all means, dress them in saris, make them wear India on their sleeves and raise the dialogue around textiles and craft. We have no objection. More than anything though, we would love to see… a new refined aesthetic, but not one where the clothes end up wearing the women. (Kashyap 2013b)

The heated debate unfolding on various forums online about the nature of Indian celebrity style, and the fashions worn at Cannes once again highlights the continued emphasis placed on women's bodies to represent national identity, as opposed to men in similar settings. In addition, Sabyasachi's revival of nationalist narratives brings to the forefront issues faced by the Indian design fraternity, as it too attempts to make its mark in a notoriously biased global fashion arena. Mukherjee's response to Kashyap's letter also sums up the dichotomous position brought about as a result of liberalization, where he states,

> India is going through a diverse movement and there are people who think that being purist Indian is regressive or alternatively, progressive. I think what [Vidya Balan] wore started off a dialogue between these two sects of people who are anyways at war with each other because it is a difference of ideology. What she did was expose the war between both. (Mukherjee 2013)[47]

Fashion blogs: Transnational spaces for re-imagining Indian fashion

Evidenced from the interaction on blogs, websites and social media sites between Sabyasachi, the local fashion press and followers of Indian fashion, the Internet plays a central role in the growing discourse around celebrity style and popular fashion in India. In addition, its creation of virtual spaces where those outside of the formal frameworks of the fashion industry can actively take part in alternate explorations of fashion and self-expression has had significant impact on fashion trends, shopping, wearing, documentation and promotion of fashion, not only in India but across the globe. Despite their initial peripheral status fashion bloggers, like Bryan Grey Yambao (www.bryanboy.com) and Tavi Gevinson (www.thestylerookie.com) for example, have come to wield significant clout within the global fashion world through their popularity (viral at times) and wide readership. The ease with which the Internet supports and relies on global flows of information and interaction (in most cases) means that blogs are inherently transnational in nature. That is, they do not have to be rooted to one geographical location—much like the fashion industry itself, that relies on globally fluid networks of design, production, consumption, retail and fashion opinion leadership.

Personal fashion blogs originating from India share multiple commonalities with their global counterparts, in that a fairly common reason cited behind starting a personal fashion blog is the need to express oneself. Some also test and review products, others give advice, as well as critique or challenge norms. Through regular posts on their outfits, bloggers actively experiment with prescribed norms, trends and ideals of fashion, and tailor them to suit their personal tastes, lifestyle, social roles, and in many cases,

[47] Cited from Kashyap (2013a).

physical shortcomings (when compared to super models). Hence, through such blogs, the Internet presents a valuable "space of empowerment through the control it grants bloggers on their own image, as well as through the alternative visions of femininity it allows them to circulate" (Rocamora 2011: 410). As a result of all these factors blogs offer exciting virtual spaces for envisioning new possibilities for urban Indian fashion that can be creatively documented and shared with a wider audience.

In mapping the size and scope of Indian fashion bloggers, blogger Purushu Arie found approximately 150 fashion blogs with an Indian connection in 2012.[48] Of these, the majority are maintained by women within the age group of 20–25, most of whom are based out of the larger metro cities (Delhi and Mumbai).[49] Most of these blogs tend to stay within global frameworks through posts featuring "new acquisitions," "rediscovery of old pieces" (Rocamora 2011) as well as innovative ways of combining new items with well-loved pieces. Through posting "selfies"[50] and creatively styled pictures taken by an accomplice, Indian bloggers feature a diverse range of style statements (casual, street, formal, fusion experimental etc.) on their sites. The majority of the photographs tend to be taken in and around the blogger's home, on the terrace, in the garden, in front of gates, or on empty streets as well as at entrances of hotels and other well-presented buildings. This makes the images more accessible and relatable as they highlight fashion in everyday contexts. Fashion trends prevalent on Indian fashion blogs also mirror global trends. For example in 2012 and 2013 these blogs featured numerous posts on maxi dresses, stripes, bright neon colors, color pop blazers, color blocking and an emphasis on the "it" bag as well as Cambridge look satchels, to name a few. A survey of these blogs also highlights a prominence of mid-market brands mixed with vintage or cheaply sourced clothing. Once again, this is not too dissimilar to Western counterparts where the high street features prominently (Woodward 2009). Comparatively, however only a few bloggers feature high-fashion designer clothes (Indian or Western) but on the whole most appear more familiar with Western brands than Indian designers, and regularly post about aspiring towards owning luxury accessories.

As per the global norm, posts featuring particular outfits are usually accompanied by a list of the items that make up for the entire look, along with additional text that explain its inspiration, the trends or the circumstances that led to an item's purchase. While this puts the spotlight on branded items with attached cultural capital, overall the development of personal style is deemed most important. In the case of Indian blogs this hinges on creative fusion between various local and global factors, as mentioned already in the previous chapter. This strategy was affirmed by Fashion Bombay bloggers Jasleen and Sonu who explain their personal sense of style, as well as what makes them distinctly Indian by saying,

---

[48] www.Purushu.com (accessed July 31, 2012).
The total number of blogs at any given point tends to fluctuate based on the regularity of posting. Due to the age group of most of the bloggers, many stop posting once they leave college and take on professional positions, unless the blog becomes their primary professional focus.

[49] Almost 29 percent of Indian fashion bloggers also came under the category of NRIs (www.Purushu.com [accessed July 31, 2012]).

[50] Self-portrait taken with [phone] camera pointed towards oneself.

We'd like to believe we are bohemian chic. Both of us are very influenced by our roots so don't shy from adding that *desi* touch to our look. Whether it's a pair of *mojris* or a set of ethnic bangles … We are big fans of recycling, so a lot of our [posts feature] different ways to use a blouse, *kurta* or a dress … (Gupta and Bohra 2012)[51]

In this way, much like other forms of fashion print media, Indian bloggers naturally localize their content to Indian tastes as a result of their social conditioning. There is a heavy focus on dressing appropriately for the Indian climate, especially the monsoon season, which according to one blogger is an "Indian blogger's biggest nightmare." Climate-related adjustments are also critical when it comes to translating global trends for India, as many items like wool skirts, heavy knits, thick stockings and fur boots don't work beyond the northern cities, which leads one Mumbai-based blogger to lament the lack of winter in her city. Terms such as *thrifting* in the Indian context are commonly used to refer to clothes purchased from popular street shopping venues like Sarojini Nagar in New Delhi and Fashion Street or Colaba Causeway in Mumbai. Bloggers also play a vital role in assisting other women with clothing and fashion-related transitions and transactions—by turning their own clothing dilemmas into solutions on how to wear heels, how to wear a skirt three ways (one of which makes it into a *salwar kameez*)[52] (Figure 4.6) or handbag to shoe matching. Indian bloggers increasingly see their role as educating the wider public about the subtleties of fashion—especially Western fashion terms and concepts, such as the pronunciation of *haute couture* or *faux pas*.[53] This mirrors the way fashion magazines position themselves as style mediators and educators, but in the case of blogs, readers often develop a more familiar and personal bond as the result of the sharing of personal tips and experiences and the general tone of posts, making their reception markedly different.

Collectively fashion blogs have added to the global visibility of Indian fashion, as well as contributed towards strengthening its fusion-centric aesthetic. Additionally, the comments section of these blogs is proof of the transnational traffic they enjoy. So while global flows of fashion can be unidirectional or imbalanced—as Indian brands rarely feature in Western blogs or fashion media—the exchange between bloggers is not so. Even though the material fashions may not cross over, the ideas about fashions do. The nature of fashion blogging in this way affirms Appadurai's observation on the new global cultural economy, which no longer relies on one central core axis. His concept of "imagined worlds," in reference to "multiple worlds, which are constituted by the histori- cally situated imaginations of people and groups around the globe" (Appadurai 1990: 297) that provide the opportunity to subvert or challenge other similar worlds, or a point of origin of a dominant discourse, is also applicable here. In the case of fashion blogs, by putting everyday ordinary people in the "forefront of fashion making" (Berry 2010)

---

[51] Jasleen Kaur Gupta and Sonu Bohra, via an email interview with the Author in 2012.

[52] "Same same but different," LTWT, http://ltwt.in/2012/09/28/same-same-but-different/ (accessed December 12, 2012).

[53] In doing so one blogger posts—"P.S I've heard enough people say fox pass..it's pronounced fau pah. Thank you!"

Figure 4.6 "Same same but different – 3 ways to wear an ethnic long skirt," September 28, 2012. From the fashion blog titled LTWT—Love the World Today…! Photographed by Ritika Saraf. Images courtesy Dipna Daryanani.

without relying on traditional fashion frameworks (designers, stylists, magazine editors) for approval, blogs succeed in a further democratization of fashion (Woodward 2009; Berry 2010; Pham 2011), where "fashion capital has been decentralized" within global networks (Berry 2010). More specifically in the case of Indian blogs, they also actively subvert racial stereotypes associated with Indian dress and fashion, and contribute towards the breaking down of Eurocentric frameworks that have led to its historic exclusion from fashion (Pham 2011).

Street fashion

> There is no street fashion in India … but there is actually fashion on the streets—from a Marathi woman wearing a *Nauvari* sari to a Maharashtran woman's unique drape or a Bhil woman wearing her traditional dress. This is what dictates Indian styling, which also gets imposed on Indian fashion. (Kathiwada 2010)[54]

Related to the emergence of fashion blogging in India, is the phenomenon of street fashion—i.e. "real fashion" spotted in real time on the street. Globally, contemporary street fashion or street style marks a shift from earlier linkages to subcultural style that was more obviously about resistance to dominant culture (Evans 1997), towards "subtly differentiated style grouping, which [increasingly] incorporate mainstream high street fashion" (Woodward 2009: 84).

In speaking about this emerging medium of sartorial self-expression, Sangita Kathiwada points to an interesting paradox on the subject of street fashion in India, which hints at two interlinked interpretations of the term. The first interpretation refers to the inherent sense of style in the clothing worn by men and women on the streets (urban or rural) across India. While by no means lacking in individualism, creativity and in many cases aesthetic sophistication, these instances of street style are out of the realm of formal fashion systems and markets, as they are worn by segments of society who do not have the means or access to high-fashion. They range from nomadic and tribal dress to everyday clothes worn on the street evident in Figure 4.7. In all my conversations and interviews with designers, stylists, writers and fashion commentators, this kind of street fashion was singled out as being indicative of Indian style in the truest sense, and deeply influential when it comes to design, especially for high-fashion and couture.[55] Yet, the lives and clothes of those who maintain this belief could not be further from those they admire.

The photographic recording of such street fashion mirrors the historic practice of methodologically recording unique sartorial styles encountered in India during colonial times by British photographers, anthropologists, illustrators and artists. They are also

---

[54]Sangita Kathiwada in an interview with the author in 2010. Ms. Kathiwada is a prominent fashion personality in India as well as the owner of premier fashion retail store Mélange in Mumbai, which opened in 1993. Mélange has not only been pivotal in giving a platform to emerging Indian designers, but also supports ethically and sustainably created fashion products.

[55]In terms of color combinations, textile use, craft, and styling of such clothing (Sangita Kathiwada, 2010).

Figure 4.7   (Left) Photograph documenting local street clothing in Shillong. From the blog post titled "Nobody wears pyjamas with shoes anymore," May 31, 2011, Wearabout.com. Image courtesy of photographer and blogger Manou. (Right) Cattle herder's wife at a cattle fair in Gwalior. Image by the author.

reminiscent of photographs taken by tourists (which include professional photographers as well as designers) who travel to India in search of inspiration, and document their fascination with the "exotic" quality of Indian costume and crafts, and clothing on Indian bodies—that appear untouched by the forces of globalization, or are worn in unabashed ignorance of global fashion trends. The celebration of such fashion and its documentation as Indian street style once again labels these "stylish" indigenous groups or those from hailing from lower segments of society as "Other." Only this time it is not through the colonial lens, but through that of fashion and re-Orientalism.

The second interpretation of street fashion features styles worn and displayed by trendy middle-class or elite global Indians at fashion weeks, art fairs, literary fests and other such events as well as on personal blogs. These individual fashion statements are indicative of wearers' acquired fashion capital as a result of their background, combined with the experience of travelling overseas, styling for a magazine, or over time through their observation of fashion via their blogs etc. Their style experimentations highlight their ability to draw from current global fashion cues, yet at the same time, present their own individual stance that often draws upon familiar traditional dress practices (Figure

Figure 4.8   Dheeman Agarwala featured in the blog post titled "Nobody wears pyjamas with shoes anymore," May 31, 2011, Wearabout.com. Image courtesy of photographer and blogger Manou. Together Figures 4.7 (left) and 4.8 highlight how clothing styles worn across India on the street, in cities, towns and villages act as inspiration for cosmopolitan constructions of Indian street style.

4.8). In doing so, Indian garments (*dhoti* pants, *kurtas* etc.) become mixed with Western styles, prints, textiles, colors and accessories, resulting in rich, vibrant, playful and original outcomes. As evident in Manou's blog www.wearabout.com that documents both afore-mentioned interpretations of Indian street style, the "Other" India is yet again a valuable source of inspiration as *lungis, gamchas*, ankle bracelets, nose rings and *banyans* get refashioned. Furthermore, the "street" is not so much a real space—made impossible by infrastructural and spatial issues commonly faced in India—but a conceptual space that puts sophisticated everyday style experimentations by urban Indians on a par with the global performance of fashion.

Conclusion: "It's all about attitude"

I think it's time to make India proud in a very stylish way ... Identify which part of the sari is the heroine ... Is it the *pallu*, border, skirt? But don't wear it the usual way ... The adventure begins when you take the *pallu* and wrap it around your waist instead of your shoulder.[56]

Film, television and the Internet together offer a mix of established and emerging platforms for the assertion of individual and collective identity through the medium of fashion. Furthermore, various style statements by urban, hip, global-*desis* within these mediums have the ability to subvert traditional and racial stereotypes about fashion in non-Western settings. As a result, they present new and exciting territories in the study of India's evolving fashion cultures, and are active sites for the production and making of shared meanings, much like the broader definition of culture—as an ongoing process and set of practices (Hall 1997: 2). These meanings are open to negotiations as they are polysemic and not straightforward or in any way fixed. Often they do not "survive intact the passage through representation" as they shift with "context, usage and historical circumstances" (ibid.: 9).

In this way, viewers, readers and fans do not receive or consume the representations of fashion discussed in this chapter passively—as it is possible that through sifting and careful selection they arrive at their own construction of fashion and self. In doing so they are able to take into consideration a number of cues offered by the formats of film, television and the Internet, and subsequently accept, reject, adapt, oppose or modify them towards crafting their wardrobes on a daily basis. Such an approach to self-fashioning is encouraged across all of these mediums, where the common message is that fashion is not about what you wear: "it is about attitude," and even as Western or global influences remain fairly ubiquitous, the assertion of local Indian identity is desirable or in some cases crucial. This is evident in the presentation of clothing on the body that is articulated strategically through a hybrid mix of local, global, Indian, and Western elements much like the bilingualism present in the Indian popular audiovisual entertainment industry (Dasgupta et al. 2012), where the use of *Hinglish* is not an indication of a lack of cosmopolitanism but can actually be "cool."

---

[56]Excerpt from Shubika Sharma's *hatke* (different, unique) ways of wearing the sari, quoted from *Style Police*, Episode 10, UTV Bindass.

5

DESI-CHIC: THE IMAGE AND IDEALS OF FASHION IN INDIAN MAGAZINES

Introduction

The evolution of a distinctive visual identity within the local fashion design industry that responds to Indian tastes, traditions and crafts, along with the presence of international fashion brands in India have not only led to a shift in the sartorial landscape, they have also had an impact on the image and representation of fashion. This was evident in the discussion over the previous chapter with regard to film, television and emerging spheres of fashion blogging, and is also mirrored in print within contemporary fashion magazines. In turn, the influx of global media and Western branded magazines like *Vogue* and *Harper's Bazaar*, for example, have further influenced the face of local publications, and contributed to the way fashion is accepted, adapted, designed, worn and imagined in India.

The role fashion magazines play in shaping sartorial tastes and body and beauty ideals through images and text has been widely examined by academics in a number of disciplines (Barthes 1985 [1976]; Jobling 1999; Hollander 1993 [1978]; Rabine 1994; Entwistle 2000, etc.). Thus, providing a strong theoretical framework for "reading" such visual constructions of fashion-ability. Despite being regarded by many historians and critics as "ephemeral and exiguous forms of cultural production" (Jobling 1999: 1), the ability of fashion magazines and the fashion photograph to represent, and through this representation further shape a collective, socially prescribed ideal of both clothing and the body cannot be overlooked. The widespread propagation of fashion image-texts and fashion magazines through "regular synchronic reading" (Edensor 2002: 7) means that "the description of the garment of Fashion … is therefore a social fact, so that even if the garment of Fashion remained purely imaginary … it would constitute an incontestable element of mass culture …" (Barthes 1985 [1976]: 9). Shaped by the collective imaginations of numerous collaborative forces, the image of fashion is as much real as it is fictional. Through their juxtaposition of images and texts, fashion magazines add meaning to certain styles of clothing, making them an "example of the way in which 'fashion'—as an abstract idea and aesthetic discourse—and 'fashion'—as the actual clothing … connects with everyday dress" (Entwistle 2000: 237).

This chapter intends to add to the existing literature on fashion in print, with particular focus on Indian magazines. Issues of global transnational modernity, which is in keeping with Indian traditions and beliefs, are central to the shaping of contemporary fashion in India. As this chapter will highlight, the same is evident when one examines the image and text of fashion in magazines, which offer idealized representations of their readers' collective aspirations, as well as act as agents of cultural change and arbitrators of national identity viewed through a global lens. Fashion image-texts in the form of editorials, photo-essays, advertorials and advertisements further impinge on the experience of fashion, beauty, gender roles and womanhood in India, as the "fantasies generated by fashion magazines ... do not confine themselves to the page ... They are actually acted out by readers on their own bodies" (Rabine 1994: 63). The direct and accessible nature of communicating various concepts linked to local, global, modernity and tradition in the case of Indian magazines, makes it possible for these images to be consumed on a daily basis through the act of viewing, and eventually play out in the "real" clothing being worn.

Fernandes (2000) and Mazzarella (2003a) highlight the importance of contemporary visual culture as critical sites for negotiating the [imaginary] line between local and global subsequent to India's economic liberalization. Fashion image-texts in particular, that are increasingly centered on class, refinement and style, become "social currency" (Brosius 2007: 118) for further status upliftment and improving lifestyles. Thus making the readers consumers of not only the images and commodities in the images, but also of the "new India produced through the meanings attached to these commodities" (Fernandes 2000: 622). Visual constructions in fashion and lifestyle magazines play a key role in promoting branded fashion as well as Indian design, and increasingly position Western clothing and designer fashion as crucial material mediums for the lived experience of global modernity. Though localizing and indigenizing Western trends, magazines also ensure they fit socially acceptable norms of modesty and respectability. In this way, strategies of localization and glocalization evident in current fashion spreads and editorial content affirm the concepts of re-Orientalism and new-*Swadeshi* introduced in the first chapter, and mirror similar strategies across other mediums of popular culture as well as Indian design.

Beyond a review of existing literature on fashion magazines and media representations of the modern Indian woman and her beauty ideals, this chapter draws its discussion from a random reading and visual analysis of mainly five English language fashion and beauty magazines currently in circulation in India. Namely—*Femina*,[1] *Vogue* India, *Elle* India, *Marie Claire* India, and *Harper's Bazaar* India.[2] In addition, some observations were also made within past issues of *Verve* and *Grazia* India, which corroborated with the aforementioned titles. The study is deliberately selective as the aim is not to focus on their differences through making comparisons (Barthes 1985 [1976]), but to highlight some key themes and scenarios that appear frequently when we view such magazines as a whole, especially in their construction of local fashion informed by global trends for

---

[1] No affiliation with any international publications with the same name.
[2] The study included issues from these magazines dating primarily from 2006 to 2010, and then less regularly till 2013. This also varies from magazine to magazine, as it depends on when the magazine entered the Indian market. For example *Vogue* entered India 2007 and *Harper's Bazaar* in 2009.

the Indian consumer. The singling out of women's fashion magazines is deliberate, due to the long-standing association of women's bodies with the representation of national culture—through wearing of traditional clothing and embodying traditional values. Much like the older visual rhetoric established during the Indian nationalist movements, women's body, beauty and fashion ideals within the image-texts in contemporary fashion magazines continue to be reshaped in order to maintain and communicate a cohesive yet simultaneously ambivalent sense of traditional and modern [global] identity. This is evident in the thematic and visual constructions of the ever-evolving modern Indian woman, which this chapter will discuss.

The chapter excludes Bollywood magazines, lifestyle magazines, Hindi language periodicals, and popular print media aimed at lower segments of Indian society, as they are beyond the scope of the book. These omissions were also seen to be justified for the purpose of the chapter's focus on the confluence of local and global within the images and ideals of high-fashion, that ultimately impact wider trends through being filtered down via celebrity style, Bollywood films, television serials etc. In addition, through their availability (though limited in the case of the more expensive magazines) in smaller towns and cities, these magazines "constitute an agency for interaction between small town and rural audiences... and their more cosmopolitan publishers, writers and reporters" (Breckenridge and Appadurai 1995: 8).

The changing face of Indian fashion magazines

Of the five magazines selected for this chapter's discussion, *Femina*, priced at Rupees 60 (launched in 1959, fortnightly) targets the lower to middle segment of the middle-class market. Due to its wide readership, spread across all cities (Tier-I, II and III) as well as major towns, *Femina* is positioned more so as a lifestyle and women's beauty magazine. In it there is added focus on cosmetics, health issues, relationship advice, food etc. and the fashion spreads and editorial material are often stronger in rhetoric and connotation. The general belief is that the reader needs to be taught or explained the nature of the product and how it fits in within their current or aspired lifestyle, and this is often spelt out through the use of leading texts and slogans that allow the visual quotations to come to life (Brosius 2007: 117). Fashion in *Femina* rarely includes exorbitantly priced high-fashion or Western luxury labels as these are mostly beyond their readers' means. In contrast, *Elle* India (launched in 1996, monthly) priced at Rupees 100, *Vogue* India (2007, monthly) priced at Rupees 125, *Marie Claire* India (2006, monthly)[3] priced at Rupees 100, and *Harper's Bazaar* India (2009, bi-monthly) at Rupees 150, are all targeted towards the middle to upper end of the middle-class market, as well as the elite upper-class market.

---

[3] In July 2013 Outlook India announced that it would no longer be renewing its contract for the *Marie Claire* India title.

These magazines are more popular in the bigger cities and large metros [*sic*] like Delhi and Mumbai.

Beyond their price points, the distinction between the magazines selected for this study and the audience they attempt to target is further evident through the types of products featured, the magazines' layouts, and in the subject matter and tone of the editorial material. Since magazines like *Vogue* India and *Harper's* [*sic*] India target a socially and economically higher audience, their content tends to lean towards denotation that assumes their readers are already "in the know" (Jobling 1999: 75). Hence, the image-texts in these magazines aim to communicate meaning through the juxtaposition of different products and scenarios that are automatically recognized by the reader. High-fashion brands, expensive luxury products and Western-fashion-spread-scenarios are the norm, in these magazines both in advertising materials as well as editorial content. Barring *Femina* all of the magazines selected for this study regularly feature international fashion spreads (with Western labels shot on Western models) sourced from their global networks. The chapter deliberately avoids these in its discussion as the focus is largely on articles and fashion spreads (image and text) written, styled and photographed with the Indian market in mind.

A review of all the aforementioned magazines demonstrates how much the "face" of fashion and lifestyle magazines in India has evolved over the past few decades, especially since the influx of international periodicals. Where previously, *Femina* and a handful of lifestyle and Bollywood magazines like *Filmfare*, *Stardust*, *Cineblitz*, *Society* etc. provided news and features on fashion alongside celebrity style reports, now it is possible to find Indian editions of all the leading international fashion publications. Besides the sheer quantity of glossy publications all targeting different segments of the market, Indian fashion magazines have undergone numerous visual and editorial changes in the past few years. The most obvious and striking of these is that on first glance they are hard to distinguish from their global counterparts, especially on the basis of cover styling, advertisements, fashion imagery, trend reports, editorial style and general visual layout. It is not my intention here to give the impression that this is entirely a new phenomenon, as "various forms of global interaction have always been with us" (Breckenridge and Appadurai 1995: 14). Even before current times, there was obvious visual cohesion between Indian and Western magazines in terms of editorial style and general fashion trends. Additionally magazines like *Femina* have for decades relied on global networks for their editorial contributions.[4] However, now there is definitely a heightened presence of Western luxury and designer brands as well as input from international media channels, which has significantly amped up the global experience in fashion magazines. Globally based publications like *Vogue* and *Elle* have the ability to bring in international contributors including those from the Indian Diaspora, along with access to global photo-shoots, and international editorial sections for their content. This allows for a blurring of boundaries, that also helps position Indian and Western design on par with each other for the Indian consumer to enjoy.

---

[4] See *Femina*, June 2009, 50th Anniversary issue.

Comparing earlier issues of the magazines selected for this study to their more recent ones, there is definitely a greater level of creative "play" with regards to visual design, layouts, photography and fashion styling in current issues. This change emerges alongside a steady inflation in their cover price as well.[5] Like their Western counterparts, Indian fashion magazines include articles on a number of topics pertaining to beauty, fashion, relationship advice, health, women's issues, styling tips, diet and food, interior design ideas, technology, social events, art and travel, along with features on "real" women and celebrities. There is strong evidence of editorial vigor, enthusiasm and the desire to connect with the Indian reader. By positioning themselves as style and "cultural intermediaries" (Entwistle 2000: 238) they offer their readers new information, helpful hints and fashion advice all in the aim of imparting "good taste" that is crucial for the upkeep of modern lifestyles. Readers are introduced to a plethora of luxury items that are now available in India, and are encouraged to experiment with their personal look and expand their horizons through the appreciation of items like Gucci clutches, Jimmy Choo shoes, as well as champagne, fondue and other such highly coveted products that were previously out of the reach of the Indian consumer. Here the general tone ranges from being quite personal and friendly, to that of authority and experience.

Despite stylistic similarities between Indian and other Western magazines, that are obvious outcomes of transnational interactions within the fashion industry, "cultural investment … is possible only if [these images are] within the means of the group to which [they are] offered" (Barthes 1985: 242). This literally means that readers need to be able to connect with the images, products and meanings that reside in those images, *before* even considering their affordability—making it crucial for fashion magazines in India to stay locally rooted and relevant to their Indian reader. *Marie Claire* India's founding editor, Shefalee Vasudev, emphasizes the role local editorial staff play in ensuring the Western content, such as trends reports on *Dandyism*, *Golden Girls* or *Studio 54* for example, become localized or effectively explained for Indian readers "without being disloyal to fashion nor to its customers."[6] This is done through featuring products and clothing that remain aspirational, while making certain that a number of these can be sourced and/or worn in India. Similarly the editor of another leading international magazine maintains that in order to connect with the Indian reader it is important to never seem condescending in the magazine's tone and content.[7] In explaining this further, she states,

People haven't grown up with a Bond street or an Avenue Montaigne. They don't necessarily know the hierarchy of brands and what sits next to what. So you need to be informative but you mustn't lecture. And you must be aware of Indian style … We *have to be* internationally Indian.[8]

---

[5]At the time of beginning this research till the time of writing this chapter all the magazines listed experienced a 50–75 percent inflation in their cover price.

[6]Shefalee Vasudev, in an interview with the author in 2010.

[7]Indian fashion magazine editor (name withheld), in an interview with the author in 2010.

[8]Ibid.

The general sense of viewing the world through the lens of locality that is packaged for the Indian reader's enjoyment and education is an underlying experience in the majority of the fashion content in these magazines. While they enshrine Western consumer items, lifestyles and ideals of beauty, they present them to Indian consumers as "commodities available for *consumption*" (Kondo 1997: 78, emphasis mine). Here "the world is at the disposal of the now powerful, much sought after [Indian] consumer" (ibid.). This translates into a general sense of empowerment that these magazines aim to offer their readers, as well as builds on the ascendancy of the East that can compete with the West in terms of material possessions through conspicuous commodity consumption (real or imagined).

The global-*desi* is yet again a key character that emerges on the pages of these magazines through their portrayal of the ideal Indian consumer who is young, hip and conscious of his or her sense of locality and simultaneously aware of global trends, while being socially mobile and financially able to indulge in them. A unique outcome of transnational flows of media, images, ideas, spaces, material artifacts, and people, thematically the construction of the global-*desi* is a "creative attempt to show and produce taste and distinction by appropriating elements from a vast array of other styles" (Bhatia 1994, cf. Brosius 2007: 122). Practically, it manifests itself into a useful medium for promoting the consumption of fashion products featured in magazines—by visually communicating to the reader how to best personalize unfamiliar or challenging styles, shop for new trends, shop anywhere in the world, manage their wardrobe while living in two different cities,[9] be confident in traditional dress, don traditional and Western clothes in cohesion or be able to select clothing that can do both in a unique way (Plate 7).

Celebrate you: The modern Indian woman

In presenting some of the common themes and scenarios that appear in the magazines selected for this chapter, I begin with the construction of the "modern" Indian woman—a common thread that also runs across the chapters in this book. Market research shows that in recent decades the profile of the modern Indian woman has changed profoundly, claiming that "the 'hedonistic' woman has at last come of age" (Munshi 2000: 78), making her part of a group that is considered to be a huge potential market for consumer products especially fashion, cosmetics and jewelry. A key distinguishing feature of Indian magazines is their unanimous effort towards presenting the "real" and "modern" Indian woman as their ideal customer who is finally seen to be "free to be ME" (*Femina*, August 12, 2006). Despite a celebration of women's liberation, the Indian woman in these magazines is constructed as "an ambivalent entity" (Thapan 2004: 12) which positions her simultaneously as a bearer of tradition *and* a site for showcasing India's globalized modernity. Such constructions of womanhood echo past paradigms of Indianness (such

---

[9]For example in *Vogue* India's, October 2011 issue designer Ritu Beri discusses managing her wardrobe living between India and Paris, and Pia Puri between Mumbai and Kuwait.

as the sari-clad image of the Indian woman), which relied on the positioning of women's bodies and clothing as a powerful site for asserting national identity.

While the rhetoric of current modernity and globalization no longer rely on older nationalist idioms that saw the West as a "space of contamination" (Chatterjee 1993), many aspects of the older construct of womanhood still hold true for the contemporary portrayal of the modern woman. This is especially true with regard to the way she is "shaped by the social and public domain which simultaneously portrays her as glamorous, independent, conscious of her embodiment and of the many forms of adornment and self-presentation available to her, and *yet* enshrined in the world of tradition through her adherence to family and national values" (Thapan 2004: 415–16, emphasis mine). While she may be "articulated or constructed by the codes and conventions of global media flows," her representation is constantly localized to suit her hybrid Indian identity (Munshi 2000: 12). Juxtapositions of past ideals, inner spirituality, tradition and collective identity signified through the medium of traditional Indian dress, with "modern" concepts of career goals, financial independence, self-preservation through commodity consumption and the sense of individual identity symbolized through Western dress, are common constructions within these magazines. Here we begin to see multiple, sometimes contradictory articulations of the Indian woman—as a mother, homemaker, lover, career professional, entrepreneur, single woman, fashionista, friend, rock-chick— all within one issue. It is important to note the growing acceptance of single lifestyles, sex-before-marriage, marital relationships built on equal partnerships, personal retail therapy and fun through fashion as seen in the editorial features. We also see a shift from magazines focusing on women's collective identity to a more individually centered approach that encourages women to *indulge in themselves* instead of on their family-related [domestic] commitments.

Equally popular is the need for magazines to [re]define what it means to be a modern Indian woman. In shaping this definition, each of the selected magazines employs its own way of identifying "who" or "what" she is or can be, which is also based on what the individual magazine needs to promote. It is not uncommon to find multiple definitions of this modern woman in editors' notes, articles and advertorials within each issue, as it appears to be a helpful reference point for the magazine (editors and contributors), as well as the readers who are presumably attempting to find their own reality within the magazines' pages.

In setting the ground for this precedent, *Femina*, India's oldest and widest-selling women's English language beauty magazine,[10] referred to this woman in its old motto as "The Woman of Substance"—with particular focus on women who lead exemplary highly visible lives or are socially active in the public sphere (Thapan 2004: 417). *Femina*'s motto has since changed to "Generation W" (where "W" stands for "woman") and more recently to "for all the women you are," which acknowledges the multiple roles the Indian woman encompasses, and the resulting ambivalence surrounding the many constructions of the ideal modern woman. These mottos also highlight how *Femina* continues to position itself

---

[10]*Femina,* June 3, 2009 (50th Anniversary Issue).

as a women's magazine that provides a platform to express one's individuality (through beauty and fashion) and showcases the struggles and achievements of "real" women of substance. In doing so, *Femina* regularly features articles on professional women active "in new spheres of work" like design, fashion etc., as well as those working in traditionally male-dominated spheres like the army, police and politics (ibid.: 417)—a feature that has defined the magazine from the very beginning. According to the Times of India group, *Femina* "has adapted to reflect [the modern woman's] changing interests from decade to decade: home and work in the 1960s; film and fashion in the 1970s; supermodels and controversies in the 1980s; global issues and the environment in the 1990s; strong women and campaigns for social justice in the new millennium."[11]

Other magazines, targeting the upper middle-class to elite reader, offer more varied and cosmopolitan constructions of the modern woman. For example, *Vogue* India defines her as one who can combine labels like Mango with high-fashion designer brands like Moschino and Gauri and Nayanika all in one look (Tanna, *Vogue* India, June 2009: 22), or travel three cities, across three countries to be able to find her personal sense of style ("Style in the City," *Vogue* India, June 2009: 56)—thereby stressing social and financial mobility and a resulting sense of global eclecticism. Since the other magazines selected for this study also target a similar high-end market, they too are more whimsical in their construction of the Indian woman—where *Verve* caters to those who have the "fashion chromosome" for whom "dressing is an art form" (Mahindra, *Verve*, September 2007: 19), and *Elle* India's editor Nomita Kalra describes her "as someone who has a flair for the dramatic," "likes to make a statement, yet ... will never lose her sense of self" (Kalra, *Elle* India, August 2006). There is a general consensus that in being modern, the Indian woman should be able to make "free" and educated choices about her sense of style, based not necessarily on Western trends, but more so on personality as well as her Indian roots. There is also a strong assertion on the need for Indian women to carefully assess how they should style themselves to suit both modern and traditional expectations. This adds to the general ambivalence, but also hints at the role fashion magazines can play in assisting women in navigating through their wardrobe dilemmas.

Fashion lessons:[12] "What do I wear?"

> Throw comfort, style, personal taste, practicality and tradition into the mix, and the result is every modern Indian woman's daily morning in-front-of-the-mirror dilemma. (Nitasha Gaurav, *Femina*, January 2, 2008)

Scenarios like the aforementioned quote from *Femina* that refer to women's sartorial dilemmas are not limited to Indian magazines, as Western magazines follow a similar

---

[11] Cited from "Best of Femina celebrates 50 years of mag's history." *Times of India,* May 22, 2009. Available from http://timesofindia.indiatimes.com (accessed January 19, 2010).
[12] A regular feature in *Marie Claire* India.

approach in constructing multiple versions of the ideal woman and identifying her clothing needs. However, in catering to the multiple roles the Indian woman can co-inhabit and the diversity of clothing styles worn in India, fashion magazines tend to offer an overwhelming variety of clothing styles, both Indian and Western, within a single issue, from which to choose from. Yet, alongside the celebration of Indian clothes—saris, *lehengas*, *kurtis*, *dhoti* pants, etc.—and numerous sections on how to wear them in fashionable ways, all of the magazines selected for this study, and indeed most other forms of visual and print media, including magazines in regional languages, associate Western or Westernized clothing with youth, fashion and the general experience of "freedom" and modernity. As Kondo has noticed in her study of Japanese fashion and fashion magazines, there is "an unproblematized enshrining of things Western, particularly in those [magazines] catering to youthful, hip, urban audiences" (Kondo 1997: 78). This is evident in the way clothing is styled and visually presented in Indian fashion spreads and further reiterated in editorial content (images and text) that actively promote Western garments as "sexy" and "fun." The notion of coming "undone" through "faded denims, canvas sneakers and a tiny black skirt" for the "rock chick" is one such representation of the fun and freedom factor of such clothing, especially for the woman who wants to channel her inner "Avril Lavigne" ("Come Undone," *Marie Claire* India, August 2006).

Multiple style columns encourage readers to experiment with new styles and offer advice and remedies on how to make informed fashion choices. These range from the simple—how to wear the tailored jacket (Figure 5.1, *Elle* India, August 2013), how to pick the right [bra] cup size ("Undercover" *Femina*, December 2006), how to sit in a tiny skirt (*Femina*, January 2, 2008), how to dress for all ages (*Marie Claire* India, October 2010, regular segment) to more status oriented—what to buy now and love forever (*Harper's Bazaar* India, 2010, regular segment). Stressing on an item's trendiness allows for some styles, such as the jumpsuit (2008 and 2009) or sequin shorts (2010), to gain greater acceptance through editorial endorsement despite some concerns about the style not suiting the Indian woman's body type. *Vogue* India's editor Priya Tanna tells readers how "being introduced to her ankles" through being introduced to the shift dress in London by *Vogue* India's editorial director Anna Harvey was a life-changing moment (Tanna, *Vogue* India, October 2007: 55); while *Marie Claire* India stylist Nikhil D shows readers ten ways to wear khaki shorts.[13] There is no indication that such styles may pose a challenge to the reader, who is assumed to be already "in the know" and is able to make free and independent sartorial choices. Magazines like *Femina*, that cater to a lower demographic, offer suggestions on how to hide problem areas and still wear Western clothes, as illustrated in the feature titled "by the cuff" (*Femina,* August 16, 2006) where sleeves are touted as the new erogenous zones that can hide body imperfections like flabby arms. Similarly, designer Priyadarshani Rao's "Style FAQs" section (previously Anita Dongre's "Style Facts") in *Femina* responds to readers' fashion dilemmas in a slightly more conservative manner to suit the target readership by considering body type, skin complexion, problem areas and at the same time carefully assesses the suitability of

---

[13]*Marie Claire* India, April 2010.

ELLEEDITS

Sorbet sweetness brightens up steely grey. These are the flats to take you from conference to cocktails.

The bucket bag is this season's must-have. Extra points for going bold and bright.

Georgette kurta, ₹ 13,250, **Pranav Mishra and Shyma Shetty for Huemn.** Woollen jacket, ₹ 17,640, **Lecoanet Hemant.** Cotton trousers, ₹ 3,999, **Marks & Spencer.** Rexine brogues, ₹ 4,500, **Shikha & Vinita for Ilk.** Chain necklace with uncut citrine, ₹ 3,200, gold-plated ring, ₹ 4,850; **both Zariin.** Rubber strap watch, ₹ 12,996, **Emporio Armani.** Leather iPad sleeve, ₹ 2,000, **Vitasta.** Leather clutch, ₹ 36,000, **Tod's.** Acrylic sunglasses, ₹ 17,500, **Marc Jacobs**

Silk shirt, ₹ 6,950, **Bebe.** Woollen jacket, ₹ 17,640, **Lecoanet Hemant.** Cotton trousers, ₹ 4,499, **Sisley.** Leather T-strap sandals, ₹ 27,500, **Stuart Weitzman.** High-waist leather belt, price on request, **Gucci.** Clic Clac H metal bracelet, ₹ 43,000, **Hermès.** Leather bucket bag, brass necklace with Swarovski ELEMENTS, price on request; both **Louis Vuitton**

how to wear

THE TAILORED JACKET

ACCESSORISES NOW

Tactic leather bracelet, ₹ 7,900, **Swarovski**

Gold and diamond earrings, price on request, **Pure Gold Jewellers**

Leather tote, ₹ 27,250, **Michael Kors**

Acrylic sunglasses, ₹ 25,639, **Fendi**

Leather pumps, ₹ 58,000, **Salvatore Ferragamo**

FOR DETAILS, SEE ADDRESS BOOK

Figure 5.1 "How to Wear The Tailored Jacket" from the Elle Edits segment, August 2013. Photographed by Farzan Randelia. Image courtesy *Elle* Magazine India.

Plate 1 Limited edition collection of saris by Hermès, 2011. Designs from left to right are titled: *Coupons Indiens*, *Fleurs d'Indiennes* and *Silk Patch*. Photographed by Rohan Shrestha. Image courtesy Hermès.

Plate 2 Film still from *Jodhaa Akbar* (2008) featuring film actress Aishwarya Rai Bachchan in a *lehenga* ensemble designed by Neeta Lulla. Image courtesy Neeta Lulla.

Plate 3 Film poster for *Aisha* (2010). Female characters styled by Pernia Qureshi. Image courtesy Anil Kapoor Films Co. Pvt. Ltd.

Plate 4 Characters Akshara (played by Hina Khan) and Naitik (played by Karan Mehra) from a publicity image for *Yeh Rishta Kya Kehlata Hai*. Image courtesy Star TV, UK.

Plate 5   Film actress Sonam Kapoor photographed along with the shoe design created for her by Salvatore Ferragamo. Image courtesy Salvatore Ferragamo.

Plate 6 Film actress Vidya Balan in an outfit designed and styled by Sabyasachi Mukherjee, at the 2013 Cannes Film Festival. (AP Images).

Plate 7 "Reunited Colors of India." Cover Image from *Marie Claire* India, June 2008. Photographed by Bruno Juminer. Image courtesy *Marie Claire* Magazine India.

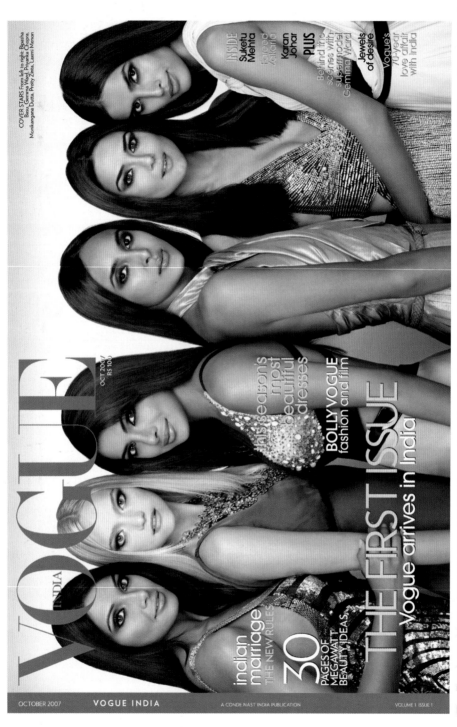

Plate 8 "The First Issue: Vogue Arrives in India." Fold out cover from *Vogue India*, October 2007, featuring from left to right: Bipasha Basu, Gemma Ward and Priyanka Chopra (top cover), and Monikangana Dutta, Preity Zinta and Laxmi Menon (inner cover). Photographed by Patrick Demarchelier. Image courtesy *Vogue* Magazine India.

Plate 9 Catwalk look from Sabyasachi Mukherjee's 2012 Couture Collection titled *New Moon*.
Image courtesy Sabyasachi Mukherjee.

Plate 10 Catwalk look from Manish Arora's Spring/Summer 2008 ready-to-wear collection showcased at Paris Fashion Week. Image courtesy Manish Arora.

Plate 11 Catwalk look from Manish Arora's Fall/Winter 2013/14 ready-to-wear collection inspired by the Burning Man Festival. Showcased at Paris Fashion Week. Photographed by Yannis Vlamos. Image courtesy Manish Arora.

Plate 12 Ritu Kumar advertising campaign, 2010. Image courtesy Ritu Kumar.

Plate 13 Sari being embroidered on the *adda* with Chinoiserie inspired motifs designed by Rajdeep Ranawat. Image by author.

Plate 14 "Imbued with the soul of Spain, huge fringed shawls, known as 'Mantón de Manila' remain a Spanish tradition and almost always depict flowers in varied hues and sizes. In harmony with the beauty of the Indian *Jamawar*, a unique collection takes birth in deep aubergines, reds and turquoises in rich silks and jacquards." (Caption provided by JJ Valaya).

An Alika jacket from JJ Valaya's 2013 bridal couture collection titled "Maharajas of Madrid." Photographed by Anand Seth. Makeup by Suchitra Bose. Image courtesy JJ Valaya.

Plate 15 "Aubergine silt, multi dimensional georgette drapes and metal embroidery." Catwalk look from Gaurav Gupta's Autumn/Winter 2011/12 ready-to-wear collection showcased at Wills Lifestyle India Fashion Week. This look highlights Gaurav's use of drape to create fluid garments that subvert aspects of traditional Indian drapes as well as metal thread embellishments. Image courtesy FDCI/Gaurav Gupta.

Plate 16 *"Vrindavan Resham"* sari by Raw Mango, from the 2012 collection titled *Birjoo* inspired from devotional cloth hangings known as *Pichhwais* that are used as backdrops for images worshipped in Hindu temples by devotees of Lord Krishna. This hand woven silk sari featuring a cow motif is woven using the *khadwa* technique from Benares. The holy town of Vrindavan in Madhya Pradesh India, referenced in the design's title, is renowned for its many temples dedicated to the worship of Radha and Krishna. *Resham* means silk. Photographed by Pranoy Sarkar. Image courtesy Sanjay Garg, Raw Mango.

Western garments over Indian dress. In case the reader is not able to wear Western garments, trendy Indian styles like the *kurti* are advised as a safer option.

Interestingly, the emphasis on Western styles within all of the Indian fashion magazines concurrent to the celebration of traditional clothes and Indian couture, means that readers are also advised on how Western garments can be styled and worn *with* traditional clothes. Thereby further ensuring traditional clothing and indigenous dress styles remain relevant to contemporary fashion.

Visualizing *desi*-chic

The image of fashion in Indian magazines is not only a useful medium for fuelling readers' desire for high-fashion brands and accessories through glamorous, fun and edgy photo-shoots, it also helps in the process of visualizing various combinations of Indo-Western fusion, plus gives context to the clothing through the use of familiar settings that further localize fashion for their readers. All of the magazines selected for this chapter's discussion play an active role in familiarizing the Indian reader with global trends as well as highlighting how they can be localized and adapted into the Indian wardrobe. This process is essential for both Indian and international brands who are vying for the same market, and visually interesting to observe as it relies on the innovative co-styling of Indian and Western elements, garments, brands and general aesthetics. Such fusion is also in keeping with the way Indian consumers already subconsciously mix and match Indian and Western garments in their wardrobes.

Creative experimentation with Indo-Western or *desi*-chic styling in fashion spreads has the added ability to transcend a "fun" element to Indian traditional dress—as "homemaker" Krati Gupta realizes when she pairs a *lehenga* with a vest[14] resulting in a "very global look" (*Femina*, December 15, 2010). Garments such as the *kurti* and the *salwar* come highly recommended due to their ability to function as an Indian garment and yet be similar to a Western shirt (in the case of the *kurti*) and trousers (in the case of the *salwar*). Style experimentations on the versatility of the "Indian fashion staple" that is the *salwar* ("Rocking the *Salwar*," *Vogue* India, August 2008), illustrated through funky images with "hip" styling (Figure 5.2) demonstrate how this often "unrecognized" garment can be transformed through playing up its "urban cool" with the "right mix" (ibid.). Teamed with leather jackets, corsets, T-shirts, and even some *kurtas,* the *salwar* in these editorial photo-shoots is once again India's fashion treasure. Revisiting Indian opulence through moderation and balance is also encouraged in fashion spreads, as features on how to wear "Maharaja Chic" (*Elle* India, June 2009) or the "Little Black Dress" "adorned with royal Indian jewelry … [to give] the iconic dress a *revamp*" (*Marie Claire* India, June 2009, emphasis mine) showcase how Indian ornamentation and dress can be styled with international designer clothing.

---

[14] Here "vest" refers to a sleeveless T-shirt or singlet.

Figure 5.2 Image from the fashion spread titled "Rocking the *Salwar*," *Vogue* India, August 2008. Photographed by Tarun Khiwal. Courtesy *Vogue* Magazine India.

Besides being a logical progression of India's long-standing tradition of sartorial fusion, the conscious featuring of Indian garments alongside Western brands as a popular visual strategy in Indian magazines could further be read in two ways. Firstly, as a way of legitimizing Indian fashion through the presence of established Western labels. An example of this is the iconic front cover of *Vogue* India's first issue from October 2007 (Plate 8, left side), where Indian fashion, in the guise of Indian models-turned Bollywood stars Bipasha Basu and Priyanka Chopra, proudly stands head to head with Western fashion, represented by world-renowned supermodel Gemma Ward. Secondly, as a way of representing the compatibility and cohesion between Indian and Western fashion systems for the global-*desi*—as highlighted in the fashion spread titled "Beyond Borders"

BEYOND BORDERS

Dolce & Gabbana
&
Vineet Bahl

This season, we found a novel way to wear traditional Indian silhouettes—by combining them with their international counterparts. The results are modern and very, very cool

Photographed by
MARK PILLAI

Styled by
DEEP KAILEY

88

Figure 5.3 Image from the fashion spread titled "Beyond Borders," Vogue India, July 2009. Featuring designs by Dolce Gabbana and Vineet Bahl. Photograph by Mark Pillai. Image courtesy *Vogue* Magazine India.

(*Vogue* India, July 2009) where Indian designer garments are styled together with those from well-known Western designer labels. The pairing of Dolce and Gabbana with Vineet Bahl (Figure 5.3), Chanel with Tarun Tahiliani, and Sabyasachi Mukherjee with Givenchy results in an outcome that is "fun," "edgy," "modern and very, very cool" (ibid.). According to *Harper's Bazaar* India's founding editor Sujata Assomull Sippy, the outcomes of such fusion is vibrant, eclectic, surprising and satisfying for the Indian palette, but also crucial in ensuring Indian clothes remain globally viable and do not get relegated to the status of "costume."[15]

Yet, as Osuri (2008) reminds us, "global" is a slippery concept and is not universally experienced as the term suggests, "as many processes of circulation do not extend across the globe" (Osuri 2008: 111). Hence, while Indian fashion is featured alongside and on par with Western fashion in Indian magazines, the same is relatively less frequent in Western fashion magazines.

"Made In India": Contours of the nation[16]

Beyond the fusion of diverse clothing styles, another distinguishing feature is the heightened emphasis on India—Indian culture, artifacts and design—which makes for an even more visually colorful and eclectic experience of fashion in these magazines.

This is evident in the editorial content, images and textual references that consciously internalize the Orientalized Western gaze and promote Indian garments, products, lifestyle, celebrities and travel destinations as exotic and timeless treasures to the readers. Here we see magazines making reference to a wide range of items, places, crafts, textiles, people, rituals, jewelry, palaces, traditional embroideries, yoga, Ravi Varma prints etc., whereby the "accumulation of historic items affirms one's prestige and taste" (Brosius 2007: 122). The strategy of self-Orientalizing or auto-exoticization, as highlighted in previous chapters, acts as a powerful medium for the assertion of distinction from the rest of the world and a celebration of Indian cultural identity. It also showcases local ingenuity and the wealth of resources India has to offer the rest of the world, such as "authentic" ornamentation, traditional dress styles, textiles and Indian color palettes; and ultimately frames these within global fashion trends. The linking of the term *couture* to high-end, made-to-measure and hand-embellished (often traditional) Indian garments, and their designers, is one such example by which a Western institution becomes indigenized and promoted as a sign of exclusivity and Indian distinction. Articles on crafts, textiles and embroideries and the importance on their preservation aim to educate the Indian consumer of the unique and exotic treasures that exist *in* India that have always been revered and respected by the West for centuries. Furthermore much of this content focuses on how these treasures can be re-vitalized and modernized for contemporary lifestyles.

---

[15] Sujata Assomull Sippy, in an interview with the author in 2010.
[16] Trivedi (2003), see footnote #19 for a detailed explanation of the source of this reference.

In addition, the magazines' local contributors see themselves as important agents for the empowerment and encouragement of the domestic fashion industry and design that is "Made in India." By providing established and emerging designers a platform to showcase their work, magazines promote their designs for consumption. To further endorse Indian design, magazines often include features on designers that showcase local talent and demystify the conceptual inspiration behind collections, and also portray design as an exciting and innovative activity. Competitions and awards, such as *Marie Claire* India's "Made in India"[17] awards and *Vogue* India's Fashion Fund, recognize India's establishing and emerging designers, as well as give special attention to those who use India as a "muse" in their designs or show "best craft revival."[18]

The need to find and promote "authentic" fashion made in India once again reminds us of the older rhetoric of Indian nationalism that sought to distinguish India from its Colonial rulers. Familiarizing the Indian reader with the wealth of local resources also bears resemblance to the way *khadi* cloth was officially incorporated into the *Swadeshi* movement by the Indian national congress and portrayed as a "material artifact of the nation" (Trivedi 2003: 13–14).[19] Interestingly, such approaches and concepts also inform Indian designers' design philosophies. The key difference now is that the West is regarded as a positive influence for modernizing Indian crafts, textiles and dress practices—with the aim of ensuring their continued relevance to contemporary culture and global markets. The ultimate message that readers receive through such image-texts is that Indian fashion allows for the greater expression of individual identity and personal creativity, which is also within the collective arena of national identity and traditional heritage—all crucial aspects within liberalized India.

The "Made in India" experience in fashion magazines goes deeper than a visual showcase of Indian design, textiles, and clothing. In exploring India's diversity and cultural highlights, editorial photo-shoots increasingly feature Indian locations presented in ways where "the masses have virtually disappeared" (Inden 1999, cf. Brosius 2007: 118) or are positioned for exotic consumption as backdrops for high-fashion and couture on fashion models. Photo-shoots such as the one in Figure 5.4 are instances whereby both the clothes and an aesthetically curated backdrop of Indian people and places are on show. Taking this one step further in its "India issue" (August 2008), *Vogue* India featured a fashion spread that combined the "season's most coveted accessories" of handbags from Hermès, Fendi, Anamika Khanna, shoes from Miu Miu and Alexander McQueen, to name but a few, with "the people, colours and sights of *authentic* [emphasis mine] India"; and allowed the reader to "take a visual journey through the streets of Jodhpur…" This feature was highly criticized in the media[20] as the "people of India" that it featured hailed

---

[17] Discontinued.

[18] Award category within the *Marie Claire* India "Made in India" Awards.

[19] Trivedi illustrates the role visual culture played during India's freedom struggle to firstly communicate messages of nationalism and promote *khadi*, and secondly to inspire "new modes of consumption," again in the aim of securing a sense of shared identity through material items, such as *khadi* clothing (Trivedi 2003: 13). Through the medium of *khadi* exhibitions Indian visitors were able to experience the "contours of the nation" through a "wide range of products [and images] drawn from different regions" (ibid.: 15).

[20] See Timmons (2008).

Figure 5.4 First page from the spread titled "Time Travel" from the Elle Lifestyle, segment, January 2013. Photographed by Farrokh Chothia. Image courtesy *Elle* Magazine India.

not from the upwardly mobile middle-class or the elite class, but a farmer and his wife in a mud hut, a family of three on a scooter, a group of village women wearing their traditional garb, among others. In doing so, it blatantly underscored the polarity of India's "split public" where it is highly likely that the income earned by these unidentified "models" over a lifetime could not equate to the cost of some of the items they were seen holding.[21] Such photo-shoots, that could easily be seen as subversive techniques of mimicry by India's fashion media, combined with regular travel features on exotic destinations within India in magazines like *Vogue,* allow readers to experience their nation through the eyes of locality, as well as through the eyes of the West via travelogues by Western designers, writers, artists, celebrities and international editors. In this manner, they are yet another way India is re-Orientalized for the reader to enjoy and consume.

Finally, there is also a sense of pride built into the notion of international fashion magazines *in* India. In *Elle* India's August 2006 issue, the editor shares a letter from Nancy Duarka in New Delhi with the readers in the section titled "Mailbonding," that describes an instance where a "foreigner" found the Indian *Elle* "more appetizing" due to its "Indian flavour" (*Elle* India, August 2006). "Here's to the pride of India, *ELLE*!" says Nancy in her letter (ibid.). Similarly, *Vogue* India's readers are reminded of how lucky they are to finally have their very own *Indian Vogue*. A dream that the magazine's editor Priya Tanna had harbored for 21 years is now a reality due to India's economic growth, international outlook and "scintillating soiree with world attention" (Tanna, *Vogue* India, October, 2007: 55). The confluence of India's modernity with international agents of good taste and high cultural capital, once again instills a sense of pride in that *Vogue, Elle, Harper's Bazaar* etc. are all finally "Made in India"!

Fair and lovely:[22] Global-Indian beauty and bodies

> India's opening up to the world 'outside' in the current economic climate of globalisation finds a symbolic parallel in the beautiful Indian woman who has become linked to the world outside through the global currency of her beauty [and her body]. (Reddy 2006: 63).

As already discussed, the Indian woman's body acts as a powerful site for the representation of the specific nature of Indian identity that is shaped by both past and present discourses of Indianness. Also mentioned earlier, the construction of the modern Indian

---

[21] *Vogue* India's editorial team responded to the criticism they received via global media channels by emphasizing the non-serious nature of such photo-shoots and fashion. Yet while such image-texts have been the norm in Western magazines for decades with editorials photographed amongst African tribes or appropriating elements from different "exotic" cultures, *Vogue* India's mimicry or appropriation of an Orientalist stance within India was not categorized in the same grouping.

[22] A popular skin fairness cream launched by Hindustan Unilever Ltd. in India in 1976.

woman as a bridge between local and global makes her body a hybrid entity that can shift seamlessly from one mold to another.

Evident in the popular ideals that emerge from the pages of Indian fashion magazines, the image of the Indian woman is a hybrid combination of the Western body-beautiful and Indian traditional inner-self. This literally translates into Western ideals of thinness, physical fitness, fair skin (or in some cases dark tanned skin, also admired in the West as being "exotic"), with Indian inner beauty achieved through being mindful of traditions, family values, issues of modesty and morality, and spirituality. When wearing global or Western styles the Indian woman is uninhibited, but in Indian clothing she dons a more graceful and timeless sense of mystique. While she retains her Western form, she embodies the centuries of tradition that makes her uniquely Indian. Much like the construction of contemporary fashion, the distinctive nature of Indian beauty lies in the fusion of these elements that allow it to be superior to the rest of the world—which Indian magazines note has been demonstrated through the numerous Miss World and Miss Universe titles won by Indian women in recent years.

It is important here to mention *Femina* and its involvement in the Miss India beauty pageant that began in 1964. Looking back, in its 50th Anniversary issue (June 2009), *Femina* credits itself for single-handedly putting Indian beauty on the map of the world, through promoting "beauty as an ideal and a goal" (Thapan 2004: 420) and grooming potential Miss India candidates to be able to cultivate this ideal through hard work, discipline and staying true to their roots. Past winners like Aishwarya Rai Bachchan[23] and Sushmita Sen[24] play a central role as global ambassadors of Indian beauty and are supported in their endeavors by *Femina*'s editorial material. Regular articles on the effort and determination these women put into maintaining their bodies alongside being exemplary Indian women bears testimony to the fact that beauty can be a full time occupation. Runkle (2004), Reddy (2006), and Osuri (2008) all examine the role *Femina* in particular has played in selecting women with an international look as Miss India winners, thus transforming the beauty industry with "a product that was fairer, taller, slimmer, straight haired, and much more likely to be well-received on the global scene" (Lal 2003 cf. Osuri 2008: 112). Thapan describes such processes as having a "re-colonizing" effect on the Indian female body that results from the combination of the "specific modernity of the postcolonial … [and] global alignments and fluidly of capital … which seeks to position women in particular ways that are not dissimilar to their positioning in colonial contexts" (Thapan 2004: 411–14).

The predominance of fair-skinned models and skin-lightening products in adver-torials poses some confusion when flipping through the pages of the Indian fashion magazines—and most cover-images reinforce this preference through the use of fair models and celebrities—who do not match the general skin coloration of Indian women. However, fairness is not a new preoccupation in India. Rituals of body beautification,

---

[23] Aishwarya Rai Bachchan was runner-up in the 1994 Miss India Contest and also won the Miss World title in the same year.

[24] Sushmita Sen won the Miss India Contest in 1994 (same year as Aishwarya) and won the Miss Universe title in the same year.

skin lightening and adornment have a deep-rooted history in the Indian woman's toilette and "middle and upper-class sections of Indian society have always privileged white or lighter skin over dark skin" (Thapan 2004: 424). These ideals continue to be projected by Indian print media through advertisements for skin-lightening products that have been around in Indian magazines for decades, as well as other forms of televisual media and films. A number of theorists (Runkle 2004; Thapan 2004; Reddy 2006; Osuri 2008 etc.) have addressed this obsession with fair skin as an Indian beauty ideal, which they link to colonial inferiorization of dark skin as "Other," which is still at play within the postcolonial psyche as it attempts to overcome this inferiority. Though not necessarily classified as mimicry, it is more so regarded as a case of adopting the language of dominance (Fanon 2001 cf. Thapan 2004: 424), which in this case is the "fair" ideal.

Recent decades have seen active and lively debates within these magazines' editorial content, challenging such ideals of fairness, as seen in *Marie Claire* India's article titled "An Unfair Debate on Fairness" (*Marie Claire* India, August, 2008). Though these discussions occur concurrent to the idealization of fairness, global recognition of Indian models like Ujjwala Raut and Lakshmi Menon has meant that darker-skinned bodies have gained greater visibility in Indian magazines. However, their representation is often typecast in exotic stylizations. The jewelry spread titled "Objects of Desire" in the first issue of *Vogue* India (October 2007)—in which two dark female models, dressed only in jewelry replicate erotic Indian visual imagery and sculptural art through their posture and choreography—is one such example where the dark female body is represented in a highly sexualized and exoticized manner. "Such narratives borrow from older, historically specific meanings that present a fusion between national tradition and global capitalism" (Fernandes 2000: 615) as well as auto-exoticize the Indian body for local and global consumption.

While the desire for fair skin has been one shared by Indian women across generations, the obsession towards achieving thin bodies is a more recent phenomenon. In 2007, The Wall Street journal claimed that "India's slimming and fitness industry now amounts to US$750 million in terms of revenue and is expected to grow 25% to 30% annually … [and] … fashion appears to be the biggest factor driving the newly weight conscious" (Cohen 2007). With slimming studios (gyms) mushrooming in even the smaller urban centers, today's media driven consumer culture mirrors Western ideals of the perfect body—perfectly shaped, toned and exercised. Achieving the ideal body through exercise and diet is heavily encouraged through numerous articles, self-help columns and advertorials that talk about women's "Leg-acy" and "Shape-scapes" (*Marie Claire* India, June 2011). The commodification of this body ideal and its fetishization in all forms of visual and print media, subsequently means that "the discipline of the body and the pleasure of the flesh are no longer in opposition to one another. Instead, discipline of the body through dieting and exercise has become one of the keys to achieve a sexy, desirable body which in turn gives *you* pleasure" (Entwistle 2000: 20, emphasis mine).

"Real" fashion and bodies in print

Much like in all other fashion magazines worldwide, the ageing or overweight body rarely has any place in the construction of high-fashion imagery in Indian magazines. When such bodies are included, it is usually for tasteful makeovers (tackling problem areas, dressing for your body type) or the portrayal of tradition and longevity presented in the collective realm—especially with regards to promoting products that are either for the home or those that are aligned with Indian rituals, festivals or traditions. The portrayal of older celebrities like the late Maharani Gayatri Devi, and actresses Sharmila Tagore and Hema Malini illustrate the commodification of the history and tradition vested in their bodies. Rarely are such bodies associated with high-fashion.

The contradiction between the real and the representation becomes highly obvious in the non-fashion related material in fashion magazines, through features and stories on the lives of inspirational, publicly active, philanthropic women; who are portrayed as the real representatives of Indian modernity. Usually preferring to wear either casual Indian styles (such as the *salwar kameez*) or less fashion forward Indo-Western clothing, these women demonstrate the gap experienced between the young, trendy ideal that magazines portray in their fashion spreads and the real modern woman that is featured alongside. The platform provided to these women, while empowering, is clearly demarcated from

Figure 5.5 From the fashion spread titled "What do I wear?," *Femina*, January 2008. Photographed by Darren Centofanti. Image courtesy Darren Centofanti/*Femina*.

Figure 5.6 "Street Style Project" spread featured in *Marie Claire* India, August 2012. Image courtesy *Marie Claire* Magazine India.

the trendier editorials that tend to focus more on body-beautiful people. Regular features on India's "best-dressed" men and women in all of the magazines selected for this chapter's study demonstrate a preference for celebrities, movie stars, designers, models, DJs and stylists as style icons, and provide a visual fantasy that everyday women can aspire towards that further offsets the real representations.

As a compromise, magazines often include features on carefully selected, stylish non-celebrities, who are either career professionals, emerging entrepreneurs or from their own editorial staff in more realistic settings—with the clear intention of resonating with readers. Evident in the photo-feature in *Femina* titled "What do I Wear?" (*Femina*, January 2008) (Figure 5.5) on "women from all walks of life"—artists, visual merchandisers, photographers, homemakers and radio jockeys—through highlighting style dilemmas of these "real" models as they relate to concerns about flabby arms, showing knees and weighty thighs the magazines turn this into yet another effective fashion lesson. More recently, current trends of fashion blogging and street fashion have opened up a new space for representations of real people and emerging fashion cultures in Indian magazines (Figure 5.6). Often sourced through the magazines' own networks, instances of sartorial fusion and juxtapositioning of local and global brands evident in Indian street style further affirm the *desi*-chic image magazines themselves have helped visually construct. The representations of real fashion on the streets is yet another way in which readers can experience the "contours of the nation" through viewing other women's (and men's) bodies, as well as experience a sense of pride through knowing Indian fashion can be at par with the rest of the world while maintaining many aspects relating to local traditions and ingenuity.

Conclusion: What is India wearing?

As a conclusion I offer the question that was posed to editorial and photographic contributors in the first issue of *Vogue*'s India edition: "If India was a woman, how would you dress her?"[25] Understandably, it generated some mixed responses that ranged from "draping her in a *sari*" "with a more contemporary look," to dressing her in "a pair of old faded jeans in the day and jewellery at night," or in "Pink [as] it's the navy blue of India," or "white," or "in a kingfisher blue *sari* [embellished] with fine threads of gold, a couple of bangles from Butler and Wilson … a classic men's Rolex Oyster … and a very small diamond on the upper lip." Thus making it clear that there is no one single mode for fashioning the ideal Indian woman.

On the pages of fashion magazines India's modern and fashionable woman finds the construction of her sartorial identity a fluid process, which is commodified through a myriad of branded items—where the past and the present, the old and the new, the local and the global, the traditional and the modern—are all critical components (Thapan 2004: 412). Also evident from these image-texts is the platform they provide for the material and visual construction of contemporary culture that stems from the vibrant confluence of India's rich national heritage and the dynamism of globalization. Through the medium of fashionable clothing wearers are [once again] able to experience the contours of the nation as well as the rest of the world towards magazines' construction of individual and collective identity. The lasting impact of the Orientalist gaze becomes reconfigured through self-Orientalizing and auto-exoticizing strategies of distinction that project India's uniqueness and authenticity through the discourses of modern, traditional, local, global fashion.

As many of the images featured on the pages of *Elle* India, *Harper's Bazaar* India and *Vogue* India convey seemingly unattainable ideals of beauty that are vastly different from the real body in print, on the street, in shops and other such regular settings, the authenticity of these images becomes an area of contention. In addition, despite the ubiquitous presence of Western clothing in metropolitan cities, it is harder to be convinced of some of the visual constructs that are portrayed in magazines, as one is also aware that beyond these cities the spread of Westernized fashion still remains limited. Banerjee and Miller (2000) in their account on the modern sari, echo a similar sentiment through their observation of clothing norms for women outside of large cities, which mainly comprises of the sari and *salwar kameez*. Nevertheless, this difference does not mean such bodies are entirely fictional. "Dressing is always picture making, with reference to actual pictures that indicate how the clothes are to be perceived" (Hollander 1993: 311) and "[in] a picture making civilization, the ongoing pictorial conventions demonstrate what is natural

---

[25] *Vogue* India, October 2007.

in human looks; and it's only in measuring up to them that the inner eye feels satisfaction and the clothed self achieves comfort and beauty" (ibid.: xii). Hence, fashion image-texts in the form of editorials, photo-essays, advertorials and advertisements contribute towards shaping their readers' sartorial tastes as "people dress and observe other dressed people with a set of pictures in mind—pictures in a particular style" (ibid.: 311). Readership of these magazines, especially *Femina*, is not limited to the big cities alone, and so while they may not always impact on "real" clothing, their construction through social forces and their consumption through viewership bears evidence of their profound impact on the "imaginations" of modern Indian women, which cannot lie wholly outside the reality that these women experience in their daily lives.

6

DARZI TO "DESIGNER": CRAFTING COUTURE AND HIGH-FASHION FOR INDIA

The year 2012 marked a special year in the calendar of Indian fashion. A number of India's most established and well-known high-fashion designers completed 25 years in the business, and at least a dozen others reached their two-decade landmark. Designers like Ritu Kumar, Tarun Tahiliani and Suneet Verma, to name a few, were not only celebrating their individual labels' longevity and design achievements, but also their collective contribution towards the growth and development of a local design industry as well as the evolution of a local design idiom.

Each of the aforementioned designers and their contemporaries share common trajectories of starting out in an environment much different to what exists today. Many began their workshops and studios out of their homes or garages; training and hiring tailors, patternmakers and embroiderers along the way; each armed with personal creativity, entrepreneurial spirit and the deep desire to succeed in a business that was at the time really only associated with the West, or oriented towards exporting products to the West that were mostly devoid of all traces of local design aesthetics. There was little talk of trends, limited access to innovative fabrics, a scattered infrastructure for sourcing crafts, lack of adequate retail space, few organized and cohesive fashion events and related fashion media, and no common local or global platform to promote "Indian" fashion design. It was a time when designers had to work hard towards convincing clients of the value of their designs and garments. The popular belief of fashion being fickle, frivolous and not deserving of serious investment (in terms of time, money or thought) was another hurdle these designers had to overcome.

And then there was the association with "ladies' tailoring" or being a *darzi* (a thriving parallel industry in India) that acted as a stereotype, which had to be challenged in the attempt to be taken seriously as a "designer."

Introduction

Over the past 20 years, the field of fashion in India has changed significantly. We see a shift from an industry that solely supported Western markets through exports, to an industry that has begun to take Indian consumers, their tastes and their potential market base into consideration. India's domestic designer-wear industry was estimated to be worth over Rupees 720 crore (US$119 million) in 2012 and projected to grow by 40 percent annually (Ghosal 2012). There are currently over 350 fashion designers registered with the FDCI[1] and several fashion design schools situated in the large metros as well as in smaller cities across India. The annual fashion calendar features a number of fashion weeks, including one dedicated to menswear and one to couture. As discussed in the last chapter there are now Indian editions of all the leading international fashion magazines that feature rich local and global content. Contributing to this content is a rapidly expanding domestic apparel manufacturing and retail sector catering to Indian consumers, as well as a growing list of international brands and luxury labels with pre-established brand loyalty and related cultural capital entering into the market.[2] In the midst of such large-scale shifts the question for Indian design is now increasingly centered on how it must differentiate itself from its global competitors to remain viable, locally relevant, and in demand.

In addressing this question, the discussion in this chapter highlights various factors that define the design of contemporary Indian fashion and contribute towards distinguishing it from other countries. The most important of these is its multifaceted relationship with the cultural contexts of increasing globalization on one hand, and indigenous Indian culture on the other—the latter of which includes traditional forms of dress, textiles and crafts that vary across the country. Though broadly similar to the emergence of design in other parts of Asia,[3] what gives Indian design its own distinctive form is its specificity to the local context through reference to India's individual history, incorporation of Gandhian values, and the revival and use of Indian crafts, textiles and traditional styles of dress. In addition, the confluence of local and global in contemporary Indian design and fashion mirrors the cultural shifts being experienced concurrently by India's urban middle and elite classes. As a result, through reading Indian design, it is possible to recognize how design acts as an ever-evolving cultural activity that reflects as well as gives "expression" (Clark 2009) to what is currently happening in India.

Indian design

The notion and practice of "design" in and for India is a complex site—one where issues of tradition, craft, heritage, Indian, Western, modernity, local, global, and national identity all come into play and together shape the designed product. Despite contemporary shifts in urban lifestyles, India's rich traditions that have evolved and passed down over many generations continue to hold their importance in daily life. Hence their application

---

[1] Fashion Design Council of India, www.fdci.org, 2013 (accessed February 10, 2013).
[2] Since economic liberalization, India is now the fourth largest economy in terms of purchasing power parity and is rated among the top 10 destinations for foreign direct investment according to the 2012 World Investment Report, UNCTAD, http://unctad.org (accessed February 12, 2013).
[3] See Clark (2009) on design in Hong Kong.

to contemporary design in new and innovative ways is crucial, as is their application to wider global and future focused materials, techniques and ideas.

Mathur (2005) and Balaram (2005) highlight various opposing design conflicts that designers from developing nations, like India, face in dealing with issues of local and national identity. This includes the perceived inability of formally trained designers to be able to create culturally rooted contemporary works, especially when compared to informally trained craftspeople whose work has collectively had significant impact on the formulation of India's visual design identity. Historically, there was no clear distinction between the fields of art and craft in India—the practices of which were evolutionary and organic processes handed down and refined over generations of craftspeople and artisans (Patel 2012). During the colonial rule "design" came to be associated with the traditional crafts practiced in villages as a result of the way the British came to view them. This was reflected in their promotion and presentation of Indian crafts at world exhibitions. Crafts were strongly demarcated from modern Western industrial production, the latter of which was considered superior, individualistic and progressive. Furthermore, the British maintained a sharp distinction between Indian craft and the canon of "fine-art." Their introduction of art schools, intended to improve Indian tastes, also promoted the superiority of Western art and artistic styles. This ultimately had a long-lasting and negative impact on local creativity and design thinking in India (Balaram 2005). Even though the premise of the *Swadeshi* movement was to reinstate a sense of pride in locally made products, craft and self-reliance in the wake of the onslaught of industrial production, Mathur (2011) argues that Gandhi's *khadi* campaign and its rhetoric of design that positioned homespun *khadi* fabric as a symbol of a self-sufficient nation in *opposition* to Western mill-made products ultimately helped reiterate the aesthetic divisions established in the colonial period.

After gaining independence India's first Prime Minister Pandit Jawaharlal Nehru (1889–1964) envisioned design as a catalyst for reinvigorating the young nation in its attempt to catch up and compete with the rest of the world. The aim was not to emulate the West but to mobilize local creativity and innovation towards furthering industrial growth and modernization. In 1958 Pandit Nehru invited Charles and Ray Eames on behalf of the Indian government to spend time in India in order to research and propose a plan for the future of Indian design. At the end of their study the Eames' presented a report titled *The India Report* that recommended an investigation into "those values and qualities that Indians hold important to a good life" and the exploration of "the evolving symbols of India" as key strategies for shaping its design practice (Eames and Eames 1997 (1958): 6). The Eames recognized the evolutionary (and not revolutionary) nature of Indian craft and design (Balram 2005) and noted that future designers needed to consider the "values that exist in commonplace things that surround them" as well as "vernacular expressions" (ibid.: 11) while finding design solutions to problems that were unique to such a rapidly industrializing ancient society (Mathur 2011). According to Vyas (2006), the report and subsequent establishment of the National Institute of Design (NID) in Ahmedabad in 1961 helped shape the beginnings of modern Indian design—with the clear objective of coexisting alongside traditional design idioms, and where the parallel mechanization and simultaneous preservation of craft processes was a distinguishing feature (Vyas 2006: 27).

It appears that in the decades following, discussions on design, such as the Ahmedabad Declaration signed between the United Nations Industrial Development Organization (UNIDO) and the International Council of Societies of Industrial Design (ICSID) in 1979[4] were largely centered on more serious fields of architecture, product or industrial design. Such fields were viewed as being closely in sync with the nation's policies directed towards creating solutions for uplifting the quality of life for India's wider population. While the fields of textile and graphic design were recognized in such policy documentation, "fashion" was not mentioned. Despite this omission, it is important to note that the recommendations listed in the Eames' report—of considering evolving national, local and cultural symbols, responding to Indians' expectations for a good standard of living; and the inclusion of vernacular expressions to shape India's design identity—have ultimately come to inform many of the conceptual frameworks that contemporary fashion designers consciously and subconsciously follow. In addition, even though the notions of luxury, couture and high-fashion as fields of design targeted at rich and upper class Indians do not match the goals and ideals of the nation prior to its liberalization phase, they have contributed significantly to the research and revival of Indian crafts and textiles[5] (and continue to do so). This ultimately aligns (albeit indirectly) fashion with older nationalist idioms as well as the viewpoint of stimulating local creativity and innovation.

A review of the collections designed by contemporary fashion designers like Sabyasachi Mukherjee, Gaurav Gupta or Aneeth Arora (Péro), each of whom offer their own interpretation of ongoing cultural shifts in India, indicate how "design can become a means of embodying or giving form to a new cultural identity—new in the sense that the identity draws upon the local and the global, and also new in the sense that the complex cultural *identity sought in or through design does not yet exist*" (Clark 2009: 12). Here tradition and modernity are both evolutionary processes as contemporary designers actively create new kinds of hybrid products that rely on different forms of dialogue between the two, to cater towards an increasingly global and fast-changing society. Through treading the delicate balance between traditional dress practices and global fashion in their work, Indian designers are able to highlight the inherent innovation within Indian traditions and crafts. Also evident is the way local cultures actively adapt to global cultural forms without being usurped by the latter, as well as the creative contextualization of global forms to suits local environments. Another emerging space within Indian design is that of globally positioned design idioms for which the post-1990s economic liberalization era has acted as a catalyst. Patel (2012) believes the multitude of creative responses to liberalization and globalization by contemporary designers across all fields is "reflective of their cosmopolitanism; their increased awareness of the world, their intercultural contact and interconnectedness" (Patel 2012).

---

[4] This declaration was followed by the UNIDO-ICSID meeting titled "Design for Development" in 1979.
[5] The preservation of Indian crafts and textiles was a key goal behind the establishment of the Indian Handicrafts Board in 1952.

Design education and fashion

Fashion, as a formal field of design in India, saw its beginnings in the 1970s and 1980s. This was around the time India's "first wave" of designers—Ritu Kumar, Rohit Khosla, Rohit Bal, and Ritu Beri, amongst others, began to set up their labels and contributed to the initial framework of a local design industry. Khaire (2011) credits three key aspects prevalent in India at the time for the emergence of India's fashion identity: Firstly, the rich traditions, crafts and textiles; secondly, the preference for traditional clothes amongst women; and lastly, the ease and affordability of tailoring services across India. Since the Indian consumer was unused to the notion of a "designer" creating exclusive and "expensive" clothing, these early designers had to work hard towards convincing clients of their design worth (Castelino 1994; Khaire 2011). For many, designing traditional clothing with heavy embellishments instead of Western clothes was an inroad to the Indian consumer, which eventually became a selling point as well as a point of difference from the average tailor or boutique (Khaire 2011). Over time these designers helped give fashion design much greater visibility through showcasing their work in fashion shows, setting up retail spaces and reviving and modernizing dying Indian crafts. Some were more provocative in their strategies of promoting fashion on the catwalk and through the media, which further pushed fashion into the limelight. As one Mumbai-based designer told me, "there was more freedom and creativity in fashion then"[6]—alluding to the fact that the relative newness of fashion design as a profession and the lack of an organized industry also had its positives.

In 1986, the Ministry of Textiles set up India's first fashion school—National Institute of Fashion Technology (NIFT)—with the intention of "developing professionals for taking up leadership positions in fashion business in the emerging global scenario"[7] and taking Indian "heritage and traditions on to a global scale … by making ancient craft modern and market-friendly from the inception stage" (Kumar cf. Sengupta 2005: 255). Prior to this point there were few options for those interested in studying fashion within India. During NIFT's establishment initial mentorship and support was sought from Fashion Institute of Technology (FIT) New York. NIFT's faculty attended various training workshops at FIT as part of the research and development phase and in the beginning NIFT's curriculum was an offshoot from FIT's model. Asha Baxi, one of NIFT's founding fashion design faculty, states that while the FD (Fashion Design) program began with FIT's curriculum they soon realized that "it was blocking out the rich content that India had to offer" and in many ways lacked "relevance to the Indian context."[8] This was when "they started looking within" in terms of designing a curriculum that responded to the local environment as well as local market needs.[9] Key changes at the time, according to Baxi, included the

---

[6] Designer Azeem Khan, in an interview with the author in 2010.
[7] NIFT homepage, www.nift.ac.in (accessed February 22, 2012).
[8] Asha Baxi, in an interview with the author in 2010.
[9] Ibid. As an example, Baxi notes the textile science course in the original curriculum. While its scientific/laboratory type content was important for the overall curriculum, the absence of content that focused on India's rich textiles and their integration with Indian lifestyles meant that there was a mismatch between the curriculum and the reality

addition of content on Indian textiles and embellishments, Indian costume history (taught alongside Western Costume history) and craft documentation.[10] In Baxi's experience, the inclusion of craft documentation in particular, definitely changed the students' outlooks. She found that the experience had a positive impact on the graduating collections, where she saw a much "better application of Indian sensibilities and materials" over the years. According to Baxi, it was important for NIFT to "create designers who had expertise at an international level (especially technical expertise), yet at the same time contribute to *Indian* fashion with an *Indian* spirit."[11] As a result, NIFT's curriculum was redesigned to encourage students to experiment with Indian elements alongside more avant-garde concepts in their work.[12]

According to Rajiv Takru, NIFT Director General in 2010,[13] since its inception in the 1980s there has been a gradual shift in NIFT's curriculum from its aim to aid the Indian industry "to access global markets" towards professional practices, entrepreneurship and design *for* India.[14] Due to the boom experienced in the domestic apparel industry and the emerging middle-classes becoming such a lucrative market for international brands and business, it was obvious for NIFT's curriculum to look inwards once again and refocus its aim towards India and encourage students to consider local markets and local resources.[15] This shift is also mirrored in the approach of independent designers as well as local brands like Pantaloons, Wills Lifestyle and Westside, who have come to realize the importance of their local customer. The promotion and glamorization of design through popular media (magazines, reality TV etc.) has also meant the demand for design education has significantly grown in recent years leading to the mushrooming of numerous design institutes across the country. By 2010, NIFT itself had 15 centers spread across the country—in Bangalore, Bhopal, Bhubaneshwar, Chennai, Gandhinagar, Hyderabad, Jodhpur, Kangra, Kannur, Kolkata, Mumbai, New Delhi, Patna, Rae Bareli, and Shillong (with the possibility of opening more) with a combined enrollment of over 2,000+ students. Through opening up less "urban centric" centers the student demographic at NIFT has also shifted.[16] Initially, as Takru recounts, when NIFT first opened its doors, it started with 20–30 students who mainly hailed from elite segments of society. Now it recruits students from all corners of the country (and some even from

---

of Indian dress and fashion that the curriculum was meant to serve. A focus on Indian textiles and crafts was subsequently added into various courses and projects—which included a surface ornamentation course while I was a student at NIFT.

[10] Craft documentation (a mandatory project when I was at NIFT) was a month or so long group project that involved first-hand study and documentation of a (preferably undocumented) craft, which students undertook in the summer semester between the first and second year. Part of the project also involved designing products using the craft as inspiration—as a way of modernizing or reinterpreting the craft through the design students' eyes.

[11] Asha Baxi, 2010.

[12] Ibid.

[13] NIFT Director General (2007–10).

[14] Rajiv Takru, in an interview with the author in 2010.

[15] Ibid.

[16] Ibid.

overseas).[17] Additionally, with the presence of NIFT centers beyond Tier-I cities, those hailing from more rural areas also have access to fashion education.

Due to the roots of its conception stemming from Western institutions, for example, the Eames Report, links with Bauhaus (NID) and FIT (NIFT), Indian design education has received criticism for blindly "aping the West." However Baxi and Takru's accounts on NIFT's shifting curriculum bear witness to the conscious awareness of local needs and realities in the ongoing evolution of design education, despite its association with the curriculum of Western centers.

The complexity of crafting design education for India not only stems from existing polarities and diversity in almost every sphere, but also "the simultaneous telescopic existence of the past traditions with the contemporary" (Balaram 2005: 12). Since many traditions have been communicated orally or through undocumented practice their documentation becomes a necessary part of design research. The need to develop design models that can relate not only to large-scale production but also to smaller scales of production applied in craft, cottage- or home-based industry models, is another challenge, especially as they contribute to the distinctiveness of Indian design. An example of the way design education in India has evolved to combat such complexities is the craft cluster initiative.[18] Already pioneered by NID, craft clusters were included in NIFT's curriculum in 2003. This occurred in tandem with the opening up of new centers beyond Tier-I cities, where the approach to design education makes a "deliberate attempt to ground [students] into Indian reality."[19] The proximity of many natural craft clusters to these new centers meant that they could be "tied" to it, and linked to the curriculum. The craft cluster program links craftspeople with students and faculty who work collaboratively towards introducing contemporary and innovative elements to the design and outcomes of the craft. The overall aim of this approach is to revive flagging crafts through design intervention in order to sustain and create further demand, as well as develop technological improvements to make craft practice more time and resource efficient—in step with the needs of growing local and global markets.[20] Balaram sees the craft documentation and cluster-based model as an important evolution within the indigenous design curriculum in that it enables students "to find new and unique design applications for older materials" (Balaram 2005: 20), and is also in keeping with the recommendation in the Eames report — as a strategy for creating designers who not only find solutions but help others find solutions. Additionally, the reference to traditional systems of Indian design training makes such cluster initiatives one of the most innovative and distinctive features of design education in India (ibid.).[21]

---

[17] Ibid.

[18] A "craft cluster" is literally the grouping of a craft for the purpose of research, documentation and design intervention. Traditionally regional crafts in India tend to be clustered close together—where artisans practice the same craft using local resources, responding to local and regional tastes and needs, as well as live and work in close proximit. Thereby making it easy to create such "clusters" based on region or specific craft.

[19] Rajiv Takru, 2010.

[20] Ibid.

[21] See Balaram (2005) for his discussion on the *Gurukul* system—an apprenticeship model of learning a craft under the tutelage of a *guru* (teacher, mentor).

Made *and* designed in India: Fashion as an emerging creative industry

Strategically, "design" and "fashion" form an integral part of national industrial and economic development in India, as it does in other countries across the world. Through their role as value-adding cultural industries, and producers of cultural goods, they also contribute towards the overall "image" of the nation. This phenomenon has already been researched and documented in relation to notable [Western] centers of fashion, commonly referred to as "fashion capitals"—namely Paris, New York, London and Milan, with the later addition of Tokyo. Each of these centers has established fashion identities built over many years that are highly symbolic of modernity and innovation, and are eventually a source of national prestige. In addition, their titles themselves have become vested with symbolic geography (Gilbert 2006). These capitals act as key sources of fashion trends that get transmitted globally through various media channels; and over time they have led to the establishment of overarching frameworks by which global fashion now functions—such as fashion weeks, magazines, trend fairs etc.—within which most designers and labels (Western, non-Western) find themselves.

Though India is an established and recognized manufacturing hub of mass fashion goods for the rest of the world, and more recently a design production and textile crafts source for multiple high-end luxury fashion brands,[22] gaining global notoriety for stand alone "Indian design" is still in its early stages. Select Indian designers, like Manish Arora have received significant global recognition in recent years, beyond the Indian Diaspora. Many others have had the opportunity to showcase their collections at international fashion weeks and trade shows, often on invitation, and accumulated international stockists. However, few have sustained a position of long-term visibility in the international scene or global media; or attracted orders large enough to rival Western designer and luxury brand conglomerates. The irony lies in the fact that even though the design and production of fashion products has become increasingly decentralized, due to such activities shifting towards countries like China and India,[23] on the surface the flow of global fashion culture and opinion leadership continues to follow Western dictates. Niessen highlights the artificiality between the East and West divide, which does not impact global fashion commodity flows as much as it does the "conceptual" boundaries between Western fashion and non-Western dress systems. Such boundaries remain strong and surprisingly impermeable, especially as experienced by Asian designers, where the appearance of Asianness in [Western] fashion does not necessarily imply the acceptance of local or indigenous Asian design (Niessen 2003: 256).

---

[22] See Prada's "Made in India" collection of products, launched in 2010. Some of the products included dresses with *Chikan* embroidery, and shoes and bags with leather rattan work.

[23] High fashion labels such as Versace as well as H&M all share this fact in common, where design teams in India for example, contribute towards various aspects of product design and development and in doing so also add to the global success of these Western labels.

Manish Arora outlines the challenges he faced in attempting to break into the Western fashion scene and gain global recognition as a valid "designer" (Ramachandran and Patvardhan 2008). While it was his over-the-top Indian kitsch design aesthetics that made him visible at London and Paris fashion weeks, to move beyond simple entertainment value towards receiving sustained critical appraisal from Western fashion observers and consumers he needed to tone down many recognizable Indian or ethnic elements in his designs. His experience bears evidence to the fact that success is sometimes only possible through the censoring of clearly ethnic or local tastes (Niessen 2003; Skov 2003). However, removing these altogether also comes at the risk of negative comparisons with established Western designers. In other words, Arora must function within his given niche without the amplification of his Indianness. His experience underscores a common barrier for designers from emerging economies who have to "grapple with the challenges imposed by their location" also known as the "liabilities of origin" (Ramachandran and Patvardhan 2008: 145), as well as poor or uninformed consumer perception about the designer's origin, some of which reiterate older colonial or Orientalist stereotypes.

The need for wider international recognition for original Indian design becomes a crucial factor for gaining legitimacy as a global center of fashion, that is also distinct from other established global fashion centers and fashion systems, which in turn will benefit designers like Manish Arora vying for wider markets. In this way, fashion, like other cultural industries, can play two roles. The first is towards furthering economic growth and development through creating employment and revenues generated by exports and in the domestic market. Since many independent designers rely on indigenous crafts and textiles, the success of Indian fashion also indirectly helps preserve and promote these handicrafts. The second role, as highlighted by Goodrum et al. in the context of New Zealand and other global centers of fashion, is that of "presenting an image" of [India] in the international marketplace, "a function seen as enhancing broader economic development goals of the country as a whole" (Goodrum et al. 2007: 187). Through the promotion and success of this image designers are more likely to attract corporate investments and build brands that have the resources to tap into international markets and secure business for designed products that can command the price and value attached to a label as opposed to providing raw materials towards Western labels. Attaining distinction is also beneficial when competing within the domestic market, where exposure and access to global media and international products has meant that the needs and desires of the Indian consumer have evolved. As a result of being able to "shop around" the Indian consumer is now in a position to demand more sophisticated renderings of local fashion that are in step with global trends and international brands. Furthermore, Rovine highlights that this image of, "fashion serves as cultural attainment" (Rovine 2009: 46). "High fashion, which might be considered sartorial 'fine art,' is visible to many, affordable to few, and a sign of elevated status ... Thus, designation of garments as *fashion* has profound implications" (ibid.: 46, emphasis mine).

Japan's entrance onto the world's fashion scene as a non-Western center, that did not conform to Western stereotypes and was comfortable deriving its framework from traditional Japanese philosophies, textiles and approach to clothing the body—is one example that is often cited in the context of India's emerging fashion identity in the hopes of reaching a similar iconic status. In addition, England's model of creative industries and the Fédération Française de la Couture, du Prêt-à-Porter des Couturiers et des Créateurs de Mode (Paris)[24] have also been influential in shaping Indian designers' collective aspirations towards bringing Indian design and couture to the forefront, as has Italy's monopoly in the world luxury market despite its size and population (Koshy 2008). In 1998, the Fashion Design Council of India (FDCI)—an independent non-profit association of fashion designers—was founded "on the premise of promoting, nurturing and representing the best of fashion design talent in the country" and propagating the "Business of Fashion" in and of India.[25] At present FDCI represents over 350 independent designers—ranging from the most established to emerging ones. Despite the fact that a number of these designers continue to face infrastructural issues and hurdles relating to government regulations (that control or inhibit setting up studios and workshops due to cities' zoning codes) and the absence of adequate retail spaces or shopping districts (such as a high street), the presence of an organization like FDCI has meant that there are gradually more formalized frameworks for showcasing Indian design on a local and global stage. Currently FDCI is instrumental in producing a calendar of fashion events across India, which include a bi-annual fashion week for womenswear Prêt-a-Porter collections that are in line with the fashion week calendar of global fashion centers like London and Paris, a men's fashion week and an annual couture fashion week. FDCI has also helped formalize various other aspects of the fashion industry through developing marketing strategies, setting industry standards, mentoring designers, inviting international buyers to fashion weeks, as well as promoting designer fashion to local consumers, many of whom would have previously not seen the value in buying "Indian."

Re-dressing Indian fashion: Establishing a design culture

While the 1980s and 1990s were important decades for India's first wave of designers in gaining visibility and validating their profession, as well as making the local customer familiar with designer fashion, the field of contemporary fashion design is now centered on giving shape and substance to India's evolving and unique fashion identity, and branding it within India as well as for international markets.

In 2010, I met Nida Mahmood—a young, emerging designer with a small studio in the centrally located Shahpur Jat village (New Delhi), situated alongside a number of similar studios, embroidery, printing and dyeing workshops, small boutiques and art galleries. Meeting Nida at her studio, where she had 10–12 tailors and embroiderers working on her sample collection, highlighted the wealth of resources available to a young designer

---

[24]This includes The Chambre Syndicale de la Haute Couture, The Chambre Syndicale du Prêt-à-Porter des Couturiers et des Créateurs de Mode and The Chambre Syndicale de la Mode Masculine.
[25]Cited from the FDCI home page, http://www.fdci.org (accessed February 10, 2013).

Figure 6.1 Hand painted blouse with *Don* (1978) inspired text and motifs that also draw from truck art, worn with a sari and jeans from Nida Mahmood's *New India Bioscope Co.* Spring/ Summer 2010 collection. Photographs by Bibhuti Bhattacharya. Image courtesy Nida Mahmood.

like her in being able to start an independent label. The collections she was working on at the time comprised of quirky jackets and other garments that had been hand painted by poster artists who had once enjoyed a lucrative career in cinema poster painting, before the advent of digitally printed film hoardings (Figure 6.1).

Nida was not only indulging her nostalgia for this iconic form of Indian street art and popular kitschy film icons from 1970s through her design, but also supporting these artists through her work by setting up a craft corpus.[26] Her collections featured other similarly nostalgic and vernacular icons, such as bicycles printed on shirts as well as saris—the latter of which she famously paired with jeans. Like most fellow emerging designers, Nida was attempting to establish a design identity for herself and her label

---

[26] Nida Mahmood, in an interview with the author in 2010.

that relied on a re-interpretation of her roots teamed with her knowledge of local crafts and awareness of global fashion.

The key distinguishing factors or "trademark" of Indian fashion that emerged through the observation of Nida's work called to mind prior (and subsequent) discussions with various Indian fashion designers, fashionistas and industry professionals over the course of my research. These are its reliance on Indian textiles, crafts, embellishments and styles of indigenous clothing; and its ability to retain it traditional and vernacular shapes and aesthetics in tandem with the incorporation of modern, Western, global and innovative design elements into its folds.

Delhi-based designer, Anju Modi, affirms this by listing four constant features of Indian fashion that she believes inform its design and help differentiate it from the rest of the world. The first being Indian drapes; and second, India's handloom fabrics. To this she adds, it is the specific color palettes favored in India that make local fashion sensibilities different from the West. Finally, craft, in all shapes and forms, is key[27] as designers actively use crafts in various capacities as way of instilling a sense of uniqueness as well as to establish an "authentic" local identity. For Modi, it is "the era that gives a fresh perspective to these elements and makes them modern."[28] Shefalee Vasudev describes Indian fashion by proposing a simple formula that she finds designers follow in different proportions: "A combination of aesthetics + ethics and cultural responsibilities (in the use of craft and indigenous textiles) + commercial success + local and/or global outlook."[29] Where some designers are more focused on aesthetics or global trends, some are more focused on the ethics of craft revival and the aesthetics that stem from that. And finally, designer Gaurav Gupta describes Indian fashion as "maximalist."[30] Not to mean overdone (though in some cases it appears to be and needs to be), but just "more," as a reflection of Indian tastes.[31]

An overall shift in focus towards an Indian consumer as a design priority, mentioned at the start of this chapter, was clearly evident at Wills Lifestyle India Fashion Week (WLIFW) Fall/Winter 2013 and Spring/Summer 2014[32] as well as at Lakmé India Fashion Week (LIFW), Summer/Resort 2013.[33] There was a prominence of traditionally styled garments and drapes in the collections showcased at these venues, combined with a rich variety of Indian textiles and embellishment techniques. Sippy (2013a) in her review of WLIFW Fall/Winter 2013 also notes this change, where earlier, for example when India fashion week first began in 2000, presenting garments like *salwar kameez, lehengas* and saris was often frowned upon, and there was a strong Western perception informing the collections (Sippy 2013a; also noted by Nagrath 2003). Now according to Sippy, there is a strong revival of the "Indian Quotient" with an open celebration of Indian textiles, patterns, crafts and "designs with an old fashioned pedigree" (Sippy 2013a). Similar to

---

[27] Anju Modi, in an interview with the author in 2010.
[28] Ibid.
[29] Shefalee Vasudev, in an interview with the author in 2010.
[30] Gaurav Gupta, in an interview with the author in 2010.
[31] Ibid.
[32] Held in Delhi.
[33] Held in Mumbai.

Suga's observation of the Japanese market, the West is no longer "an exotic product or concept" (Suga 1995: 98). This is true for many Indian designers as well as for a large number of urban consumers who have long since accepted Western or global dress into their wardrobes. Designers are also conscious of various social and cultural factors that inform local clothing preferences and tastes and design accordingly. For example, the fact that women continue to be conservative in their clothing choices means that strategies such as net sleeves (in place of sleeveless styles), cleverly cut necklines and the placement of embroidery in areas to create interest, or in some cases to divert interest, are well-established design techniques. In all these cases designers' familiarity and understanding of local needs, realities and desires act as a design edge when compared to the international brands entering India—the latter of which have to put in much greater effort and research to fully understand the cultural realities of doing business in India.

Current visual and design practices used by designers working in couture, high-fashion as well as for mid-level mass market brands like Pantaloons, Wills Lifestyle and Westside show an active experimentation with hybridity in new and innovative contexts that seamlessly fit global fashion trends. Resulting outcomes can range from the deliberate application of re-Orientalist and auto-exoticizing strategies (Ritu Kumar, Sabyasachi Mukherjee, and JJ Valaya), to designing products for a cosmopolitan and "hip" Indian identity that employ local, vernacular and familiar cultural forms and practices, such as the *chai ka* cup[34] (Nida Mahmood), holy cows (Raw Mango), *chawls*[35] (Play Clan) and Tamil script (Masaba) recast within a more globalized framework. Additionally, in the case of an emerging group of designers, their design reflects the optimism and global connectedness of contemporary post-liberalized India and presents new possibilities for Indian fashion that position it within a larger culture of design—a deterritorialized space—that is not determined or confined to geographical boundaries nor is it dictated by fixed nodes or national centers.

The following sections elucidate some of the central themes and approaches that emerge from a review of contemporary Indian ready-to-wear (*prêt*) and couture. The discussion inevitably excludes many notable labels, as it is impossible to include the entire gamut of fashion designers whose work is deserving of mention within the framework of a chapter. This may irk local fashion historians, designers and other professionals familiar with India's recent fashion landmarks. However through focusing on a few select exemplars, my aim is to highlight the overall essence of India's design idiom, and through this encourage the reader to delve more deeply into a detailed study of Indian designers.

---

[34]*Chai*—Cup of tea.
[35]*Chawl* is a style of building typically found in Mumbai (Bombay) comprising of 4–5 stories of tiered family housing. Each story is made up of many small apartments that share a common front balcony.

Nostalgia for the past: India exotic

Sabyasachi Mukherjee

The most notable conceptual strategy that emerges from the observation of couture and high-fashion ready-to-wear collections by Indian designers is that of re-Orientalism and auto-exoticization—as a process of design that in essence appropriates the Western Orientalist gaze and refocuses it back towards India—i.e. Indian dress, textiles, crafts etc. Through this approach Indian designers (as well as consumers) begin to adopt a "distanced, self-Orientalizing perspective on the charms of their [real and] imagined ethnic heritage" (Jones and Leshkowich 2003: 282). Stemming from the lasting legacy of the imbalances and viewpoints established by Orientalism itself (Kondo 1997), that led to the labeling of India and Indian artifacts as timeless, exotic, luxurious and "Other," this approach to design is further emphasized over the past century through the success of Western designers who have worked with Indian and other non-Western cultures as exotic inspiration for their collections.[36] Such instances not only strengthen the impression of the powerful or superior Western designer, they have also come to determine the framework within which Indian designers come to find themselves (ibid.). As a result they too come to regard their own culture, traditions, dress and crafts as unique sources of inspiration. However, as discussed in the book's introduction, instead of viewing this stance as a position of inferiority or simple mimicry, it is important to consider its benefits, and the empowerment it provides Indian designers who have the added confidence of working with their roots and the intention to "take back" some lost ground in the arena of global design.

The strategy of design using tradition and history as a reference point has been central to the rise of design culture in India, and continues to inform the collections and related visual strategies (photo-shoots, advertisements, store design etc.) of many leading designers like Ritu Kumar, Tarun Tahiliani, JJ Valaya, and Sabyasachi Mukherjee, who incorporate and revive historic Indian styles, textiles, and embellishments in their garments. The style or silhouettes of clothing designed mostly tend to mimic Indian, Indo-Western fusion or fairly basic Western cuts, where the emphasis is usually on embellishments and use of textiles. These include various iterations of the *salwar kameez* (*anarkalis, churidars,* Patiala *salwars*), *lehengas, cholis*, saris, tunics or *kurtis,* kaftans and basic dresses, jackets, and blouses. Popular themes that get reinterpreted into contemporary fashion range from references to India's past—courtesans, the nationalist movements, historic figures, Mughal royalty, Maharajas and their wardrobes, regional dance costumes, and tribal tattoos; to the research and revival of craft—vintage textiles and embroideries; as well as looking at instances of current regional or tribal dress as "exotic" street style. Nagrath (2003) frames the last of these as the "Othering" of those within the nation, for whom the designers may never actually create clothes, despite their being style inspirations for these collections. While such strategies of design are not

---

[36]Recently evident in Chanel's Pre-Fall 2012 collection titled *Paris-Bombay* and Marchesa's Spring Summer 2013 ready-to-wear collection.

unique to India or non-Western designers,[37] what makes them unique is the combination of colors, embellishments and cuts of clothing suited to the Indian palette. Additionally, such design has helped ensure Indian crafts and clothing remain relevant to contemporary design and fashion practice.

Kondo theorizes a third phase as part of the cycle of re-Orientalizing design, which is evident in the way Indian designers also source similarly exotic inspiration from other histories, countries and cultures for their collections. She sees this as an evolution from the phase of self-Orientalizing, where designers take on a position of power and in turn Orientalize others (Kondo 1997). Sabyasachi Mukherjee's 2012 couture collection titled *New Moon*[38] offers a visually extravagant example of this, where both Indian and Western dress cultures get exoticized through his combination of "the straitjacket discipline of New York, the classic nostalgia of the British Raj in Kolkata, the subversive decadence of Berlin, the incredible romance of Paris and the bohemian flair of Barcelona."[39] (Plate 9) The collection features Russian needlepoint, Boutis from Provence (France), *Zardozi* from Agra, *Kantha* from Bangladesh, block printing from Bengal and Rajasthan, intricately embroidered *Pashmina* from Kashmir, Chintz from the United Kingdom, and Toile de joy from France, alongside rhinestone, baubles, bows and "the finest quality of embroidery" in ways that are "exuberant yet disciplined."[40] In doing so, the collection represents accurately the cosmopolitanism of India's emerging elite and upper middle-classes who are financially, socially and culturally able to be connoisseurs of the best the world has to offer, in India. In addition, it also provides a powerful social commentary on Indian design as it attempts to assert itself through highlighting its ability to speak a sophisticated design language that selectively fuses (and strategically positions) local with the global.

In light of this, no discussion on contemporary Indian fashion would be complete without a deeper exploration of Sabyasachi Mukherjee's work and his approach to designing from and for India. This closely fits the mold of re-Orientalizing strategies as well as aligns with nationalist ideals. A graduate from NIFT (1996–9), Sabyasachi's work follows from that of India's first wave of designers, including Ms. Ritu Kumar, who initiated the research and revival of Indian textiles (and themes) as a valid approach to design, and also stipulated it to be a *responsibility* of Indian designers. His journey as a designer has seen him single handedly build a successful brand from very humble middle-class roots to reaching celebrity status and winning numerous accolades along the way, using nostalgia and staunch revivalist idealism as his business model.[41]

---

[37] Teunnisen (2005) reminds us that designers like McQueen and Westwood also turned to their own dress history for design reference, and the reliance on the "Orient" for inspiration has been a regular feature on Western catwalks.

[38] Showcased at PCJ Delhi Couture Week 2012, presented by FDCI.

[39] Cited from the press release for *New Moon*, provided by VTY to the author on behalf of Sabyasachi Mukherjee.

[40] Ibid.

[41] In 2010 Sabyasachi won the British Council's most outstanding young Designer of India award. His foray into designing costumes for Bollywood films, notably Sanjay Leela Bhansali's *Black* (for which he received the National Award for the best costume designer for a feature film in 2005), and styling film stars like Rani Mukherjee, Vidya Balan and Sridevi, as well as his appearance on the NDTV show *Band Baajaa Bride* (a combination of *Say Yes to the Dress* and *Extreme Makeover* but for weddings) has also meant that he is currently one of the most loved, sought after and copied designers in India.

Indian dress and textiles were a motivation for Sabyasachi even in his initial (critically acclaimed) collections that helped shape his design philosophy, which celebrates the "personalized imperfection of the human hand."[42] It is common to hear words like *vintage*, *hand-stained*, *aged* and *bohemian* used to describe his garments, and he himself states that, "antique textiles and cultural traditions of his home town, Kolkata have been a lifelong inspiration."[43] These have led him to mix unusual combinations of fabrics, textures and details (as seen in his multi-border saris featuring checks, velvets, embroidered panels, and other non-traditional colors and handloom textiles), painstakingly detailed hand embellishments (for example, *Zardozi,* Kashmiri embroidery and Parsi style *Gara* sari borders etc.) in a fusion of Indian traditional and Western styles for his collections, which he describes as having "international styling with an Indian soul."[44] The continuing themes across his collections reinforce a re-Orientalizing approach to design. Season after season he looks to past instances of iconic Indian style and costumes combined with other historic global influences (such as Frida Kahlo). His first couture collection, titled *Chand Bibi* (LIFW 2007) took its influence from the costumes of Royal India, the *zenana*[45] and the *purdah* system, old enamel utensils, the by-lanes of Karachi and "dilapidated royalty." The collection exuded nostalgia through his use of antique brocade coats, *Zardozi* embroidered *ghagharas*, vintage-look jackets and dresses, vegetable dyed silk and net saris, fluid silk trousers and heavily embroidered silk and cotton *kalidars*. Mukherjee regularly touches upon nationalist themes, as highlighted in my introductory sketch in Chapter 1 of his 2010 couture collection, as well as in his Fall/Winter Festive Collection in 2011, that presented a "North West Frontier Province" (now part of Pakistan) look with models wearing Gandhi *topis* and old-fashioned Patiala *salwars*. In addition, the names of his collections—*Peeli Kothi, Nair Sisters, Aparajito,* and *Kora* for example, all mirror his penchant for nostalgic and historic references that rely on the viewer's familiarity with the same towards appreciating his muses. This is further accentuated by the presentation and styling of his collections, more recently through the use of vintage photographs, prints, mirrors, and clocks clustered en masse on his catwalks, as well as in his flagship stores—meant to resemble the interiors of old ancestral properties (Figure 6.2).

Beyond the celebration of Indian textiles and indulgent layering of traditional cuts of clothing, another overriding common characteristic visible in Sabyasachi's design sensibility is the modesty quotient of his pieces and the way his collections are styled. Not by any means prudish or conservative; yet his garments rarely rely on overexposing the female body. Instead they appear almost Victorian—covered but still hinting towards the body underneath through strategic use of fabrics, for example in his sheer saris that highlight the embroidered petticoat beneath. Sabyasachi's emphasis on modesty, combined with his fusion of historic Indian and European (Victorian) costume, styled with

---

[42] Cited from Sabyasachi's personal biography from his website, www.sabyasachi.com (accessed March 26, 2013).

[43] Ibid.

[44] Ibid.

[45] Part of the house reserved for the women of the household.

Figure 6.2 Sabyasachi Mukherjee's Hyderabad store. Image courtesy Sabyasachi Mukherjee.

geeky spectacles, multiple *odhnis* and nationalist caps, is geared towards asserting a distinctive identity for Indian fashion as well as making a statement on taste. This inevitably leads to a comparison between his design ethos and the birth of the modern style of sari in the late nineteenth century, which at the time of its conception was a fusion between regional Indian (Bengali, Parsi, Gujarati) and British clothing, and indicative of the levels of taste, refinement, traditions and dress modesty expected of the educated middle-class *bhadramahila*—who was markedly different to her Western counterparts.

Sabyasachi's design ideals also highlight parallels with the ethos of the *Swadeshi* movement, as he is passionately committed to emphasizing the role design must play in improving and empowering local craftspeople, traditional dress and handloom textiles. In a recent interview he evokes Gandhian ideals by stating, "I want to raise the bar of people's tastes … if a woman shifts from polyester to *khadi* then I believe it's a contribution well-made" (Mukherjee 2010).[46] Yet, even though he is admired for succeeding commercially through the medium of *khadi,* his designs have increasingly come under criticism for appearing too much like "costume," regressive and in opposition to the globalized direction contemporary India is heading towards (Tewari 2013). This critique is further fuelled by his conscious avoidance of Western fashion weeks and his approach to styling film actress Vidya Balan at the Cannes Film Festival in 2013 (ibid.), mentioned in Chapter 4. However as Sabyasachi notes, his designs as well as their copies continue

---

[46]Cited from Pratap-Shah (2010).

to thrive—alluding to the fact that his linking of design with older rhetorics of dress and difference resonates deeply with many Indians (Mukherjee 2013).[47]

Mind it ... We are like this only!—Celebrating the vernacular and everyday

Manish Arora, Play Clan, Nida Mahmood

In contrast to the representation of royal India and other such exotic themes incorporated in elaborate fashion collections that have been known to wow Indian audiences, equally successful are designers' fresh, kitschy, and quirky interpretations of everyday cultural practices and vernacular products. Multiple graphic and textual references to Indian cities, rickshaws, elephants, *chai*, *chappals* (sandals), and *chawls* have the ability to tickle and please Indian and international consumers through tapping into their familiarity and nostalgia for these age-old icons. Such strategies for creating recognizably *Indian* design are still linked to the aforementioned approach of re-Orientalism, nostalgia for the past and use of local crafts, but often presented in ways that are more aligned to global trends and aesthetics.

The roots of this style stem from MTV (India) and Channel [V]'s early attempts in the 1990s to connect with the Indian viewer through creating a visual pastiche of Indianness that only Indians, (in India or within the Diaspora), could relate to. In its early years, MTV, which initially struggled to appeal to Indian audiences, quickly realized that it needed to consider the tastes and preference of its local viewers, who at the time showed a preference for *masala* films and *filmi* music. It also needed to make its global programming locally relevant and relatable to Indians. Such strategies had already worked for Channel [V], that had developed characters like "Quick Gun Murugan" and "Udham Singh" with catch lines like "we are like this only" and "mind it," and a smorgasbord of 1960s, 1970s and 1980s Bollywood film clips and iconic symbols that stemmed from familiar or everyday items (lotus, rickshaw, cycle, Ambassador car, political party signs, Hindu gods and holy cows) layered into kitschy prints with vibrant color palettes that were used for advertisements and video clips. The strategy of "Othering" was (and still is) at play, as many of the symbols or references were sourced from the lives and realities of those who were not the target audience of these channels. The birth of this new visual style enabled global music channels to tailor content towards the Indian palette, as well as connect with their vast middle-class audience. In turn, the vivid celebration of all things Indian and the incorporation of familiar humor sourced from everyday scenarios packaged in a global format provided globally linked, young cosmopolitan Indians the opportunity to connect back to their local roots. Unlike older generations the tastes of this generation in clothing, food, films and music for a large part were no longer identifiable as solely "Indian." In some cases they were indistinguishable (at least on the surface in terms of

---

[47] Cited from Kashyap (2013a).

clothing and fashion) from their global counterparts, thereby creating an inherent fear of homogenization and the deep desire to retain a sense of distinction, without turning back the clock of globalization.

The development of this new aesthetic parallels the trajectory of fashion designer Manish Arora, alumni of NIFT (graduated in 1994). His use of Indian iconography and gaudy color palettes reflected a celebration of Indian tastes that were, at the time, outside of the ethnic-chic look as well as the non-ethnic, sophisticated impressions of fashion that his peers were attempting to create. Manish's self-titled label launched in 1997 and diffusion label, aptly named Fish Fry[48] founded in 2002, featured bold graphics, kitschy prints, appliqués and embroideries that mirrored mass-market tastes that had never been applied to high-fashion in India before. Referring to himself as a modern-day *darzi*—the same title that the Indian fashion fraternity was trying to shake off—Manish positioned himself as a locally grounded provocative designer who was unafraid to challenge elitist norms. In doing so, he did not shy away from embracing the bold and neon colors, shiny fabrics and over-the-top embellishments featuring popular religious icons that were usually dismissed as being lower class by upper middle-class and elite Indians. In one of his early collections Arora made reference to the work of Roy Lichtenstein (Plate 10) in marking the conceptual and visual parallels between his themes and Pop Art's alignment with mass culture and anti-elitism in the West. Arora differed from his design contemporaries by focusing on edgy Westernized garments in his collections. He also focused heavily on brand collaborations (Reebok and Swatch) as well as creating wearable Western garments (t-shirts, skirts, tights, shift dresses) that complemented his riotous aesthetic, but also appealed to a global fashion risk taker.

Manish Arora's subsequent global success[49] has led him to consciously avoid overdoing the Indian kitsch stereotype he himself began, as he attempts to evolve towards making garments that are in step with Western trends through focus on developing the cut and silhouette of his clothes, in order to succeed in the global market (Plate 11). However traces of his vibrant visual style still exist in his use of color, embellishments and overall maximalist approach—that Western markets have come to expect from him. His contribution to the wider field of Indian fashion has definitely been the initiation of a humorous and tongue-in-cheek bold design aesthetic, teamed with an unapologetic celebration of local pop-culture that many emerging designers have since further explored in their work.

Almost two decades after its inception, Indian kitsch remains a highly successful and increasingly mainstream visual design strategy—evident in numerous products ranging from fridge magnets, paperweights, tote bags, home wares, T-shirts, underwear, and even saris—such as those designed by Play Clan. Ex-NIFTian, Nida Mahmood's designs also fit this broad umbrella, as she "uplifts and dramatizes the mundane" and works on

---

[48] In reference to local food and a popular spicy fried fish dish.

[49] In 2005 Manish Arora was invited to showcase his work at London Fashion Week and since then his work has gained global recognition and earned him praise from some of Western fashion's harshest critics. He now showcases his collections at Paris Fashion Week every season and was also invited to design for Paco Rabanne's initial re-launch collections in 2012.

Figure 6.3 *Kathakali* print T-shirt (top) and "the *Koti* with *Pagri*" (waistcoat with turban) (bottom) by Play Clan. Images courtesy Play Clan.

themes relating to the everyday, *filmi* popular culture and local colloquialisms.[50] These range from her *High on Chai* collection, centered on the importance of a cup of tea, to the *New India Bioscope Co.* collection (refer to Figure 6.1) inspired by iconic films from the 1960s and 1970s—a familiar time period for Indians of her generation to feel nostalgic about. While Play Clan, founded in 2008 by Himanshu Dogra (also from NIFT), does not fall under the category of high-fashion, its exploration of everyday objects rendered in contemporary graphic styles that fuse semiotic and design cues from local and global vocabularies have resonated strongly not only with Indians, but also amongst tourists and expats (Dogra 2012).[51] These include Lego-style prints of Indian gods, t-shirts printed with illustrations of Mumbai's iconic *chawls*, *Kathakali* make-up (Figure 6.3), turbans and

---

[50] Nida Mahmood, 2010.
[51] Cited from Shah (2012).

moustaches, limited edition artworks of kitsch *masala* film icon Rajnikanth,[52] references to *Mughal-e-Azam* and the Mughal dynasty, and the great Indian *shaadi* (wedding). Play Clan's use of Indian colloquialisms and *Hinglish*—such as the phrases *Aam Aadmi* (common man), Mumbai Local (Mumbai's local train network), *Bindaas* (chilled out, cool) etc.—parallel similar strategies evident in other forms of popular culture. Even though Play Clan's design strategies perpetuate the "Othering" of the common man in India, its recasting of the vernacular into locally specific yet globally relevant products act as successful mediums of experiencing national pride for India's global-*desis;* as well as quirky keepsakes for visitors and tourists.

What both the aforementioned strategies of re-Orientalism and reinterpreting the vernacular share in common is their reliance on nostalgia for India's past, as well as for the Other India that has been pushed further away or out of sight from contemporary cosmopolitan lifestyles—"that regular stuff that no one sees anymore." [53] Such nostalgic images subdue any negative elements that could be associated or experienced in real terms (dirt, dust, poverty), instead turning them into pleasurable experiences that can be consumed, as well as symbols that reinforce identity, and belonging. While observing similar design strategies in Hong Kong, Huppatz (2009) notes that the use of nostalgia asserts a sense of stability. In the context of India this relates to recent social, cultural and economic transitions, along with "mixed legacies of colonialism, nationalism and capitalism" (Fiss 2009), as well as the seismic shifts occurring within the fashion industry as it negotiates its position within global fashion, and asserts its presence through local fashion.

Crafting fashion

Revivalist re-design: Ritu Kumar

It becomes obvious while examining contemporary fashion collections that indigenous craft techniques and textiles form the backbone of design in India. Through lending themselves to numerous visual outcomes and innovations textile crafts additionally serve as mediums of authenticity and distinction for Indian fashion. Designers David Abraham and Rakesh Thakore believe that crafts and handloom fabrics offer a unique advantage to designers, especially in the wake of globalization that has brought the best of Western and international labels into the market—brands that are not only vested with globally recognized cultural capital, but are also in a better position to promote their products through international fashion magazines and advertising tie-ups (Abraham and Thakore cf. Ghose 2010).

The history of designing with craft in the forefront has deep roots in the evolution of design education in India. As already mentioned, institutions like NID and NIFT

---

[52] Popular film actor who has acted in both South Indian and Bollywood films.
[53] Nida Mahmood, 2010.

emphasize craft collaboration in their curriculum. Such initiatives are in keeping with other government agencies, NGOs and independent bodies, like the Craft Council and Dastkar, that aim to support craftspeople with infrastructural support, retail avenues, craft festivals, business acumen, and design and technology input in the hope of preserving and further developing crafts to ensure they remain contemporary and relevant to both Indian and global markets.

The need to safeguard craft along with indigenous dress also has older historical precedents that are worth noting, as like the aforementioned re-Orientalizing design strategies, they too become re-inscribed through contemporary design processes. During the nineteenth and early part of the twentieth century, the idea that "certain things *could* properly represent the 'traditions, instincts, and beliefs of the [Indian] people'" (McGowan 2005: 264) became firmly lodged in the colonial psyche and projected via the Orientalist gaze. Attempts were made to study, classify and make detailed records of Indian artifacts by the British to ensure there existed reference points by which dress and textiles, among other things, could be better understood and authenticated. From the perspective of the British, Indian cloth and clothing had a strong "mystic" and "exotic" appeal, which they were keen to preserve. In some cases they actively encouraged Indians to dress in an "oriental manner" (Cohn 1989) to ensure a clear distinction between them and their Indian subjects. During the same time, Indian nationalism and the *Swadeshi* movement sought to mobilize (and through this revive) Indian craft through the promotion of spinning and weaving of *khadi,* along with indigenous clothing styles, as forms of political resistance, national unity and visual symbols of national distinction. Furthermore, safeguarding Indian handloom from the wake of industrial production and Westernization was not only a key agenda item during India's independence movement, but also a focal point subsequent to its independence.

While Westernization is no longer a threat to the future of Indian crafts, current challenges continue to stem from the competition posed by industrial mass production (both nationally and internationally) and shifting tastes within the domestic market. In addition, certain crafts have tended to stagnate over time—where the technology, design, color combinations and raw materials have all stayed the same. Thus making them difficult to align with contemporary cycles and demands of modern fashion. The time-intensive nature of some crafts means that the prices are extremely high, but if additional new designs are rare, they become relegated to one-time purchases.

Ritu Kumar's contribution to the revival of craft is important to highlight here, as she provided an important framework for Indian design by proving the compatibility of craft and fashion as well as helped initiate an indigenous fashion vocabulary and visual identity that was commercially and conceptually successful. Ms. Kumar, who began her career in the mid-60s fuelled by a desire to see the continuance of crafts that were in danger of being extinguished or had already been lost due to the prominence of machine-made goods and cheap imports, undertook significant research on older and traditional motifs, dyes, embroideries and craft techniques, that she then subsequently attempted to revive through her designs. Her aim was not only to revive craft and make it relevant to modern times, but also to educate both the Indian and the international consumer of these valuable treasures—a sentiment that is also echoed across her books, exhibitions and visual promotional materials.

Her early experiences taught her that a simple revival of motifs or prints was not enough, as customers actively looked for subtle design intervention (trends, colors, fresh cuts) if purchasing "designer" fashion. Ms. Kumar has since worked with a number of craftspeople reviving various forms of block printing, *Zardozi*, leatherwork, *Kalamkari, Phulkari, Kantha*, and *Chikankari*. In many cases her interventions have encouraged craftspeople to consider older techniques and authentic methods, such as in the case of using real metal thread, as opposed to Lurex, in *Zardozi*. Ms. Kumar believes that maintaining a commercial angle in her revivalist work was advantageous, as it meant that she and other designers like her were motivated to continue nurturing the crafts they had begun working with. This was not only to ensure their own label's growth but also the growth of the crafts—so they met the needs of future generations and maintained a sustained demand for their designs, and indirectly for the craft (Kumar 2000: 55). A review of Ritu Kumar's collections over the decades makes clear her philosophy of revival through a sensitive injection of design that despite her introduction of new fabrics, colors, motifs and patterns applied on Indian and Western styles, does not veer away from the original format or discipline of the craft itself (refer to Figure 2.8 on p. 43 and Plate 12). In other words rarely does she de-contextualize the craft.

Craft and fashion: Issues of balance

In contrast to more historically sensitive approaches of working with crafts, equally successful are alternate design approaches that stretch the limits of a craft technique in order to achieve a non-traditional look or product that is in line with the designer's own personal aesthetic, and also in keeping with global trends. Seeing as embroidery is a permanent feature and an easily accessible craft technique for Indian designers, its evolution and applications away from traditional forms is a natural outcome of the way designers tend to develop their collections in their studios. Metal thread embroidery and *Ari* work, as well as a range of hand stitches, sequin work and appliqué together comprise the most commonly used techniques across various designer collections. Designer Rajdeep Ranawat believes the freedom India's embroidery resources offer to express various inspirations (which in his case range from exotic flowers, Chinoiserie (Plate 13), Italian architecture, etc.) are unsurpassable and an important part of the creative process.[54] Through consciously "refashioning" crafts into innovative, exciting and unpredictable outcomes, designers are able to make bold statements about their aesthetic and awareness of Indian techniques as well as more subtle iterations that are still distinctive and unique. Designer Rajesh Pratap believes that Indian textiles "are [often] not compatible with stitched/constructed garments" that current fashions demand (Pratap, cf. Sethi 2010).[55] Hence, for those designers wanting to pursue global trends it

---

[54] Rajdeep Ranawat, in an interview with the author in 2010.

[55] Rajesh Pratap himself has worked in Benaras to produce finer fabrics, blending cotton with silk and fine Cashmere with silk to create double cloths. He says, "it is vital for people like us to contribute, to make them relevant for our times … Just making silk saris, which are not worn as much today, will not help to keep the traditions alive" (Pratap cf. Sethi 2010).

Figure 6.4   An example of Manish Arora's recontextualization of the Banarasi brocade from his Spring/Summer 2013 ready-to-wear collection showcased at Paris Fashion Week. Photographed by Yannis Vlamos. Image courtesy Manish Arora.

becomes important to consider refashioning aspects of the technology and raw materials as well as the aesthetics of indigenous crafts. In many cases such design interventions can help further evolve the craft towards new frontiers and open it up to a wider market — as evident in Manish Arora's redesign of the Banarasi brocade to create zebra like stripes for his Spring/Summer 2013 ready-to-wear collection (Figure 6.4) showcased at Paris Fashion Week in 2012.

    In spite of the long history of design intervention and commercial success of many traditional crafts through the medium of fashion, the link with contemporary design has also fuelled much criticism. The main critique being that designers have not done enough to ensure the exchange between traditional crafts and contemporary design occurs on an equal footing (Jaitly 2010). The realities of the fashion system make such a balance, where the craftsperson and the contemporary designer connect at a creative and egalitarian level (ibid.), hard to conceive in most cases. Fashion, as we already know, is all about change, influenced by seasonal trends and equally unpredictable market forces. This is true for fashion in India as well, and leads to questions relating to how such trends impact crafts-people that need sustained orders beyond a single season or year to earn their livelihood. When seasonal changes occur, do designers use the same textiles in their subsequent collections, and in doing so continue to support the same crafts? In some scenarios, is it prudent to revive a craft when it's highly likely the demand will only be for one collection, with no guarantee that local patronage will be able to support it once the style is out of vogue? There are also conceptual issues of ownership and tradition due to the way the injection of "design" shifts and re-positions craft into a new arena with its own aesthetic demands that can often have little to do with the craftsperson and the original roots, meanings and aesthetics of the craft itself. In the case of designers the challenges of working with craft are also many, ranging from sourcing, employment, quality control and mass production. Hence, maintaining a balance between fashion and craft gets caught up in various issues pertaining to notions of tradition versus modernity, trend versus longevity and the cultural practice of a craft versus its practice for purely commercial purposes.

Swarup Dutta, who has collaborated with various indigenous crafts during his career, believes that many craftspeople, especially those based in rural areas, feel insecure and isolated as they are further and further away from the markets they create products for. Since they rely on the designer's input to make products that are commercially viable, not being able to see these products in the context they are worn or used makes it hard for them to gauge how to make new work that is reflective of their own cultural identity.[56] This brings about concerns about whether the craft still reflects the craftsperson's own sense of creativity, especially if designers change the core elements which characterize the craft, without considering its cultural significance and history. Furthermore, there are similar concerns when a craft that is closely linked to local culture, such as *Phulkari* or *Kantha,* changes from being a leisure activity undertaken within the household to becoming industrialized into a per-piece labor activity. In other words they shift from being a "craft" to a "technique." Such changes not only have cultural significance but also impact issues of quality and design—as mass manufacturing tends to dilute time intensive motifs and techniques in favor of affordability. Indian crafts are often not techno-logically equipped to deal with mass production—and when they are, it is not possible to ensure the exact sameness of each item due to the irregularities and imperfections of the hand. This is both an endearing quality, as well as an issue for those attempting to supply to global markets.

From the perspective of indigenous craftspeople there is a deep polarity when comparing their wages to design professionals. The former continue to suffer due to

---

[56] Swarup Dutta—Kolkata-based photographer, designer and former Dean of Undergraduate studies at the Indian Institute of Crafts and Design (IICD), Jaipur—in a phone interview with the author in 2013.

middlemen, low pay and rising costs—where for example the retail price for handloom items remains the same, as do wages, but the cost of silk or cotton yarn and other raw materials continue to increase. Adding to the risk of preserving crafts, is the recently launched Mahatma Gandhi National Rural Employment Guarantee Act that guarantees people in rural areas at least 100 days of unskilled employment per year by the Indian government at a fixed wage of Rupees 125 a day (US$2) on infrastructure projects, such as road works, building sites etc. In some cases the promise of paid employment is more lucrative than practicing certain time and cost intensive (high risk, low pay) craft activities. The eminent danger of losing trained craftspeople as a result of a government policy, named after a key figure in Indian history who was instrumental in mobilizing craft as a symbol of national pride through the *Swadeshi* movement, is sadly ironic.

Sustainable design in the context of craft and fashion

Rahul Mishra, Aneeth Arora (Péro)

Technopak's report on Indian Apparel and Textiles in 2012[57] projects eco-fashion and sustainable design to become a greater concern for Indian consumers as the market matures over the next ten years. Jaipur-based label Anokhi is already an example of an established model that is built on well-balanced and sustainable relationships between craft revival and design, craftspeople and designers—as it supports local communities and crafts in Rajasthan through providing a fulfilling environment for craftspeople, while offering a quality designed product that is not too affected by trends.[58] Even though crafts are undoubtedly prominent in the work of most Indian designers, more recently a number of emerging designers are putting sustainable and ethical methods of craft collaboration in the forefront of their design philosophies.

Approaches that follow on from the craft cluster educational models I mentioned earlier, as well as a desire to create sustainably designed products are both central to Rahul Mishra and Aneeth Arora's design ethic. They share a passion for Indian crafts, but are also keen to ensure that the craftspeople that make their textiles are supported in the long term. Mishra's key focus has been giving handloom textiles like *Chanderi* (cover Image) and cotton Kerala *mundus* (Figure 6.5) extra prominence, though he also works with other forms of *khadi*, *Ari* embroidery and tie-dye. Aneeth has worked with an impressive array of textiles for her label Péro—ranging from *Jamdani, Ikat,* tie-dye, all forms of block-prints, extra weft techniques (from Assam), *Chikankari*, Madras checks, and Himachali[59] wools to name but a few (Figure 6.6). Both designers are unified in their

---

[57] Page 38, "Textile & Apparel Compendium 2012," report prepared by Technopak (2012), www.technopak.com (accessed December 15, 2012).
[58] See Dwyer (2006) and the Anokhi's website, www.anokhi.com.
[59] From the state of Himachal Pradesh.

Figure 6.5 A catwalk look from Rahul Mishra's *Kerala Reversible* Spring/Summer 2013 Collection. The collection features Kerala handlooms and supports Padma Shri awarded Master Gopinathan in his pursuit to employ and empower rural weaver women of Balarampuram. The garments in the collection are reversible and can be worn inside out for a completely new look. Image courtesy FDCI/ Rahul Mishra.

Figure 6.6 A catwalk look from the label Péro by Aneeth Arora. Spring/Summer 2011 collection showcased at Wills Lifestyle India Fashion Week. Featuring a cotton *khadi* scarf, worn over a *Jamdani* blouse and checkered *ikat* bottom. Image courtesy FDCI/Aneeth Arora.

approach towards ensuring they work with the same crafts over multiple seasons and years in order to support the craftspeople as well as strengthening their own networks and fluency with the craft. Beyond this, Mishra's larger goal is to secure the future of Indian handloom production through designing "systems"[60] by which craftspeople can become independent entrepreneurs, and cast designers as consultants. Taking his work with Kerala handloom as an example, he has proposed various strategies that help build design repositories for the craft, impart education and training to new craftspeople and attach local tailoring establishments to craft production so that it is locally self-sufficient in creating finished products.[61] He also believes linking craft to tourism helps create a

[60] See Ranjan (2007). Mishra applies aspects of the IICD Model of "Craft as an Industry in India" developed in 1991, included in Prof. Ranjan's post.
[61] Rahul Mishra, in a phone interview with the author in 2013.

mutually beneficial relationship, where one will boost the other.[62] Ultimately, however, Mishra feels that high-fashion and couture, with their exorbitant prices, are sometimes the only way certain time-intensive handicrafts *can* remain viable to practice.[63] Thus, despite being unattainable for the masses and contextually divorced from those who practice crafts, the upward flow of luxury indirectly benefits the revival and use of many fine handicraft and weaving techniques, which would otherwise have been lost over time.

Even though fashion shows and seasonal collections are the reality of the fashion system both these designers find themselves in, Aneeth tries to maintain a balance in favor of the culture of the crafts she works with—through strategies like ordering fabric in bulk before she determines its use (a risky approach) as well as working a year in advance (as opposed to six months) to give weavers enough time to develop her textiles.[64] When it comes to retail, Mishra does not follow the notion of planned obsolescence or the rule of only selling one collection per season. Instead he offers a variety of collections across his stockists with a mix of classic pieces along with some that relate to his catwalk shows.[65] In terms of design, Rahul Mishra and Aneeth Arora both follow from the framework of design established by Ritu Kumar where they are mindful of the cultural contexts and traditional aesthetics of the textiles they use. Through reviewing their collections it is evident that both designers are eager to design clothing that is globally relevant, however their design interventions tend to rely on their ability to work closely within the textile craft's creative boundaries as they introduce innovative colors, "tweak" motifs, and suggest technological improvements to yarns and fibers. While Aneeth's garments follow simple and classic cuts that compliment and give prominence to the textiles she works with, Mishra designs his cuts according to the way the fabric is woven, and in some cases has his fabric woven to compliment his cuts. In this way, through their reliance on fashion systems, as well as the subversion of the same, both these designers are able to craft their own systems to ensure that traditional crafts remain feasible to practice as well as fashionable to wear.

Indian couture: Modern Maharajas

JJ Valaya

> I am essentially a couturier … We have our own dyers, we have our own weavers, embroiderers, we even have people who cut gemstones to size for us. (Valaya 2010)[66]

The term "couture" and the symbolic status it brings may be a recent entrant amongst

---

[62] Once again it is important to note Anokhi's Museum of Hand Printing situated in the once-dilapidated Chanwar Palkiwalon ki Haveli (Anokhi Haveli) in Jaipur. Featuring regular exhibitions and workshops this initiative successfully links crafts with tourism.
[63] Rahul Mishra, 2013.
[64] Aneeth Arora, in an interview with the author in 2013.
[65] Rahul Mishra, 2013.
[66] JJ Valaya, in an interview with the author in 2010.

the terminology of Indian design, however its association with handcrafted, made-to-measure, exclusively designed garments is not new in the context of Indian dress. This is especially true for the kinds of embellished clothing created for special occasions and bridal trousseaus that undergo the same process outlined under various definitions of *haute couture*—the design and manufacture of fashionable clothes to a client's specific requirements and measurements, with high attention to design, detail, craftsmanship, quality and exclusivity. Much of women's clothing made and worn in India historically, and to a large extent even to this day tends to be individually tailored. As already mentioned, the ease and availability of tailoring services and women's preference for ethnic clothing were key factors that gave shape to India's emerging fashion industry in the 1980s (Khaire 2011). Designers' ability to create heavily embellished traditional garments that were superior to what an average tailor could provide, in terms of quality and with input of exclusive design, made designer clothing more prestigious to own and wear. Through the years this took on the distinction and label of Indian "couture." Designers like JJ Valaya, Tarun Tahiliani and Sabyasachi Mukherjee have successfully built luxury couture brands on this framework, and their reliance on and prominence of India's wealth of craft-based resources sets Indian couture apart. Beyond weddings, Indian tastes in clothing rely on many couture techniques that have also come to inform designers' approach to ready-to-wear. Indian couture has also ensured the preservation of traditional motifs applied on fairly traditional garment styles—as even though many Indians may no longer wear traditional clothes like the sari on a daily basis, when it comes to weddings most women, young and old, still prefer wearing saris and *lehenga cholis.*

In 2010, I met with one of India's most well-known couture designers, JJ Valaya, at his soon-to-be-opening luxury showroom outside of New Delhi. Known for his opulent wedding wear that exudes luxury, Valaya's collections offer twists on the concept of modern royalty in India (he refers to himself as a lost [modern] Maharaja), through fusing traditional motifs, embellishment techniques and classic Indian cuts with modern details, digital prints, Swarovski crystals and distressed foils and at times even "rock star elements." In outlining the meaning of couture in India and how it differs from its Western counterparts, Valaya states that, "a beautiful, well-cut [simple] jacket is couture in France. This does not drive the Indian market."[67] In India, couture buyers need to see value for their money and so the term "couture" most commonly refers to elaborately embellished traditional clothes and bridal ensembles.[68] Valaya believes Indian weddings—a cultural phenomenon that are in no danger of vanishing or becoming less flamboyant—have the ability to once again capture the essence of India's royal past through their pomp and splendor.[69] In keeping with this statement and the expectations of the Indian client, the majority of the themes that inform the design of Indian couture collections incorporate

[67] JJ Valaya, 2010.
[68] While this is an acknowledged fact, it is also a bone of contention amongst the Indian design fraternity as many do not want to be associated with the label of "bridal" designers and are keen to design couture away from that stereotype, and at par with the West.
[69] JJ Valaya, 2010.

strategies of self-Orientalizing and that of Orientalizing other cultures (Plate 14)—as they are most suited towards such traditionally styled and elaborate outfits.

Despite the absence of any official requirements for Indian couture, Valaya stresses his adherence to building a couture brand through a combination of four factors that were hallmarks of Western couture labels. These are namely—brand identity, longevity, luxury and craft, but in the case of India, "craft" becomes further expanded due to the craft resources at hand.[70] His label "Muse" epitomizes all of these factors, and at the time of my interview with him, it was the most exclusive label and experience the house of Valaya offered. The trademark of the Muse experience, beyond its high cost,[71] is the personal attention the client receives and their involvement at every possible stage of the design and creation of the garments. According to Valaya, a Muse client's experience begins with a meeting with him to discuss the design of the piece she (or he) would like to order. Then follow numerous fittings to ensure the piece is perfect, with a guarantee that the design will never be repeated for another client and nor will a replica piece, segment or design be openly exhibited. To stress on this exclusivity, the Muse client receives a certificate of authenticity as well as the khakha[72] from which the garments are made.[73] However, protecting their designs and copyright in the wake of countless imitations that can easily be sourced in local markets like Chandni Chowk (Old Delhi), for up to 50–70 percent less than the designer price tag, is one of the key challenges couture designers face in India.[74] Valaya has developed what he calls the "Daison"—a logo that confirms the authenticity of his garments. But the challenge of protecting motifs, patterns and embellishment techniques—such as the paisley or metal thread zari embroidery placed along lehenga panels—in designs that are familiar, culturally ingrained and form the basis of centuries of craft evolution is questionable as well as difficult. It is possible that certain interpretations and techniques allow them to be distinct, but for the untrained eye it can be challenging at times to distinguish one from another. In addition, unlike the few French couture houses, access to Indian crafts and craftspeople is not limited to the larger established fashion houses and labels. Thus making it possible for anyone to copy or lay claim to the label of couture—leading to a proliferation of Indian couturiers.

The heightened success of couture following India's liberalization, that continues to thrive despite frequent economic fluctuations, has meant the emergence of more formalized frameworks for promoting and showcasing couture garments (that go beyond wedding wear) through various exhibitions and an annual fashion week organized by FDCI. The success of couture in India, from a monetary and cultural perspective compared to its much-publicized demise in the West brings attention to another theory

---

[70] Ibid.

[71] The "Muse" experience starts at around Rupees 15,00,000 (US$ 24,700) (JJ Valaya 2010).

[72] A khakha is like the "blue print" pattern of an embroidery design on tracing paper—which is used to trace the pattern onto the fabric through the process of making small holes on the paper and then dusting white chalk or a temporary blue dye.

[73] JJ Valaya, 2010.

[74] In 2006 Ritu Kumar won a landmark case under the Copyright Act, 1957, against an individual copying her designs. The case took nine years to resolve, and though the ruling was in her favor, issues of copyright continue to be designers' constant nightmare.

that can be applied here—and that is of a sort of "reverse colonization." Those who were previously excluded from the very classification of fashion and *haute* couture, are now vested with its success—both from a design as well as a consumption standpoint Indians are a growing customer base for domestic as well as Western luxury couture. Getting official recognition for Indian couture globally is a different matter.

India modern

Abraham and Thakore

Our intention was to present a point of view that clearly states that it is possible for a woman, particularly a fashionable urban professional, to look at traditional Indian garments, such as the sari, the *dupatta*, *salwar kameez*, *churidar* and, of course, the *kurta*, as viable modern fashion alternatives. We wanted to present clothing that could express the timelessness of fashion, yet retain the spirit of tradition, as well as coexist with the spread of western labels. (Abraham and Thakore cf. Ghose 2010)

… a *rani* pink saree with a little lime green edge – that is Indian minimalism. (Garg 2013)[75]

The challenges of creating culturally rooted design within the existing polarities and diversity of India opens up an exciting space for multiple design idioms to emerge that represent this diversity. As highlighted in the discussion up to this point, on one hand there is the vivid celebration of Indianness through Indian themes, traditional garments, couture and a vibrant recasting of vernacularisms. On the other, there is also a significantly pared down aesthetic, one that increasingly responds to the realities of modern India—its dust, its climate, its traditions, crafts and subtleties of everyday life. Such an approach shares many aspects in common with the strategies discussed earlier, as it too relies on nostalgia, Indians' familiarity with indigenous cloth and clothing traditions, craft and local resources but recasts them into more minimal interpretations of fashion.

The quote at the start of the section by designers David Abraham and Rakesh Thakore (Abraham and Thakore) points towards their approach in creating clothing that is "low key and finely crafted" and offers "a modern design expression drawn from rich tradition of Indian textiles and craft"[76] (Figure 6.7). Fabric, cut and finish are the hallmarks of such non-embellished fashion that Asha Baxi describes as comfortable, well-constructed garments incorporating Indian patterns and cuts made from Indian textiles with subtle textures or embroideries.[77] The prominence of patternmaking techniques that focus on the

---

[75] Sanjay Garg, cited from "Raw Mango: A Conversation with Sanjay Garg." *Park Magazine*, Vol. 8, 2013, "Color," pg 31. Available from http://www.theparkhotels.com/living-magazine.html (accessed July 17, 2013).
[76] Cited from Abraham and Thakore's official webpage, http://www.abrahamandthakore.com (accessed March 10, 2013).
[77] Asha Baxi, in an interview with the author in 2008.

Figure 6.7 Blouse and pants, worn with a scarf, crossbody bag and *mojri* platform shoes from Abraham and Thakore's Spring/Summer 2011 collection. Image courtesy Abraham and Thakore.

linear seams of a *kurta*, fit of a *bandhgala* jacket or use of *kalis*, for example, teamed with subtle details, such as pin-tucks, minimal embroideries and finishing details that rely on fine craftsmanship incorporated into basic garments denote "India's version of modernism."[78] Here Baxi's observation points to the parallels such design shares with the recommendations in the Eames' report, as well as the trajectory of modern design and design education that arose in response to these recommendations—that take into consideration "some of the values that exist in the commonplace things," the "history of the country and all its social mores," its weather, "local resources, the productivity of the land—its probable future" and share a "concern for the quality of things" (Eames and Eames 1997 [1958]: 11–17).

Abraham and Thakore's exploration of Indian minimalism influenced by this ethos for modern design creates a very specific aesthetic, which has enjoyed a discerning clientele in India since their label's inception. The challenge at the outset was to win over popular Indian tastes for flashy "design," a stark opposition to the simplicity reflected in everyday dress. Only recently has such design come into the forefront in India—encouraged by an influx of young designers with a familiarity of global fashion and a deep desire to

[78] Ibid.

create no-fuss, zero-bling fashion that challenges common stereotypes of ethnic design, and allows them to rescue it from the confines of kitsch and the cultural exuberance of couture. A simple *kurta*, a crisp *sari*, a fine *Chanderi*, a perfect pintuck on a simple *kurta* or the understated elegance of gold *butis* on ecru are characteristics that could easily share a similar cultural language with design emanating from countries like Japan (Cicolini cf. Kaul 2012). A recent blog post refers to this as the "anti-glamour" movement,[79] further epitomized in the work of upcoming labels like Bodice, 11.11CellDSGN and Raw Mango, whose collective design explorations encompass a rediscovery of the minimalism inherent in Indian textiles and cuts of clothing, driven by the need to find a balance between Indian identity and global fashion in globally compatible [wearable] ways. Once again, conceptually, not too dissimilar to the juncture at which modern Indian clothing found itself a century ago.

Conclusion: *Indian* design beyond India

Gaurav Gupta, Kallol Datta 1955

> When I set up shop 5 years back, there was an influx of designers moving base to India. Each and every one of these designers was technically trained in universities (primarily Europe). They had work experience with fashion houses and then kick started their labels. So we had a group of 5-10 designers; newbies [*sic*] if you may, creating clothes that were deemed "alternative" by the viewers in India. To be part of this ongoing phenomenon where being "experimental" is part of the norm is a very exciting time in Indian fashion. (Datta 2013)[80]

While the majority of this chapter's discussion aligns itself with the evolutionary nature of local design, India's post-liberalization era has acted as a catalyst for the emergence of new revolutionary design concepts and processes that are not directly visually or culturally rooted to one place, and go beyond interpretations of Indian themes. NIFT and Central Saint Martins alums—Gaurav Gupta and Kallol Datta, though visually and conceptually poles apart, are both part of this ongoing shift that is tipped to be the future of Indian design in the twenty-first century. Both these designers share a deep desire to challenge the norms that have come before them and bring new ideas to the forefront that are provocative, subversive and at times confrontational, but have also been successful in bringing their work to light.

Gaurav, who chose to return to India after working in Europe, has been credited with reinvigorating the design scene by the Indian fashion press through his exploration of more globally focused design trajectories. His philosophy from the start was to design the way *he* wanted to design, as opposed to fitting into a pre-existing mold that required him to adhere closely to Indian tastes. Also keen to apply the conceptual design

---

[79] Malhotra (2013).
[80] Kallol Datta, in interview via email with the author in 2013.

methodologies that he had become accustomed to during his stint in Europe, Gaurav wanted to "make people think." [81] On the surface Gaurav's garments appear to maintain strong visual links to India, as seen in his use of bold colors, showmanship, reference to traditional garments like the sari and *lehenga*, use of embellishments and adherence to Indian couture's focus on bridal. [82] But on closer inspection it is clear that none of these appear where or how they are usually found—as he consciously subverts rules of balance, symmetry, beauty and even the application of drape usually found in traditional Indian clothing. He often uses knits (which were not the norm when he first began his label) and materials associated with performance sportswear alongside softer feminine fabrics. Gaurav's approach to design has been likened to that of Alexander McQueen, or India's version of "punk," as he dismantles traditional embellishments, reassembles paisleys, peacocks and jumbled up *Zardozi* with a heavy dose of metal chains and imperfect Swarovskis, and places them across his garments in unpredictable ways (Plate 15). His use of drape brings fresh vision to the long valued tradition and techniques of wearing fabric on the body in India, but in his interpretation the drapes, pleats and tucks are stitched and secure. Gaurav's saris are more like gowns, and his *lehengas*, like his saris are one-piece, zip-up garments.

In comparison, for Kallol, "India's heaviest designer"[83] and self-proclaimed "fresh breath of darkness,"[84] the theme of "they [the media, fashionistas, bling designers, fashion weeks] don't get it" appears to be a conceptual driving force. His collections do not follow the bright color palettes popular in India. He is fundamentally opposed to pretty or decorative "bling" embroideries and fussy detailing. His prints are abstract, sketchy and linked to random musings and ideas that filter into his collections. These include a combination of line drawings and text that range from origami folding instructions, "this is not a garment," mating snails, toilet signs, amputated legs, shoe prints, and most recently a caricature of a screaming man with the words "losing my sanity never was part of the plan." Kallol's clothes also do not conform to the shapes that are frequently featured on Indian catwalks—there are no *anarkalis* or *lehengas*. Instead the majority of his pieces follow unfitted or anti-fashion[85] amorphous silhouettes—where shape and volume, and the development of innovative cuts through patternmaking are key. Keen to create same-size-fits-all garments, as well as challenge popular notions of what is flattering and what is not, his Autumn/Winter 2013/14 womenswear collection was made out of a man's size 40 block (Figure 6.8). In India where most men and women still prefer to buy clothes that are close fitting in the assumption that these are most flattering, Kallol's work comes as a shock to some, and a breath of fresh [dark] air to others.

In concluding this chapter's discussion on contemporary Indian design, I highlight the question raised by Scotford on, "what happens to cultural identity and social communities when the designers mix local practices and vernacular forms with elements

---

[81] Gaurav Gupta, 2010.
[82] These have definitely contributed to his success beyond the more discerning fashion crowd.
[83] Datta's brief bio on his Twitter profile in 2013.
[84] Sinha (2012).
[85] A term often used to describe Kallol and his work.

Figure 6.8   "Senegalese Kaftan" from Kallol Datta's Autumn/Winter 2013/14 titled *Abandon*.
All the garments in this collection were developed using a menswear size 40 pattern block.
Photographed by Ronny Sen. Image courtesy Kallol Datta 1955.

imported from the increasingly pervasive culture of globalization" (Scotford 2005: 1). As
this chapter demonstrates, the space that her question opens up offers the possibility
to realize something new and hybrid in terms of a contemporary design identity, which
is not a simple "homogenization due to globalization" model and nor is it limited to one
kind of outcome. Both Gaurav and Kallol's work, though aesthetically varied, when
viewed together represent a confidence that directly responds to the optimism stemming
from India's recent economic progress. They are also in keeping with the lifestyles and
opportunities that have become possible since, as more and more Indian designers
move internationally as part of their studies or careers, in tandem with similar transnational collaborators—photographers, stylists, fashion journalists, models designers,
textile artists—who flock to India to be part of Indian fashion and give it new meaning,

expression and identity. As a result, while Indian design and designers enter into yet another critical phase of establishing clearer design idioms by which to define themselves locally and internationally, they also begin to strengthen the necessary argument and frameworks in favor of Indian fashion centers with distinct fashion cultures—where traditionally influenced fashion is not one-dimensional and nor is it the only option.

7

CONCLUSION: "WRAPPING IT UP"

The evolution of modern styles of dress and fashion in India over the last century and a half served as a key point of departure for the discussion on contemporary fashion in this book. This is because some of the broader themes and concepts established during the period of British rule, Indian nationalism and India's independence from the British, as well as instances of self-fashioning that relied on the fusion of various local and global factors, continue to play out in the way fashion is shaped by and for Indians in current times. Various Eurocentric and Orientalist frameworks that established their stronghold at the time, as well as the ability of clothing to act as visual and material mediums of social mobility, social acceptance, political resistance, national identity and a modernizing society also continue to impact the way Indians view their clothes, textiles and crafts, and traditions. This is especially so within the field of fashion design. In addition, the challenges of finding the right balance between tradition and modernity and [re]defining individual and collective identity that hinge on the act of mediation and assertion of distinction seem to resonate strongly with India's emerging urban classes— whose image and role as cultural mediators forms a critical part of India's current global trajectory.

During my research and discussions with designers and other fashion professionals, as well as urban consumers of fashionable clothing such issues of balance and the creation of an "authentic" identity in times of increased global influences remained at the forefront. This sentiment was echoed by veteran designer and craft revivalist Ritu Kumar, who is of the strong belief that since Indian fashion has devised its own unique visual identity, it now needs to develop its own vocabulary—on its own terms, to support its growing dynamism, cultural nuances and commercial success. According to Ms. Kumar, such a vocabulary cannot solely be devised using foreign terms and definitions.[1] Instead she suggests words like *odhni*, *angrakha* and bridal *jodhas* etc., that have long been part of the evolution of Indian dress as starting points for establishing such a set of terms,[2] which can further be mixed with global terms and concepts; much like the way Indian dress has for centuries maintained its ability to adapt and adopt global influences in its own locally infused, sometimes subversive manner.

---

[1] Ritu Kumar, in a phone interview with the author in 2010.
[2] Ibid.

At first this sounds like an impossible task, especially as we consider the East/West imbalances that Niessen (2003) cautions us about with regard to one-sided global flows of fashion opinion leadership (but not goods), teamed with the runaway success of global brands like Zara in India. How then does Indian fashion maintain or build, or rebuild its own design vocabulary? Yet, as this book has highlighted through its discussion on fashion innovation and instances of creative self-fashioning that actively include traditional dress styles, the evolution of such a vocabulary is a natural process that already exists. This was evident in Nirad Chaudhuri's account of wearing the European coat sans-shirt (or *kurta*), with a shawl thrown over the shoulder or *dhoti* draped like a cravat in Chapter 2, as well as in the image in the same chapter's conclusion of the fashionable couple (Figure 2.9 on p. 46) who clearly had a flare for crafting their individual sartorial identity to represent their cosmopolitanism and local roots; to most recently in the way Sanjay Garg, (who designs and owns Raw Mango) has developed his entire color palette not on the basis of the universal pantone shade card and related nomenclature, but by using Indian color terms like *rani* pink and *tota* green while simultaneously popularizing the sari as a "designer garment." Garg affirms this by stating,

> When I say *Rani* Pink to you, you get it. I don't have to explain the shade to you. Your *dadi* or your *nani* would have passed it on to you.[3] You know it consciously and unconsciously. (Garg 2013)[4]

Furthermore, the forces of contemporary globalization have in turn brought such concepts back into the forefront.

Saving the sari

The sari's future remains a popular topic for current debate and speculation in India, especially as young, urban women who belong to the post-liberalization generation become less inclined towards wearing saris beyond special occasions, and most forms of popular culture emphasize Western dress or fusion styles. Newspaper and magazine headlines on the sari outliving its relevance in urban cities are contrasted with those that announce its newfound elevated status—as India's Birkin.[5] While the sari is not a central point of focus for this book, much like past instances of its re-fashioning, its current state and status serves as a useful metaphor, or more accurately a visual and material medium, for highlighting and summarizing past as well as current shifts in Indian fashion. By discussing the status of the sari my aim is not to perpetuate the linking of nationhood on women's bodies, though this is somewhat inevitable and still prevalent, but to demonstrate how traditions can simultaneously be modern, just as modernities

---

[3]*dadi*–paternal grandmother, *nani*–maternal grandmother.
[4]Cited from "Raw Mango: A Conversation with Sanjay Garg." *Park Magazine*, Vol. 8, 2013, "Color," p. 31. Available from http://www.theparkhotels.com/living-magazine.html (accessed July 17, 2013).
[5]Sippy (2013b).

can differ depending on the time period and location of their production (Breckenridge and Appadurai 1995). The sari is globally revered not only for its textiles and innovative drapes, but also its resilience as a draped garment that has held its own amongst more seemingly functional and modern stitched contenders. It has been documented in numerous books and inspired countless fashion trends, as well as fashion collections across the globe. It is beyond question traditionally Indian, but the transitions and fashions it has witnessed in its design demonstrate the ability of the garment to be modern and shift and change according to the times.

Here it is interesting to note that in 1987 British designer Zandra Rhodes was invited to present a collection inspired by India and the sari. For this special "Indian Saree" collection she presented various design interpretations and experimentations that ranged from removing sari borders and replacing them with pearls on the hem, enhancing the *pallu* with large appliqués, to shortening the length of the sari as an option for "daywear" that could be worn with a short Lycra bodice (Figure 7.1). According to Khan (1992) these interpretations were met with moral outcry in India due to the way

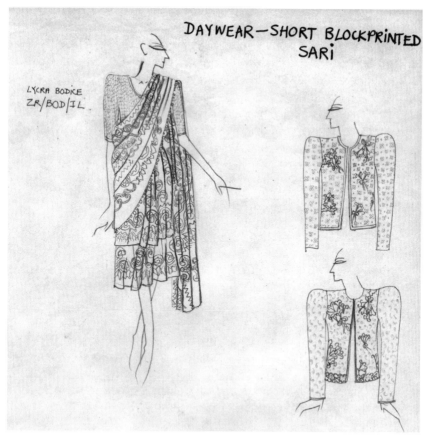

Figure 7.1 "Daywear—short block-printed sari worn with Lycra bodice". Sketch by Zandra Rhodes for the 1987 "Indian Saree Show," December 1987. Image courtesy VADS: the online resource for visual arts. Copyright Zandra Rhodes.

Rhodes had treated the sari—a hallmark of the Indian woman. "Ripped, shredded at the edges, scattered with strategic holes, it constituted, people felt, not a design but an assault" (Khan 1992: 61). Recounting the same incident, Castelino notes that at that time the designer price tag for Rhodes' elaborate and dramatic creations was off-putting for most women who preferred updating their saris through their own subtle modifications (Castelino 1994: 83).

Comparing Rhodes' experimentation with the sari's more recent transformations— showcased at India's fashion weeks, on the pages of *Vogue* India magazine or on popular serials on television—there is no surprise that fashions have changed, as have attitudes towards the sari. This is not to say that it is only recently through globalization that such traditional garments have begun to experience fashion change, or that the sari [read tradition] has been in opposition to fashion [read modernization]— but change must be relevant to the socio-cultural context within which it takes place for it to become fashion in the truest sense. This was apparent in the way the *Nivi* style emerged in the late nineteenth century, as a fashionable representation of Indian modernity through fusing Indian and European elements, that became popular not only amongst the middle-class, but also suited women's changing roles in society at the time. Similarly in the 1980s, the then modern sari retained its drape but its fabrication shifted towards the vibrant floral printed synthetics offered by the infamous Garden Sarees, designed and created by Surat's Praful Shah. It must also be noted that at the same time Shah collected and curated the impressive Tapi Textile Collection as a personal design resource for his business, but also in an effort to ensure India's valuable textile traditions were preserved, documented and accessible as a resource for future generations of crafts and craft enthusiasts. The paradox presented by this example—whereby Shah could be seen as giving rise to the very textiles and fashions that go against or contradict the traditional techniques and textiles he has attempted to preserve and conserve—is wholly logical in the Indian context as its modernity never breaks from the past, and allows for a critical reflection on the inherent contradiction that is "fashion."

Now, while questions of whether the sari will survive the onslaught of Western brands and formal gowns are rife, the Indian sari industry appears strong as it accounts for the largest market share in womenswear retail[6] and bears witness to numerous design innovations—targeted both at the mass market, as well as urban elites. Sanjay Garg vehemently believes the sari cannot be saved or revived on the basis of sympathy alone.[7] Instead, it is only through the injection of design that considers the tastes and aspirations related to contemporary lifestyles that can keep it relevant. Proof of this lies in the success of his saris that draw upon the uniqueness of Indian color palettes, set against the simplicity and respite of Indian weaves that have reinvigorated an interest in the sari amongst urban fashionistas—as modern Indian women find themselves more accurately represented in his subtle, zero-bling designs (Plate 16).

---

[6] Accounting for close to 18 percent of the market size in 2011 (Technopak 2012).
[7] Sanjay Garg, in a phone interview with the author in 2013.

Figure 7.2 From the fashion spread titled "Song of the Sari," *Harper's Bazaar* India, October 2010. Featuring: *Chhotu* sari and *choli* by Sabyasachi Mukherjee, vest by Abu Jani & Sandeep Khosla, necklace (worn as headband) by Gaurav Gupta, clutch by Jimmy Choo, earrings by Zoya and lamp by Bungalow 8. Hair and makeup by Daniel Bauer. Photographed by Farrokh Chothia. Image courtesy Farrokh Chothia/*Harper's Bazaar* Magazine India.

On the other end of the visual spectrum, Sabyasachi Mukherjee is reported to have made 45 percent of his US$11 million turnover in 2012 through the sale of his elaborate couture saris. Other contemporary avatars include the denim sari[8] and *jodi pattu,*[9] the

---

[8]Denim print on silk-feel (synthetic) saris by Sri Kumaran Silks, Chennai.
[9]A sari-shirt combination—where the sari comes along with a matching shirt piece that can be tailored for the husband. Also by Sri Kumaran Silks, Chennai.

bailou sari,[10] as well as the pre-pleated and stitched sari-gown by Gaurav Gupta, which is literally a sartorial and cultural hybrid between a sari and a gown. Nowadays the sari can be worn with jeans or teamed with JJ Valaya's limited edition Alika jacket. Sabyasachi has introduced his version of the *chhotu* (short) sari (Figure 7.2) that appears to be a hybrid between a tribal woman's typically shorter sari, a dress and a *ghagara*. Pacman printed saris sell like hotcakes,[11] Masaba's redesign of Satya Paul's iconic art saris have once again brought the label into the forefront, and *Vogue* India's fifth anniversary issue (2012) featured 50 other such style inventions and interpretations of the sari by Indian designers. Examples of craft and textile revival are equally vibrant and numerous, such as Wendell Rodricks' revival of the *Kunbi*—a style of sari weaving that had not been practiced in Goa for decades, which he used in his Spring/Summer 2011 collection. Saris can now be rented or bought online. It is also a known fact that some online sari sellers Photoshop faces of glamorous models atop their inhouse models as a way of increasing sales. There are numerous blogs and YouTube videos dedicated to television serials' saris and other *hatke* (different) ways of tying the sari. Bollywood actresses Sridevi, Vidya Balan and Rani Mukherjee all support the designer sari. In some cases, while the sari in its most recognizable "traditional" state may be outmoded, its basic framework (textiles and shape) allow for reinterpretation—either in the form of gowns, bikini wraps or textile inspiration for new types of garments. The key point being that the sari is not only relevant to a vast majority of Indians, but it *is* also now India's new Birkin.

In Sabyasachi's case the iconic status of his label and passionate following in India (as a result of his television show and design for films) meant that he was able to conceive of the "Save the Saree" campaign (Figure 7.3). Launched alongside his 2010 couture collection, the designer took up the initiative to support handloom weavers across India as well as revive the wearing of the sari on the wings of his label's success. The saris, packaged in large vintage styled tins, retailed from Sabyasachi's flagship stores and through being priced at around Rupees 3,000 (US$50) they were a steal for a loyal consumer or fan follower. In 2010, the campaign featured Murshidabad saris, but his aim going forward was to feature as many different types of indigenous weaves over time at affordable prices, where proceeds from the sales go entirely to the weaver. In addition to this, Sabyasachi's costumes for Sridevi in the film *English Vinglish* (2012) saw her wear saris throughout the film, fashioned to mirror the rhythm of the story as she moves to New York and learns English. Positioned amongst other designer-styled Bollywood films that usually feature Westernized fashion, the only exception in Sridevi's wardrobe throughout the film was a trench coat—but that too was worn over a sari. For Sabyasachi saving the sari is not only about just saving the wearing of the sari, but also a strategic coinage of a design philosophy that emphasizes Indian over everything else—as a point of distinction, rebellion, and strength.

Yet, despite current moments of heightened innovation that appear to be taking place in the sari industry, it is probable that its use for everyday wear will steadily decline over the next few generations—for whom switching from jeans to saris will not be an easy

---

[10] Kolkata based store founded by Bappaditya Biswas that offers saris and scarves with traditional weaves in contemporary design and colors.
[11] Designed under the label Surendri by Yogesh Chaudhary.

Figure 7.3 Sabyasachi Mukherjee's "Save the Saree" campaign tin along with a Murshidabad handloom sari, 2010. Image by the author.

transition. So it is quite possible that the sari is destined to become like the Kimono, in terms of being relegated to costume or fashionable references in designer collections. This cannot be forecasted as a certainty, but if past instances are anything to go by, it will be interesting to see how Indian fashion will adapt and innovate to counter this shift.

Looking to the future

The complexity of writing a book like this lies in the fact that fashion is not a stationary phenomenon. The core essence of fashion is change, hence it is only possible to offer a snapshot of what it comprises of or encompasses at a given point. Not only is this true for the general cycle of short-term trends in India, but also more so now because of the way fashion is a dynamic, ever-evolving field fuelled by economic growth, market changes and a maturing fashion industry that have helped new fashion cultures emerge, strengthen and formalize their own independent systems and related centers.

Economic and market-related forecasts continue to paint the Indian market in a positive light as a destination for international labels. From that perspective, the future for fashion customers in India is bright as the world is now at their doorstep. New modes of advertising and promotion teamed with systems of seasonal change and formats for presenting fashion that have been established by Western centers of fashion, have become layered over India's own festive and seasonal style impetuses—making fashion in India a unique global-local hybrid. India's young generation of fashion consumers, who have grown up in a post-liberalized environment exposed to global media via satellite television and the Internet 24/7, increasingly view their clothing choices in a different light—as they draw their influences from a variety of places that cut across local borders and many hierarchies of scale (Massey 1998 cf. Edensor 2002). As we move into the future, their style experimentations (already evident on blogs and magazines), in tandem with the maturing of Indian retail and the design industry, will create new paradigms by which multiple style identities and fashion subcultures may emerge.

In the case of design, many now believe that the future lies in achieving global success, which in turn also impacts success in local markets. Global success is a complex concept to define, as it relates both to commercial success as well as the assertion of an "image." Many Indian designers have attracted stockists across various global markets, significantly in the Middle East, where there is the added bonus of shared aesthetic tastes, especially for traditional styles and Indian couture. Instances of globally revered fashion forward celebrities such as Lady Gaga wearing an Alpana and Neeraj ensemble or a Little Shilpa hat are now more commonplace. A number of designers and labels like Aneeth Arora's Péro and Play Clan have successfully built their own niche markets overseas. Others have had more prominent exposure—most notably Manish Arora whose collections at Paris Fashion Week have received positive reviews, and whose garments have been worn by prominent stars like Katy Perry as well as featuring regularly in global print media. And at the time this manuscript was in its final stages, Rahul Mishra became the first Indian designer to win the prestigious 2013/14 International Woolmark Prize. All of these accomplishments further promote the positive image and distinctiveness of Indian fashion. In addition, showcases on Indian design across the globe are on the rise. Beyond invitations to fashion weeks and global competitions, exhibitions like *Global Local* (as part of *Import Export*) in 2004,[12] *India Fashion Now* at ARKEN Museum of Modern Art, Denmark (August 2012–January 2013), *New India Designscape* at the Triennale Design Museum, Milan (December 2012–February 2013) all featured numerous examples of fashion products, and in 2014 the Victoria and Albert Museum will hold a prominent exhibition on Indian Design, for which the museum has actively sourced key pieces from contemporary designers to be included in its permanent collection. Such opportunities are extremely encouraging for Indian designers, as they highlight growing recognition of India as a legitimate fashion

---

[12]Which also travelled to India, and caused some controversy due to Manish Arora's use of Hindu god appliqués when exhibited in Bhopal.

center. Within India, numerous fashion events and awards have also raised the profile of local designers, with the hopes that one day they will achieve wider recognition through such promotion. Various organizations, like KHOJ[13] for example, actively inspire young designers to engage with new approaches, and find for themselves their own definition of design. The opportunities possible through large financial investors, brand conglomerates and business collaborations, that are inevitable in the not too distant future, will also project brand India or Indian brands further into the global limelight—this is a crucial and unwritten part of accessing fashion capital, even for established designers in the West.

On the other hand, the Indian design industry has received harsh criticism from within, as well as from various global commentators, for having too many design identities that appear incohesive (revivalist, traditional, Indo-Western fusion, Western, bridal, etc.), too many conflicting fashion events (two, sometimes three concurrent fashion weeks for a season), as well as many other unofficial ones vying for the same designers and audience. The lack of adherence to trends is also a concern, as is designers' emphasis on craft, color and embellishment, with relatively lesser focus on new cuts or silhouettes. Often the re-inscription of traditional forms becomes typecast as regressive, costume or too alien-like by fashion media in the West—a critique that bears resemblance to older Orientalist viewpoints.

However, as has been experienced in most parts of the world, fashion in the late twentieth and the beginning of the twenty-first century is clearly distinct from earlier times—as the flows of fashion information, knowledge and opinion leadership is decentralized through the Internet, the production and consumption of fashion is more globalized, and the pace of fashion (fast fashion) has increased. The last of which has led some to question the logic behind fashion weeks that preview collections meant for future seasons when customers increasingly want to access products immediately and globally, a phenomenon made possible via the Internet. Despite the continued authority of the fashion capitals established in the last century, they too are increasingly focused on glocalizing their design approaches to move beyond familiar fashion markets, towards wooing customers in India and China for example. As one reviewer of Karl Lagerfeld's India-inspired *Paris-Bombay* 2012 Pre-Fall collection for Chanel wrote, "while the setting was historical, the reason behind the spotlight on India is very much rooted in the present" (Cartner-Morely 2011).

The imposition of a model of fashion—systems and cycles—that emerged elsewhere, without considering the local flavors of non-Western centers of dress, are yet to be openly challenged by the fashion industry in India. Though signs of such opposition are already very much there in the lack of adherence for the "rules" of fashion, along with the positioning of traditional design narratives by designers like Sabyasachi who firmly believes in maintaining focus on the domestic Indian market, as well as through emerging blogs, journals and other voices that call to action the search of culturally relevant design that claims its own space as an individual fashion capital.

Without doubt, Indian fashion is yet again at a very exciting juncture.

---

[13] An international arts organization based in India (http://khojworkshop.org/).

BIBLIOGRAPHY

Ahluwalia, R. V. (2012). "Bollywood and Luxury," in G. Atwal and S. Jain (eds), *The Luxury Market in India: Maharajas to Masses* (pp. 164–78). London: Palgrave Macmillan.

Appadurai, A. (1990). "Disjuncture and difference in the global cultural economy." *Theory, Culture & Society, 7*, 295–310.

Bahl, V. (2005). "Shifting boundaries of 'nativity' and 'modernity' in south Asian women's clothes." *Dialectical Anthropology* (29), 85–121.

Baizerman, S., Eicher, J. B., and Cerny, C. (2000). "Eurocentrism in the Study of Ethnic Dress," in *Visible Self: Global Perspectives on Dress, Culture, and Society* (2nd edn). New York: Fairchild Publications.

Bajpai, S. (1997). "Thoroughly modern misses; women on Indian television." *Women: A Cultural Review, 8*(3), 303–10.

Balaram, S. (2005). "Design pedagogy in India: a perspective." *Design Issues, 21*(4), 11–22.

Banerjee, M. and Miller, D. (2003). *The Sari*. Oxford: Berg.

Barthes, R. (1985 [1976]). *The Fashion System*, trans. M. Ward and R. Howard. Worchester and London: Trinity Press.

Bayly, C. A. (1986). "The Origins of Swadeshi (Home Industry): Cloth and Indian Society, 1700-1930," in A. Appadurai (ed.), *The Social Life of Things: Commodities in Cultural Perspective* (pp. 285–322). Cambridge: Cambridge University Press.

Bean, S. S. (1989). "Gandhi and Khadi, the Fabric of Indian Independence," in A. B. Weiner and J. Schneider (eds), *Cloth and Human Experience*. Washington, DC: Smithsonian Institution Press.

Beinhocker, E. D. and Farrell, D. (2007). "Next big spenders: India's middle class." *Newsweek International*.

Beinhocker, E. D., Farrell, D., and Zainulbhai, A. S. (2007). "Tracking the growth of India's middle class." *The McKinsey Quarterly, 51*–61.

Beng-Huat, C. (2000). "Consuming Asians: Ideas and Issues," in C. Beng-Huat (ed.), *Consumption in Asia: Lifestyles and Identities*. New York: Routledge.

Berry, J. (2010). "Street-Style: Fashion Photography, Web Logs and the Urban Image." Paper presented at the Fashion: Exploring Critical Issues, Oriel College, Oxford.

Berry, S. (2001). "Fashion" in T. Miller (ed.), *A Companion to Cultural Studies* (pp. 454–70). Oxford: Blackwell Publishers.

Bhachu, P. (2004). *Dangerous Designs: Asian Women Fashion the Diaspora Economies*. New York and London: Routledge.

Bhatia, N. (2003). "Fashioning women in colonial India." *Fashion Theory, 7*(3/4), 327–44.

Boroian, M. and Poix, A. D. (2010). *India by Design: The Pursuit of Luxury & Fashion*. Singapore: Wiley.

Borthwick, M. (1984). *The Changing Role of Women in Bengal, 1849–1905*. Princeton, NJ: Princeton University Press.

Breckenridge, C. A. and Appadurai, A. (eds) (1995). *Consuming Modernity: Public Culture in a South Asian World*. Minneapolis: University of Minnesota Press.

Breidenbach, J., Pál, N., and Županov, I. (2004). "Fashionable Books." *Identities: Global Studies in Culture and Power, 11*, 619–28.

Brosius, C. (2007). "The Enclaved Gaze: Exploring the Visual Culture of 'World Class' Living in Urban India," in J. Jain (ed.), *India's Popular Culture: Iconic Spaces and Fluid Images*. New Delhi: Marg.

Bruzzi, S. and Gibson, P. C. (eds) (2000). *Fashion Cultures: Theories, Explorations and Analysis*. London and New York: Routledge.

Brydon, A. and Niessen, S. (1998). "Introduction: Adorning the Body," in A. Brydon and S. Niessen (eds), *Consuming Fashion: Adorning the Transnational Body*. Oxford and New York: Berg.

Cannon, A. (1998). "The Cultural and Historical Contexts of Fashion," in A. Brydon and S. Niessen (eds), *Consuming Fashion: Adorning the Transnational Body*. Oxford and New York: Berg.

Castelino, M. (1994). *Fashion Kaleidoscope*. New Delhi, Bombay and Calcutta: Rupa.

Chakrabarti, S. and Baisya, R. K. (2009). "The influences of consumer innovativeness and consumer evaluation attributes in the purchase of fashionable ethnic wear in India." *International Journal of Consumer Studies, 33*, 709–14.

Chatterjee, A. (2005). "Design in India: the experience of transition." *Design Issues, 21*(4–10).

Chatterjee, P. (1993). *The Nation and it Fragments: Colonial and Postcolonial Histories*. Princeton: Princeton University Press.

Chaudhuri, N. C. (1976). *Culture in the Vanity Bag*. Bombay: Jaico.

Chowdhary, U. (1984). *Fashion Process as Related to Media Exposure, Social Participation, and Attitude Toward Change Among College Women in India*. Ohio: Ohio State University.

Chowdhary, U. and Dickey, L. (1988). "Fashion opinion leadership and media exposure among college women in India." *Home Economics Research Journal, Vol. 16, No. 3*, 183–94.

Clark, H. (2009). "Back to the future, or forward? Hong Kong design, image, and branding." *Design Issues, 25*(3), 11–29.

Cohen, M. (2007, September 28). "India's New Beauty Ideal is a Wisp of Its Former Self." *Wall Street Journal*.

Cohn, B. S. (1989). "Cloth, Clothes and Colonialism: India in the Nineteenth Century," in A. B. Weiner and J. Schneider (eds), *Cloth and Human Experience*. Washington: Smithsonian Institution Press.

Craik, J. (1994). *The Face of Fashion: Cultural Studies in Fashion*. London: Routledge.

Cullity, J. (2002). "The global desi: cultural nationalism on MTV India." *Journal of Communication Inquiry, 26*(4), 408–25.

Cunningham, P. A. and Lab, S. V. (1991). "Understanding Dress and Popular Culture," in P. A. Cunningham and S. V. Lab (eds), *Dress and Popular Culture* (pp. 5–18). Bowling Green: Bowling Green State University Popular Press.

Dasgupta, S., Sinha, D., and Chakravati, S. (2012). *Media, Gender, and Popular Culture in India: Tracking Change and Continuity*. Los Angeles and London: Sage.

Derné, S. (2000). *Movies, Masculinity, and Modernity: An Ethnography of Men's Filmgoing in India*. Westport, CT: Greenwood Press.

—(2008). *Globalization on the Ground: New Media and the Transformation of Culture, Class, and Gender in India*. New Delhi: Sage.

Dhir, A., Sachdeva, P., and Jain, R. (2010). "Trends in India's domestic fashion market." *Technopak Perspective, 4*, 36–55.

Donner, H. (2008). *Domestic Goddesses: Maternity, Globalization and Middle-class Identity in Contemporary India*. Aldershot and Burlington, VT: Ashgate.

—(ed.) (2011). *Being Middle-class in India: A Way of Life*. New York: Routledge.

Dudrah, R. and Desai, J. (2008). "The essential Bollywood," in R. Dudrah and J. Desai (eds), *The Bollywood Reader* (pp. 1–20). New York: Open University Press.

Dwyer, C. (2006). "Fabrications of India: Transnational networks and the making of 'East/West' fashion," in C. Breward and D. Gilbert (eds), *Fashion's World Cities*. Oxford and New York: Berg.

Dwyer, R. (2000a). "Bombay Ishtyle," in S. Bruzzi and P. C. Gibson (eds), *Fashion Cultures: Theories, Explorations and Analysis*. London and New York: Routledge.

—(2000b). *All You Want is Money, all You Need is Love: Sexuality and Romance in Modern India*. New York: Cassell.

Dwyer, R. and Patel, D. (2002). *Cinema India: The Visual Culture of Hindi Film*. New Brunswick: Rutgers University Press.

Eames, C. and Eames, R. (1997 [1958]). *The India Report*. Ahmedabad: National Institute of Design. (N. I. o. Design o. Document Number)

Eckhardt, G. M. and Mahi, H. (2004). "The role of consumer agency in the globalization process in emerging markets." *Journal of Macromarketing, 24*(2), 136–46.

Edensor, T. (2002). *National Identity, Popular Culture and Everyday Life*. Oxford and New York: Berg.

Eicher, J. B., Evenson, S. L., and Lutz, H. A. (2000). *Visible Self: Global Perspectives on Dress, Culture, and Society* (2nd edn). New York: Fairchild Publications.

Eicher, J. B., and Sumberg, B. (1995). "World Fashion, Ethnic, and National Dress," in J. B. Eicher (ed.), *Dress and Ethnicity*. Oxford and New York: Berg.

Entwistle, J. (2000). *The Fashioned Body: Fashion, Dress and Modern Social Theory*. Malden, MA: Polity Press.

Evans, C. (1997). "Street style, subculture and subversion." *Costume, 31*, 105–10.

Featherstone, M. (1990). *Global Culture: Nationalism, Globalization and Modernity.* London: Sage.

Fernandes, L. (2000). "Nationalizing 'the global': media images, cultural politics and the middle class in India." *Media, Culture and Society, 22*, 611–28.

—(2006). *India's New Middle Class: Democratic Politics in an Era of Economic Reform*. Minneapolis and London: University of Minnesota Press.

Finnane, A. (2008). *Changing Clothes in China: Fashion, History, Nation*. New York: Columbia University Press.

Fiss, K. (2009). "Design in a global context: envisioning postcolonial and transnational possibilities. *Design Issues, 25*(3), 3–10.

Flugel, J. C. (1971 [1930]). *The Psychology of Clothes* (2nd edn; paperback). New York: International Universities Press.

Ganguly-Scrase, R. and Scrase, T. J. (2009). *Globalisation and the Middle Classes in India: The Social and Cultural Impact of Neoliberal Reforms*. London and New York: Routledge.

Ganti, T. (2012). "No longer a frivolous singing and dancing nation of movie-makers: the Hindi film industry and its quest for global distinction." *Visual Anthropology, 25*, 340–65.

Gehlawat, A. (2012). "'*Aadat Se Majboor*'/'Helpless by Habit': metrosexual masculinity in contemporary Bollywood." *Studies in South Asian Film & Media, 4*(1), 62–79.

Ghose, A. (2010). "Interview (with David Abraham)." *India Seminar* (609).

Gilbert, D. (2006). "From Paris to Shanghai: The Changing Geographies of Fashion's World Cities," in C. Breward and D. Gilbert (eds), *Fashion's World Cities* (pp. 3–32). Oxford and New York: Berg.

Goodrum, A., Larner, W., and Molloy, M. (2007). "Auckland as a Globalizing Fashion City," in L. Welters and A. Lillethun (eds), *The Fashion Reader* (pp. 185–90). Oxford and New York: Berg.

Goody, J. (2007). *The Theft of History*. Cambridge: Cambridge University Press.

Gopal, A. and Srinivasan, R. (2006). "The new Indian consumer." *Harvard Business Review, 22–3*.

Hall, S. (1997). *Representation: Cultural Representations and Signifying Practices*. London: Sage (in association with the Open University).

Hannerz, U. (1996). *Transnational Connections: Culture, People, Places*. London: Routledge.

Hollander, A. (1993 [1978]). *Seeing Through Clothes*. Berkeley, Los Angeles and London: University of California Press.

—(1994). *Sex and Suits: The Evolution of Modern Dress*. New York: Knopf.

Huppatz, D. J. (2009). "Designer nostalgia in Hong Kong." *Design Issues, 25*(2), 14–28.

Ingale, M. K. and Chandorkar, M. (2010). "In film Branding – An Emerging Trend." Paper presented at the "Services Management: The Catalyst" – Fifth International Research Conference on Services Management, Kohinoor Business School and Center for Management Research, Khandala, India.

Jaitly, J. (2010). "Crafting fashion." *India Seminar* (609).

Jin, B., Park, J. Y., and Ryu, J. S. (2010). "Comparison of Chinese and Indian consumers' evaluative criteria when selecting denim jeans." *Journal of Fashion Marketing and Management, 14*(1), 180–94.

Jobling, P. (1999). *Fashion Spreads: Word and Image in Fashion Photography Since 1980*. Oxford: Berg.

Jones, C. and Leshkowich, A. M. (2003). "What happens when Asian chic becomes chic in Asia?" *Fashion Theory, 7*(3/4), 281–300.

Joshi, O. P. (1992). "Continuity and Change in Hindu Women's Dres," in R. Barnes and J. B. Eicher (eds), *Dress and Gender: Making and Meaning*. Oxford and New York: Berg Publishers.

Kabir, N. M. (2001). *Bollywood: The Indian Cinema Story*. London: Channel 4 Books.

Kapoor, K. and Pinto, R. (2012). *The Style Diary of a Bollywood Diva*. New Delhi: Shobhaa Dé Books [Penguin Books Ltd].

Karlekar, M. (2011). "Reform and sartorial styles in 19th-century Bengal." *Marg: A Magazine of the Arts, 62*(4), 66–71.

Kawamura, Y. (2005). *Fashion-ology: An Introduction to Fashion Studies*. Oxford and New York: Berg.

Khaire, M. (2011). "The Indian fashion industry and traditional Indian crafts." *Business History Review, 85*(02), 345–66.

Khan, N. (1992). "Asian Women's Dress: From Burqah to Bloggs – Changing Clothes for Changing Times," in J. Ash and E. Wilson (eds), *Chic Thrills: A Fashion Reader*. Berkeley: University of California Press.

Kondo, D. (1997). *About Face: Performing Race in Fashion and Theatre*. London: Routledge.

Koshy, D. (2008). *India Design Edge*. New Delhi: Roli Books.

Koskinen, I. (2005). "Semiotic neighborhoods." *Design Issues, 21*(2), 13–27.

Kumar, R. (2000). "Will the Handwoven Saree and Other Handcrafted Textiles be on our Endangered List in the Next Millennium?," in V. Bhandari and R. Kashyap (eds), *Evolving Trends in Fashion: The NIFT Millennium Document – 2000* (pp. 53–63). New Delhi: NIFT.

Kumar, S. (2010). *Postcolonial Identity in a Globalizing India: Case Studies in Visual, Musical and Oral Culture*. Iowa: University of Iowa.

Lakshmi, C. S. (1988). "The Educated Woman in Modern Tamil Literature," in K. Chanana (ed.), *Socialisation, Education, and Women: Explorations in Gender Identity* (pp. 274–81). London: Sangam Books.

Lau, L. and Mendes, A. C. (2011). "Introducing re-Orientalism: a new manifestation of Orientalism," in L. Lau and A. C. Mendes (eds), *Re-Orientalism and South Asian Identity Politics: The Oriental Other Within* (pp. 1–18). London and New York: Routledge.

Leopold, E. (1992). "The Manufacture of the Fashion System," in J. Ash and E. Wilson (eds), *Chic Thrills: A Fashion Reader*. Berkeley: University of California Press.

Liechty, M. (2003). *Suitably Modern: Making Middle-Class Culture in a New Consumer Society*. Princeton, NJ: Princeton University Press.

Lipovetsky, G. (1994). *The Empire of Fashion: Dressing Modern Democracy*. Princeton, NJ: Princeton University Press.

Loomba, A. (1997). "The long and saggy sari." *Women: A Cultural Review, 8*(3), 278–92.

Lukose, R. A. (2009). *Liberalization's Children: Gender, Youth, and Consumer Citizenship in Globalizing India*. Durham, NC: Duke University Press.

Mathur, G. (2005). "Signboards as mirrors of cultural change." *Design Issues, 21*(4), 80–93.

Mathur, N. (2010). "Shopping malls, credit cards and global brands: consumer culture and lifestyle of India's new middle class." *South Asia Research, 30*(3), 211–31.

Mathur, S. (2011). "Charles and Ray Eames in India." *Art Journal, 70*(1), 34–53.

Maynard, M. (2004). *Dress and Globalisation*: Manchester: Manchester University Press.

Mazzarella, W. (2003a). *Shoveling Smoke: Advertising and Globalization in Contemporary India*. Durham and London: Duke University Press.

—(2003b). "'Very Bombay': contending with the global in an Indian advertising agency." *Cultural Anthropology 18*(1), 33–71.

McGowan, A. (2005). "'All that is rare, characteristic or beautiful' – design and the defense of tradition in colonial India, 1851–1903." *Journal of Material Culture, 10*(3), 263–87.

—(2006). "An all-consuming subject? women and consumption in late-nineteenth and early-twentieth-century western India." *Journal of Women's History, 18*(4), 31–54.

Misra, B. B.(1961). *The Indian Middle Classes: Their Growth in Modern Times*. Delhi and London: Oxford University Press.

Mitra, B. (2005). *The Influence of Television Commercials on Clothing in India*. Worcester: University of Worcester.

Mohan, R. and Gupta, C. (2007). "Consumer Preference Patterns in Apparel Retailing in India." Paper presented at the Fourth Asia Pacific Retail Conference, College of Management, Mahidol University, Bangkok, Thailand.

Munshi, S. (2000). "Marvellous Me: The Beauty Industry and the Construction of the 'Modern' Indian Woman," in S. Munshi (ed.), *Images of the 'Modern Woman' in Asia: Global Media, Local Meanings* (pp. 78–93). Richmond: Curzon.

Nagrath, S. (2003). "(En)countering Orientalism in high fashion: a review of India fashion week 2002." *Fashion Theory, 7*(3/4), 361–76.

Niessen, S. (2003). "Afterword: Re-Orienting Fashion Theory," in S. Niessen, A. M. Leshkowich, and C. Jones (eds), *Re-Orienting Fashion: The Globalization of Asian Dress*. Oxford and New York: Berg.

Niessen, S., Leshkowich, A. M., and Jones, C. (eds) (2003). *Re-Orienting Fashion: The Globalization of Asian Dress*. Oxford and New York: Berg.

Osuri, G. (2008). "Ash-coloured whiteness: the transfiguration of Aishwarya Rai." *South Asian Popular Culture, 6*(2), 109–23.

Pal, C. (1968). *A Dictionary of Fashion & Beauty for Indian Women*. Bombay: Jaico Publishing House.

Patel, D. (2012). "Contemporary Design from India: An exhibition of…?" Paper presented at the M+ Matters. Asian Design: Historied, Collecting, Curating. Available from http://www.mplusmatters.hk/asiandesign/paper_topic9.php?l=en (accessed January 31, 2013).

Pathak, A. (2006). *Indian Costumes*. New Delhi: Roli Books.

Pham, M.-H. T. (2011). "Blog ambition: fashion, feelings, and the political economy of the digital raced body." *Camera Obscura, 26*(1(76)), 1–37.

Polhemus, T. and Proctor, L. (1978). *Fashion & Anti-fashion: An Anthropology of Clothing and Adornment*. [London]: Thames and Hudson.

Purdy, D. L. (ed.) (2004). *The Rise of Fashion*. Minneapolis: University of Minnesota Press.

Rabine, L. W. (1994)." A Woman's Two Bodies: Fashion Magazines, Consumerism, and Feminism," in S. Benstock and S. Ferriss (eds), *On fashion*. New Brunswick, NJ: Rutgers University Press.

Ramachandran, J., and Patvardhan, S. (2008). "In conversation with fashion artiste Manish Arora." *IIMB Management Review, 20*(4), 143–54.

Rao, S. (2010). "'I need an Indian touch': glocalization and Bollywood films." *Journal of International and Intercultural Communication, 3*(1), 1–19.

Reddy, V. (2006). "The nationalization of the global Indian woman: geographies of beauty in *femina*." *South Asian Popular Culture, 4, No. 1*, 61–85.

Rocamora, A. (2011). "Personal fashion blogs: screens and mirrors in digital self-portraits." *Fashion Theory, 15*(4), 407–24.

Rocca, F. (ed.). (2009). *Contemporary Indian Fashion.* Bologna: Damani.

Rodricks, W. (2012). *The Green Room*. New Delhi: Rupa Publications.

Rovine, V. L. (2009). "Colonialism's clothing: Africa, France, and the deployment of fashion." *Design Issues, 25*(3), 44–61.

Roy, D. and Saha, G. (2007). "Changes in women's dress preference: an in-depth study based on lifestyle and age." *South Asian Journal of Management, 14*(2), 90–105.

Runkle, S. (2004). "Making 'Miss India': constructing gender, power and the nation." *South Asian Popular Culture, 2*(No. 2, October 2004), 145–59.

Saavala, M. (2012). *Middle-class Moralities: Everyday Struggle over Belonging and Prestige in India*. New Delhi: Orient Blackswan.

Sahni, V. (2010). "The 'brand' new fashionable Indian." *India Seminar* (609).

Said, E. (1995 [1978]). *Orientalism: Western Conceptions of the Orient*. London: Penguin.

Scotford, M. (2005). "Introduction: Indian design and design education." *Design Issues, Volume 21*(4), 1–3.

Sengupta, H. (2005). *Indian Fashion*. Delhi: Pearson Education.

Sethi, J. (2010). "The magician and the monk (interview with Manish Arora and Rajesh Pratap Singh)." *India Seminar* (609).

Sheth, K. K. and Vital, I. (2007). "India: shopping with the family." *The McKinsey Quarterly,* 74–5.

Shukla, P. (2005). "The study of dress and adornment as social positioning." *Material Culture Review, 61*, 4–16.

—(2008). *The Grace of Four Moons: Dress, Adornment, and the Art of the Body in Modern India*. Bloomington: Indiana University Press.

Simmel, G. (1904). "Fashion." *International Quarterly, 10*, 130–55.

—(1957). "Fashion." *The American Journal of Sociology, 62*(6), 541–58.

Singh, J. A. (1966). *Modern Draped Sari Replaces Traditional Costumes of Educated Women and the Relationship of this Change to the Development of Education and Communication in India*. Pennsylvania: Pennsylvania State University.

Skov, L. (2003). "Fashion-Nation: A Japanese Globalization Experience and a Hong Kong Dilemma." in S. Niessen, A. M. Leshkowich, and C. Jones (eds), *Re-Orienting Fashion: The Globalization of Asian Dress*. Oxford and New York: Berg.

Slade, T. (2009). *Japanese Fashion: A Cultural History*. Oxford: Berg.

Sridharan, E. (2004). "The growth and sectoral composition of India's middle class: its impact on the politics of economic liberalization." *India Review, 3*(4), 405–28.

Suga, M. (1995). "Exotic West to Exotic Japan: Revival of Japanese Tradition in Modern Japan," in J. B. Eicher (ed.), *Dress and Ethnicity*. Oxford and New York: Berg.

Tarlo, E. (1991). "The problem of what to wear: the politics of khadi in late colonial India." *South Asia Research, 11*(2), 134–57.

—(1996). *Clothing Matters: Dress and Identity in India*. Chicago: Chicago University Press.

Teunissen, J. (2005). "Global Fashion/Local Tradition, On the Globalisation of Fashion," in J. Brand and J. Teunissen (eds), *Global Fashion/Local Tradition: On the Globalisation of Fashion* (pp. 8–23). Arnhem: Terra.

Thapan, M. (2004). "Embodiment and identity in contemporary society: *femina* and the 'new' Indian woman." *Contributions to Indian Sociology, 38*(3), 411–44.

—(2009). *Living the Body: Embodiment, Womanhood and Identity in Contemporary India*. New Delhi, Thousand Oaks and London: Sage.

Thomas, R. (2008). "Indian Cinema: Pleasures and Popularity," in R. Dudrah and J. Desai (eds), *The Bollywood Reader* (pp. 21–32). New York: Open University Press.

Trivedi, L. (2003). "Visually mapping the 'nation': Swadeshi politics in nationalist India, 1920–1930." *The Journal of Asian Studies* (no. 1 (February 2003)), 11–41.

—(2007). *Clothing Gandhi's Nation: Homespun and Modern India*: Bloomington: Indiana University Press.

Varma, P. K. (1998). *The Great Indian Middle Class*. New Delhi: Penguin Books.

Vasudev, S. (2012). *Powder Room: The Untold Story of Indian Fashion*. Noida: Random House India.

Veblen, T. (1894). "The economic theory of woman's dress." *The Popular Science Monthly, 46*, 198–205.

Vyas, H. K. (2006). "Design history: an alternative approach." *Design Issues, 22*(4), 27–34.

Wilkinson-Weber, C. M. (2005a). "Tailoring expectations: how film costumes becomes audience's clothes." *South Asian Popular Culture, Vol 3*(No. 2), 135–59.

—(2005b). "Behind the seams: designers and tailors in popular Hindi cinema." *Visual Anthropology Review, 20*(2), 3–21.

—(2010). "From commodity to costume: productive consumption in the making of Bollywood film looks." *Journal of Material Culture, 15*(1), 3–29.

—(2011). "Diverting Denim: Screening Jeans in Bollywood," in D. Miller and S. Woodward (eds), *Global Denim*. Oxford and New York: Berg.

—(2013). *Fashioning Bollywood: The Making and Meaning of Hindi Film Costume*. London: Bloomsbury Academic.

Wilson, E. (2003 [1985]). *Adorned in Dreams: Fashion and Modernity*. New Brunswick, NJ: Rutgers University Press.

Woodward, S. (2009). "The myth of street style." *Fashion Theory, 13*(1), 83–102.

Further Reading

Adamson, G., Riello, G., and Teasley, S. (eds) (2011). *Global Design History*. London: Routledge.

Ahmed, D. A. (2012). "Women and soap-operas: popularity, portrayal and perception." *International Journal of Scientific and Research Publications, 2*(6), 1–6.

Anjaria, U. and Anjaria, J. S. (2008). "Text, genre, society: Hindi youth films and postcolonial desire." *South Asian Popular Culture, 6*(2), 125–40.

Appadurai, A. (1996). *Modernity at Large: Cultural Dimensions of Globalization*. Minneapolis: University of Minnesota Press.

Asthana, S. (2003). "Patriotism and its avatars: tracking the national-global dialectic in Indian music videos." *Journal of Communication Inquiry* (27:4), 337–53.

Athavankar, U. (2002). "Design in search of roots an Indian experience." *Design Issues, 18*(3) (Summer 2002), 43–57.

Balaram, S. (2009). "Design in India: the importance of the Ahmedabad Declaration." *Design Issues, 25*(4), 54–79.

Barnes, R. and Eicher, J. B. (eds) (1992). *Dress and Gender: Making and Meaning*. Oxford. New York: Berg.

Bhandari, V. (2007). "Fashion in India," in L. Welters and A. Lillethun (eds), *The Fashion Reader* (pp. 387–91). Oxford and New York: Berg.

—(2011). "Interview with designer Sabyasachi Mukherjee." *Fashion Practice, 3*(2), 253–64.

Bhandari, V. and Kashyap, R. (eds) (2000). *Evolving Trends in Fashion: The NIFT Millennium Document – 2000*. New Delhi: NIFT.

Breward, C. and Gilbert, D. (eds) (2006). *Fashion's World Cities*. Oxford and New York: Berg.

Chakrabarti, S. (2010). "An empirical analysis of the influence of consumer evaluation attributes in the purchase of fashionable ethnic wear in India." *Journal of Marketing & Communication, 6*(1), 4–9.

Chanana, K. (ed.) (1988). *Socialisation, Education, and Women: Explorations in Gender Identity*. London: Sangam Books.

Chaudhuri, M. (2001). "Gender and advertisements: the rhetoric of globalisation." *Women's Studies International Forum, 24*(3/4), 373–85.

Chittenden, T. (2010). "Digital dressing up: modelling female teen identity in the discursive spaces of the fashion blogosphere." *Journal of Youth Studies, 13*(4), 505–20.

Das, L. K. (2005). "Culture as the designer." *Design Issues, 21*(4), 41–53.

Dewey, S. (2008). *Making Miss India Miss World: Constructing Gender, Power, and the Nation in Postliberalization India*. Syracuse, NY: Syracuse University Press.

Dwyer, R. (2000c). "The erotics of the wet sari in Hindi films." *South Asia, 23*(1), 143–59.

Dwyer, R. and Pinney, C. (2001). *Pleasure and the Nation: The History, Politics, and Consumption of Public Culture in India*. New Delhi: Oxford University Press.

Eicher, J. B. (ed.) (1995). *Dress and Ethnicity*. Oxford and New York: Berg.

Harvey, S. (ed.). (2007). *Trading Culture: Global Traffic And Local Cultures in Film And Television*. Bloomington: Indiana University Press.

Hendrickson, H. (1996). *Clothing and Difference: Embodied Identities in Colonial and Post-colonial Africa*. Durham: Duke University Press.

Jackson, P. (2004). "Local consumption cultures in a globalizing world." *Royal Geographical Society*, 165–78.

Jacob, D. M. (1996). "Salwar Kameez: Winds of change." *The Indian Textile Journal, 106*(9), 66–70.

Jain, J. (ed.). (2007). *India's Popular Culture: Iconic Spaces and Fluid Images*. New Delhi: Marg.

Jaitly, J. (2005). "Craft as industry." *India Seminar* (553).

Joshi, S. (2004). "How to watch a Hindi film: the example of *Kuch Kuch Hota Hai*." *Education About Asia, 9*(1), 22–5.

Kasbekar, A. (2006). *Pop culture India!: Media, Arts, and Lifestyle*. Santa Barbara, CA: ABC-CLIO.

Kasturi, P. B. (2005). "Designing Freedom." *Design Issues, 21*(4), 68–77.

Kavoori, A. P. and Punathambekar, A. (eds) (2008). *Global Bollywood*. New York and London: New York University Press.

Khare, A., Parveen, C. and Mishra, A. (2012). "Influence of normative and informative values on fashion clothing involvement of Indian women." *Journal of Customer Behaviour, 11*(1), 9–32.

Kretz, G. and Valek, K. d. (2010). "'Pixilize me!': digital storytelling and the creation of archetypal myths through explicit and implicit self-brand association in fashion and luxury blogs." *Research in Consumer Behavior, 12*, 313–29.

Kumar, R. and Muscat, C. (1999). *Costumes and Textiles of Royal India*. London: Christie's Books.

Kumar, S. and Curtin, M. (2002). "Made in India: in between music television and patriarchy." *Television and New Media, 3*(4), 345–66.

Lal, R. and Fuller, V. (2008). *Shoppers' Stop Group (SSG)*: Harvard Business School. Document Number.

Lau, L. E. J. (2006). "The new Indian woman: who is she, and what is 'new' about her?" *Women's Studies International Forum, 29*, 159–71.

Lemire, B. (2010). "Introduction: Fashion and the Practice of History," in B. Lemire (ed.), *The Force of Fashion in Politics and Society: Global Perspectives from Early to Modern to Contemporary Times* (pp. 1–20). Farnham: Ashgate.

Mandoki, K. (2003). "Point and line over the body: social imaginaries underlying the logic of fashion." *Journal of Popular Culture, January*, 600–22.

Mankekar, P. (1993). "National texts and gendered lives: an ethnography of television viewers in a north Indian city." *American Ethnologist, 20*(3), 543–63.

—(1999). *Screening Culture, Viewing Politics: An Ethnography of Television, Womanhood, and Nation in Postcolonial India*. Durham, NC: Duke University Press.

—(2004). "Dangerous desires: television and erotics in late twentieth-century India." *The Journal of Asian Studies, 63*(2), 403–31.

Mathur, S. (2007). *India by Design: Colonial History and Cultural Display*. Berkeley and London: University of California Press.

McCracken, G. D. (1988). *Culture and Consumption: New Approaches to the Symbolic Character of Consumer Goods and Activities*. Bloomington: Indiana University Press.

McMillin, D. (2001). "Localizing the global: television and hybrid programming in India." *International Journal of Cultural Studies, 4*(1), 45–68.

McMillin, D. and Fisherkeller, J. (2009). "Local identities in globalized regions: teens, everyday life, and television." *Popular Communication, 7*, 237–51.

Mehta, N. (ed.) (2008). *Television in India: Satellites, Politics and Cultural Change*. Abingdon and New York: Routledge.

Mills, J. H. and Sen, S. (eds) (2004). *Confronting the Body: The Politics of Physicality in Colonial and Post-Colonial India*. London: Anthem Press.

Mishra, V. (2002). *Bollywood Cinema: Temples of Desire*. New York and London: Routledge.

Munshi, S. (2004). "A Perfect 10 – 'Modern *and* Indian': Representation of the Body in Beauty Pageants and the Visual Media of Contemporary India," in J. H. Mills and S. Sen (eds), *Confronting the Body: The Politics of Physicality in Colonial and Post-Colonial India* (pp. 162–82). London: Anthem Press.

Nagrath, S. (2005). "Local Roots of Global Ambitions: A Look at the Role of India Fashion in the Development of the Indian Fashion Industry," in J. Brand and J. Teunissen (eds), *Global Fashion/Local Tradition: On the Globalisation of Fashion* (pp. 54–81). Arnhem: Terra.

Nanda, B. R. (1976). *Indian Women, from Purdah to Modernity*. New Delhi: Vikas Publishing House.

Osella, C. and Osella, F. (2006). *Men and Masculinities in South India*. London and New York: Anthem Press.

Patel, M. C. (2005). "Search for vernacular identity." *Design Issues, 21*(4), 32–40.

Paulicelli, E. and Clark, H. (eds) (2009). *The Fabric of Cultures: Fashion, Identity, and Globalization*. London and New York: Routledge.

Sengupta, H. (2009). *Rampup: The Business of Indian Fashion*. Delhi: Pearson Education.

Shukla, R. P., Walke, S. G. and Medhekar, A. A. (2010). "Product Placement in Hindi Movies and its Influence on Audience." Paper presented at the "Services Management: The Catalyst" – Fifth International Research Conference on Services Management, Kohinoor Business School and Center for Management Research, Khandala, India.

Singh, R. (2011). *The Fabric of Our Lives: The Story of Fabindia*. New Delhi: Penguin Books.

Singh, S. (2011). "Rise of the Indian middle class." *India Now, 01*, 10–17.

Sinha, M. (1995). *Colonial Masculinity: The 'Manly Englishman' and the 'Effeminate Bengali' in the Late Nineteenth Century*. Manchester: Manchester University Press.

—(2000). "Refashioning mother India: feminism and nationalism in late-colonial India." *Feminist Studies, 26*(No.3), 623–44.

Slater, D. (1997). *Consumer Culture and Modernity*. Oxford: Blackwell Publishers and and Cambridge, MA: Polity Press.

Smedly, E. (2000). "Escaping to Reality: Fashion Photography in the 1990s," in S. Bruzzi and P. C. Gibson (eds), *Fashion Cultures: Theories, Explorations and Analysis*. London and New York: Routledge.

Sondhi, N. and Singhvi, S. R. (2006). "Gender influences in garment purchase: an empirical analysis." *Global Business Review, 7*(1), 57–75.

Sukumar, S. (2007). "The bra and the Indian woman's notion of sexuality." *Journal of Creative Communications, 2*(3), 267–78.

Throsby, D. (2008). "Modelling the cultural industries." *International Journal of Cultural Policy, 14*(3), 217–32.

Weiner, A. B. and Schneider, J. (eds) (1989). *Cloth and Human Experience*. Washington: Smithsonian Institution Press.

Williams-Ørberg, E. (2008). *The 'paradox' of being young in New Delhi: Urban middle class youth negotiations with popular Indian film.* Lund: Lund University.

Fashion Magazines

Elle*
Femina
Grazia*
Harper's Bazaar*
Marie Claire*
Verve
Vogue*

(*Indian Editions)

Webliography

Amed, I. (2013). Right Brain, Left Brain | Will India Fulfill Its Luxury Potential? *BOF – Business of Fashion*, April 23, 2013. Available from http://www.businessoffashion.com/2013/04/right-brain-left-brain-will-india-fulfill-its-luxury-potential.html (accessed July 9, 2013).

Amin-Shinde, A. (2009). My sister will get very jealous when she sees the shoes. *Mid Day*, March 6, 2009. Available from http://www.mid-day.com/specials/2009/apr/050409-Kareena-Kapoor-Aki-Narula-fashion-statement-Kambakth-Ishq-Mehboob-Studio-Play.htm (accessed May 2, 2013).

Arwind, D. (2009). Gangs Attack Women in Western Attire. *The Hindu,* February, 26, 2009. Available from, http://www.thehindu.com/2009/02/26/stories/2009022658410300.htm (accessed October 19, 2012).

Bagchi, S. (2012). Living Life King Size: A Glimpse at the Regalia of Royalty. *Luxpresso*, October 5, 2012. Available from http://luxpresso.com/news-time-n-style/living-life-king-size-a-glimpse-at-the-regalia-of-royalty/16294 (accessed October 19, 2012).

Balakrishnan, D. (2009). Man who fended off attackers threatened. *IBN Live*, February 2, 2009. Available from http://ibnlive.in.com/news/man-who-fended-off-attackers-in-mangalore-threatened/84235-3.html (accessed October 19, 2012).

Cartner-Morley, J. (2011). Karl Lagerfeld shows off his Mad Hatter streak at launch of collection for India. *The Guardian*, December 9, 2011. Available from http://www.theguardian.com/fashion/2011/dec/09/karl-lagerfeld-mad-hatter-india (accessed July 30, 2013).

Dutta, D. (2012). 2012 – Will India Sizzle or Fizzle for International Fashion Brands? *Third Eyesight*, March 13, 2012. Available from http://thirdeyesight.in/blog/2012/03/13/2012-will-india-sizzle-or-fizzle-for-international-fashion-brands/ (accessed July 23, 2013).

—(2013). India's Luxury Love Affair: It's Complicated! *Third Eyesight*, February 24, 2013. Available from http://thirdeyesight.in/blog/2013/02/24/indias-luxury-love-affair-its-complicated/ (accessed July 23, 2013).

Ghosal, S. (2012). Designer wear industry to reach Rs 11K crore mark by 2020: ASSOCHAM. *The Economic Times*, February 2, 2012. Available from http://articles.economictimes.indiatimes.com/2012-02-02/news/31017418_1_indian-designers-assocham-fashion-institutes (accessed July 9, 2013).

Harris, G. (2012). After Life in New York, Banker Returns to India for Turn at Fashion. *The New York Times*, September 14, 2012. Available from http://www.nytimes.com/2012/09/15/world/asia/after-stint-in-new-york-banker-turns-to-fashion-in-india.html (accesssed September 16, 2012).

Karmali, N. (2012). India's 100 Richest Have Mixed Year, Eke Out Small Gain. *Forbes*, October 24, 2012. Available from http://www.forbes.com/sites/naazneenkarmali/2012/10/24/indias-100-richest/ (accessed January 25, 2013).

Kashyap, M. V. (2013a). Sabyasachi Mukherjee. *Border & Fall*, Issue No. 4. Available from http://www.borderandfall.com/journal/no-4-covenant/sabyasachi-mukherjee/ (accessed July 23, 2013).

—(2013b). An Open Letter to Sabyasachi. *Mumbai Boss*, May 21, 2013. Available from http://mumbaiboss.com/2013/05/21/an-open-letter-to-sabyasachi/ (accessed July 18, 2013).

Kaul, M. M. (2012, February 29). Global Local: Mayank Mansingh Kaul Interviews Alice Cicolini. *TAKE on Art.* Available from http://takeonart.wordpress.com/2012/02/29/global-local-mayank-mansingh-kaul-interviews-alice-cicolini/ (accessed March 30, 2013).

Malhotra, S. (2013). The Anti-Glamour Movement. *So Then*, July 21, 2013. Available from http://www.sothen.in/?p=335 (accessed July 23, 2013).

Nair, S. (2009). The evolution of MTV India. *afaqs!*, April 22, 2009. Available from http://www.afaqs.com/news/story/23859_The-evolution-of-MTV-India (accessed June 2, 2012).

Pratap-Shah, M. (2010). From Kolkata to Sobo. *The Times of South Mumbai*, September 3, 2010. Available from http://www.mumbaimirror.com/article/35/20100903201009011254073855 11ee0dd9/From-Kolkata-to-Sobo-.html (accessed March 19, 2013).

Raghavendra, N. (2013). Indian TV soaps become serial hits across the world, demand for television content jumps in new markets. *The Economic Times*, January 25, 2013. Available from http://articles.economictimes.indiatimes.com/2013-01-25/news/36548364_1_indian-soaps-serials-uttaran (accessed June 4, 2013).

Ranjan, M. (2007). New Education Strategies in the Context of the National Design Policy. *Design For India*, October 30, 2007. Available from http://design-for-india.blogspot.com/2007/10/new-education-strategies-and.html (accessed February 3, 2013).

Sarkar, A. (2013). Television: Twists and Turns'. *afaqs!*, May 1, 2013. Available from http://www.afaqs.com/news/story/37360_Television:-Twists-and-Turns (accessed June 4, 2013).

Shah, G. R. (2012). Saris: No Longer Under Wraps. *The New York Times*, September 7, 2012. Available from http://www.nytimes.com/2012/09/09/fashion/09sari.html (accessed December 9, 2012).

Shah, S. (2012). Serious Play. *The Hindu*, June 15, 2012. Available from http://www.thehindu.com/features/metroplus/serious-play/article3532540.ece (accessed July 10, 2013).

Sinha, C. (2012). The Anti-Designer. *OPEN Magazine*, October 27, 2012. Available from http://www.openthemagazine.com/article/art-culture/the-anti-designer (accessed January 12, 2013).

Sippy, S. A. (2012). Fresh From Kolkata, 'Bengali Style' Emerges. *The New York Times*, May 29, 2012. Available from http://india.blogs.nytimes.com/2012/05/29/fresh-from-kolkata-bengali-style-emerges/ (accessed December 18, 2012).

—(2013a). Embracing Tradition at Indian Fashion Weeks. *The New York Times*, March 12, 2013. Available from http://india.blogs.nytimes.com/2013/03/12/designers-embrace-tradition-at-indias-fashion-weeks/ (accessed March 18, 2013).

—(2013b). Sari as the New Birkin. *The Times of India – The Crest Ediition*, April 13, 2013. Available from http://www.timescrest.com/life/sari-as-the-new-birkin-10148 (accessed April 16, 2013).

Susan, N. (2009a). Valentine's Warriors. *Tehelka*, February 28, 2009. Available from http://archive.tehelka.com/story_main41.asp?filename=Op280209valentine_warrior.asp (accessed July 22, 2012).

—(2009b). Why we said pants to India's bigots. *The Guardian*, February 14, 2009. Available from http://www.theguardian.com/commentisfree/2009/feb/15/india-gender (accessed July 22, 2012).

Tewari, B. (2012). India Inc. | Thinking Beyond the Cashmere Crowd. *BOF –- Business of Fashion*, March 2, 2012. Available from http://www.businessoffashion.com/2012/03/india-inc-thinking-beyond-the-cashmere-crowd.html (accessed January 2013).

—(2013). Cannes, Capitalism, the Red Carpet and India. *BOF –- Business of Fashion*, May 30, 2013. Retrieved 07/09/13, Available from http://www.businessoffashion.com/2013/05/cannes-capitalism-the-red-carpet-and-india.html (accessed July 9, 2013).

Timmons, H. (2008). Vogue's Fashion Photos Spark Debate in India. *The New York Times*, August 31, 2008. Available from http://www.nytimes.com/2008/09/01/business/worldbusiness/01vogue.html?_r=0 (accessed January 1, 2013).

Trebay, G. (2005). India Fashion Week; More is more, with a dollop of too much. *The New York Times*, May 5, 2005. Available from http://www.nytimes.com/2005/05/05/fashion/thursdaystyles/05indfash.html (accessed July 9, 2007).

Unknown (2009). Best of Femina celebrates 50 years of mag's history. *Times of India*, May 22, 2009. Available from http://timesofindia.indiatimes.com/city/mumbai/Best-of-Femina-celebrates-50-years-of-mags-history/articleshow/4562240.cms (accessed January 19, 2010).

—(2013). Raw Mango: A Conversation with Sanjay Garg. *Park Magazine*, Vol. 8, "Color". Available from http://www.theparkhotels.com/living-magazine.html (accessed July 17, 2013).

Vasudev, S. (2010). Free to Wear Anything Country. *Indian Express*, October 17, 2010. Available from http://www.indianexpress.com/news/freetowearanything-country/698459/0 (accessed July 23, 2013).

—(2013). Why we love Zara. *Live Mint & The Wall Street Journal*, July 11, 2013. Available from http://www.livemint.com/Leisure/Haij1kOiMie8BvJdVgeFqJ/Why-we-love-Zara.html (accessed July 23, 2013).

INDEX

References in italics denote a figure